Rising China and Internet Governance

Riccardo Nanni

Rising China and Internet Governance

Multistakeholderism, Fragmentation and the
Liberal Order in the Age of Digital Sovereignty

Riccardo Nanni ⓘ
Digital Commons Lab
Fondazione Bruno Kessler
Trento, Italy

ISBN 978-981-97-0356-2   ISBN 978-981-97-0357-9 (eBook)
https://doi.org/10.1007/978-981-97-0357-9

© The Editor(s) (if applicable) and The Author(s), under exclusive license to Springer Nature Singapore Pte Ltd. 2024

This work is subject to copyright. All rights are solely and exclusively licensed by the Publisher, whether the whole or part of the material is concerned, specifically the rights of translation, reprinting, reuse of illustrations, recitation, broadcasting, reproduction on microfilms or in any other physical way, and transmission or information storage and retrieval, electronic adaptation, computer software, or by similar or dissimilar methodology now known or hereafter developed.
The use of general descriptive names, registered names, trademarks, service marks, etc. in this publication does not imply, even in the absence of a specific statement, that such names are exempt from the relevant protective laws and regulations and therefore free for general use.
The publisher, the authors and the editors are safe to assume that the advice and information in this book are believed to be true and accurate at the date of publication. Neither the publisher nor the authors or the editors give a warranty, expressed or implied, with respect to the material contained herein or for any errors or omissions that may have been made. The publisher remains neutral with regard to jurisdictional claims in published maps and institutional affiliations.

This Palgrave Macmillan imprint is published by the registered company Springer Nature Singapore Pte Ltd.
The registered company address is: 152 Beach Road, #21-01/04 Gateway East, Singapore 189721, Singapore

Paper in this product is recyclable.

To my family

Preface

Pupil: *"Teacher, who's the current President of China?"*
Teacher: *"I don't know"*
[Awkward silence]
Teacher: *"Do you guys think us teachers know everything?"*

In 2011, I was an eighteen-year-old about to graduate from secondary school. The conversation above took place between a fellow classmate of mine and a supply teacher as we were reviewing some basic history of Maoist China. No one knew the answer to that very simple and straightforward question: "Who is the current President of China?"—not even the teacher!

Fast forward to 2018, when the doctoral research that informs this book was started, a conversation like that in a school would have been unthinkable: President Xi Jinping had already become a household name in most countries around the world. In 2018, Italy, the country where I was born and raised and where I currently live, was about to sign a Memorandum of Understanding on the Belt and Road Initiative (from which Italy had already pulled out by the time the first draft of this book was finalised). For the signature of the Memorandum in spring 2019, President Xi Jinping received the highest forms of institutional welcoming and the country's media broadcast every detail of his visit and the political discussion around the Memorandum. Xi Jinping himself was even hosted with an op-ed on Corriere della Sera, one of Italy's most popular newspapers. By that time, I had personally spent two six-month periods in China, first in Guangzhou as a student and then in Beijing as a trainee at the EU Delegation to China.

Long story short, in less than ten years, China had become a much more popular destination for European students and workers (although this trend has changed after the Covid-19 pandemic), while the name of the Chinese President went from being observers' knowledge to a household name in most countries. This is not only due to Xi Jinping's stronger political personalisation compared to his predecessors Hu Jintao and Jiang Zemin, but also to China's undebatable rise to superpower status. This pushed everyone into having an opinion about China, about its government, and about its (foreign) policy choices. It forced observers (whether journalists, scholars, or policymakers) to build their own views about China and the future of China's relations with the rest of the world, its emerging global role, and the consequences of such renewed Chinese power. This led to the emergence of an unprecedented number of China experts, but also had the nefarious side effect of producing innumerable opinionated China observers with no prior knowledge of China's history, domestic political system, and cultural specificities. This, in turn, has led to a growing number of misguided opinions and policies vis-à-vis China. Such views have grown catastrophist when applied to the digital realm, where China and its domestic companies have definitely become major world players. This is especially true after Donald Trump's repeated attempts at depicting China and Chinese technologies as a security concern—whether warranted or not—since which alarmist media reports and policies have mushroomed. What these often have in common is the general idea that Chinese industry, state apparatus, and society at large are tightly and inextricably controlled by the Chinese Communist Party. While the Party's authoritarian rule is undeniably constituted by strong elements of societal control and coercion, it would be brutally simplistic to imagine a monolithic China whose domestic (digital) industry's levers were fully handled by the Party and whose society was fully controlled and socially engineered.

On this ground, this book humbly tries to interpret China's and Chinese stakeholders' engagement with Internet governance at the global level, actively rejecting simplistic depictions and trying instead to do justice—as far as possible—to the complexity of China's domestic stakeholder ecosystem and its relationship with a global Internet governance complex whose rules predate the rise of China (and of its industry) to superpower status. This book is the result of a project which dates back to 2018: it is a doctoral research conducted at the University of Bologna that has been elaborated into a thesis, while bits and pieces of it have been published in the form of academic articles. This book brings the pieces back together and adds new insights into the evolution of China's domestic Internet governance ecosystem to better interpret the involvement of Chinese stakeholders with Internet governance at the global level.

In short, through its pages this book (for which I thank the editorial team, the anonymous reviewers, and the proofreader Rosemary Claire Burnham) addresses some open questions about the relationship between two realms people must gain awareness of: China and the global governance of the Internet.

Trento, Italy   Riccardo Nanni

Acknowledgements

I thank Sonia Lucarelli and Matteo Dian for supervising this research during my years as a Ph.D. student and George Christou for his advice and mentorship. I would also like to thank Jamal Shahin and Joe Burton for their invaluable comments on this work when it still was at the doctoral thesis stage. Furthermore, I wish to thank the twenty-nine interview participants, without whom this research would have not been possible.

A special thanks goes also to Mauro Santaniello, Claudia Padovani, Farzaneh Badii, Milton Mueller, Bhawna Pokharna, Sung Chull Kim, Andrea Ghiselli, Simone Dossi, Tatiana Tropina, Ashwin Mathew, Elisa Oreglia, Shaun Breslin, Francesco Niccolò Moro, Giampiero Giacomello, Andrea Calderaro, Lorenzo Zambernardi, Niels ten Oever, Christoph Becker, and Antonio Fiori who all gave valuable comments to this work, whether at the thesis or the book stage.

Finally, a special personal recognition goes to my parents, Massimo and Roberta, and my partner Rosie, for firmly and unquestionably supporting me through a learning and professional path made of many unknowns and very few certainties.

Competing Interests

None. This research was fully funded by the University of Bologna through a Ph.D. scholarship.

Ethics Approval

This study was performed in line with the principles of the Declaration of Helsinki. The author followed all the legal and institutional rules applicable to this research. The author also abided by the research-oriented ethical guidelines available in the European Union to the best of his knowledge. Informed consent was obtained from individual interview participants. The form in which direct quotes are presented has been agreed upon between the author and the individual interview participant ad hoc.

Contents

1 Introduction 1
   1.1 *A Few Open Questions…* 1
   1.2 *China's Rise and the Future of the Liberal International Order* 4
   1.3 *Internet Governance, Chinese Stakeholders, and the Liberal Order* 8
   1.4 *In This Book* 10
   1.5 *What This Book Is Not About…* 12
   1.6 *Book Structure* 13
   References 15

2 China, Internet Governance, and the Liberal International Order 21
   2.1 *Introduction* 21
   2.2 *China's Rise, the Liberal International Order, and Contestation in Global Governance* 22
   2.3 *Global Internet governance: What It Entails and Why It Matters* 23
   2.4 *The Question of Multistakeholderism: What Is at Stake for the Liberal Order* 33
   2.5 *Internet Fragmentation: A Challenge to the Liberal Order in Its Global Reach?* 38
   2.6 *A Few Notes on Policy- and Standard-Making Functioning* 42

		2.6.1	Internet Corporation for Assigned Names and Numbers	42
		2.6.2	Internet Engineering Task Force	42
		2.6.3	Third Generation Partnership Project	43
		2.6.4	One Final Remark	45
	2.7	A Short Note on Theory and Methods		46
	2.8	Conclusion		48
	References			49
3	Situating Chinese Engagement in Internet Governance: China's Domestic Digital Policy Reviewed			57
	3.1	Introduction		57
	3.2	Phase 1: 1994–2008. Information Control and Capital Deregulation		61
	3.3	Phase 2: 2009–2016. Information Control and Platform Bans		66
	3.4	Phase 3: 2016–ongoing. Internet sovereignty and Common Prosperity		71
	3.5	Analysis and Discussion		77
	3.6	Conclusive Remarks		79
	References			79
4	On the Normative Impact of Chinese Stakeholders in the Governance of Critical Internet Resources: A Document- and Interview-Based Analysis			87
	4.1	Introduction		87
	4.2	Chinese Stakeholders' Actions at the Core of Internet Governance		88
	4.3	Chinese Stakeholders and Multistakeholder Governance at ICANN		91
	4.4	Chinese Actors and the IETF: Public–Private Relations in Standard-Making		97
	4.5	What Is at Stake?		105
	4.6	Conclusion		108
	References			112
5	On the Normative Impact of Chinese Stakeholders in Mobile Internet Standard-Making. A Document- and Interview-Based Analysis			119
	5.1	Introduction		119

5.2	Road to 3G: Domestic Constraints, Market Drivers, and Chinese Stakeholders' Early Engagement in 3GPP	121
5.3	A Change in Strategy: Drivers and Implications of China's Approach to 4G	125
5.4	5G: Chinese Companies' Catch-Up in Telecommunications	129
5.5	The Rise of China (and Chinese Industry) in Telecommunications: Normative Implications	131
5.6	Conclusion	134
	References	138

6 The Rise of China, Internet Fragmentation, and the Future of Multistakeholderism: Implications for the Liberal International Order — 143

6.1	Introduction	143
6.2	Chinese Actors in 3GPP: What Consequences for Multistakeholderism, Interoperability, and Internet Fragmentation?	145
6.3	Observing Multistakeholderism and Fragmentation at the Core: Chinese Actors in the IETF and ICANN	149
6.4	Final Remarks	157
	References	158

7 Conclusion — 165

7.1	Recap	165
7.2	Empirical Findings and Their Academic and Policy Relevance	166
7.3	Theoretical Implications and Their Relevance	168
7.4	Caveats and Future Venues for Research	170
7.5	Final Remarks	173
	References	173

Appendix A	177
Appendix B	199
Index	203

About the Author

Riccardo Nanni is a researcher in Data Governance at the Digital Commons Lab of Fondazione Bruno Kessler, a research institute based in Trento, Italy. Previously, he obtained a Ph.D. in Political and Social Sciences at the University of Bologna. His Ph.D. thesis informs this book. Furthermore, Riccardo Nanni is an active member of the Global Internet Governance Academic Network (Giganet), one of the world's main academic associations of Internet governance scholars, and participates in the Internet Governance Forum mainly at national and regional levels. Previously, he published articles in international journals such as *Telecommunications Policy* and *Information, Communication and Society* and co-edited the book *Quo vadis, sovereignty? New conceptual and regulatory boundaries in the age of digital China* published by Springer. He spent two six-month periods in China in 2016/2017 and 2018/2019, first as an exchange student at Guangzhou University and later as a trainee at the European Union's Delegation to China. His plans to conduct field study in China during his Ph.D. were hampered by the Covid-19 pandemic, so research activities were moved online. Nonetheless, he hopes to have the chance to conduct research in China in the near future.

LIST OF TABLES

Table 2.1	Key moments in Internet governance history for China	25
Table 2.2	'Multistakeholder' and 'multilateral' Internet governance in sum	33
Table 2.3	The TCP/IP model (Harcourt et al., 2020; Russell, 2013)	38
Table 2.3	The TCP/IP model (Harcourt et al., 2020; Russell, 2013)	144
Table A.1	A summary of this book's research methods and their objectives	192

CHAPTER 1

Introduction

1.1 A Few Open Questions...

Will China fragment the Internet? Is China bringing authoritarian state influence in the governance of the Internet's resources? Is China rewriting the protocols (and rules) of the global Internet?

These questions are widespread in the media, academic, and policy environments alike (see for example: Murgia & Gross, 2020; Hoffmann et al., 2020; Segal, 2018). The trade competition between the United States (US) and China that exploded under the Trump administration affected the development of digital technologies and led to new and increasing protectionist measures, especially on the US side with the exclusion of Huawei from the US infrastructure market and the various (more or less successful) bans on Chinese platforms (Ciuriak, 2019; Poggetti, 2021). China, on the other hand, has enhanced its spur for technological self-sufficiency while many foreign investors have left the country (Lubin, 2023). This fired up the media and policy debates around China's role in Internet governance. However, sectors of academia and the technical communities demand more nuanced views (Mueller, 2017; Negro, 2020; Sharp & Kolkman, 2020), rejecting polarised conclusions on the aforementioned questions and observing the ongoing technological and market developments from a political and economic standpoint.

More formally, this book addresses the following research questions: *(To what extent) are Chinese stakeholders reshaping the rules of Global*

Internet Governance?. And more in particular: (i) (To what extent) are Chinese stakeholders contributing to increased state influence in multistakeholder fora?; (ii) (how) is China contributing to Internet fragmentation?; and (iii) what are the main drivers of Chinese stakeholders' stances?

Critical views have emerged in the literature throughout the last two decades warning against oversimplified views of the Internet and its politics (Morozov, 2011). Indeed, the definition of "Internet Governance" is itself debated (Mueller & Badiei, 2020). This debate is better illustrated below, while this book is mainly concentrated on the making of technical connectivity standards (both essential Internet standards and Internet connectivity infrastructures such as 5G) and the distribution of critical Internet resources (namely IP addresses and domain names).[1] Regarding the oversimplification of Internet-related political debates, the liberational expectations on cyberspace that characterised US cyber-libertarianism in the 1990s, with a view of the Internet as a democratising and people-empowering force, were followed by disillusionment over the failure of online platforms to serve as a safe space for progressive civil society organisations, such as during the Arab Springs (Wolfsfeld et al., 2013). In their aftermath, the PRISM scandal revealed a massive surveillance programme in a liberal democracy such as the US (Bauman et al., 2014), while new scandals connecting social media with surveillance in totalitarian states and unethical meddling in democratic elections (such as the Cambridge Analytica case) raised calls for platform regulation and increased control on online activities by the public authority (Hinds et al., 2020; Radu, 2019).

Beyond the level of platforms and their public role, literature has been systematically observing a turn to infrastructure in Internet governance. This concept entails that technical matters related to the backbone of the Internet, including its addressing system as well as the physical infrastructure, have become politicised and have been used for political ends by state actors (DeNardis & Musiani, 2016; Musiani, 2013). In this context, China has often been portrayed as a state actor ready to detach from the global Internet by establishing a national *splinternet* while promoting a more state-centric Internet governance model internationally (Hoffmann et al., 2020; Segal, 2016, 2018). This view however is contested

---

[1] See Sect. 1.5 for further clarification of this book's thematic boundaries.

in literature (Creemers, 2020; Negro, 2020), as will be further argued throughout the book.

This book is principally grounded in International Relations (IR) literature, bringing this discipline into dialogue with China Studies and Science and Technology Studies. It observes the interaction of Chinese public and private actors in selected core aspects of Internet governance to interpret the normative impact and drivers of their actions.

Observing the rise of China in the realm of Internet governance is of utmost importance as it strikes at the very heart of the Liberal International Order.[2] As a US creation, the Internet's predecessor Arpanet is representative of Washington's Cold-War era technological leadership, which in turn is a tool for hegemony (Carr, 2015). The establishment of multistakeholder governance mechanisms for the Internet in the 1990s under US guidance is epitomical of the US's hegemony in the so-called 'unipolar decade'. The prominent role recognised by private actors in the governance mechanisms of critical Internet resources (the essential elements of a technology that now connects several billion people all over the globe) represents the global spread of the Liberal Order in its free-market tenet (Santaniello, 2021; Scholte, 2017). At the same time, the growing attempts by governments across the world—including among liberal democracies—to establish some form of regulatory control on big tech's activities has spurred a new debate on digital sovereignty and other related, partially overlapping concepts (Haggart et al., 2021).

Through this analysis, this book explores whether, why, and how Chinese stakeholders contest or adapt to existing norms in Internet governance, including the Internet's core protocols allowing global interconnectivity. This research brings a twofold conclusion. First, Chinese public and private stakeholders have adapted to (and, at times, adopted) the existing normative order of multistakeholder global Internet governance. This is the case because they have built their major influence within it, hence facing no need to engage in remaking the governance mechanisms anew. Second, China is not pushing for Internet fragmentation. On the contrary, Chinese stakeholders are involved in Internet standardisation with a view to retaining global technical interoperability to maximise their economic advantage, while the Chinese government seeks to foster online societal control by ruling data and information flows domestically.

---

[2] For further discussion on the origins and definitions of the Liberal International Order, see Sect. 1.2 and Chapter 2.

This carries implications around the resilience of global Internet governance and the Liberal International Order at large. These statements are illustrated and motivated throughout the book.

The next section introduces the debate on the future of the Liberal International Order amid the rise of China. Section 1.3 then builds on the previous section to contextualise the debate on Chinese stakeholders in Internet governance. Sections 1.4 and 1.5 set the boundaries of the debates addressed in this book, while Sect. 1.6 illustrates the book structure.

1.2 China's Rise and the Future of the Liberal International Order

The Liberal International Order is the international order established after World War II under US leadership based on free market and international law, institutionally represented in such organisations as the World Trade Organisation (WTO) and the United Nations (UN) respectively (Parsi, 2021). Normatively, the Liberal International Order is state-centric and sovereignty-based in the Westphalian tradition but allows and recognises actorness to non-state actors in its free-market characterisation (Ikenberry, 2018). This latter element grants non-state actors a strong influence in certain normative aspects. Indeed, the concept of global governance, conceived as 'governance without government' (Rosenau, 1992), features a transnational element that entails non-state actors across national lines interacting in policymaking. After all, the UN itself grants corporations and non-governmental organisations a role in several of its agencies' policymaking processes (Beisheim & Simon, 2018; Clapham, 2022).

While after World War II the Liberal International Order could be seen as mainly a 'club' of Western nations (inasmuch as the communist bloc did not participate in a globalised free market) from the 1990s onwards, the Liberal Order achieved global reach (Parsi, 2021). This, of course, does not entail global acceptance of liberal normativity at all national levels and the fadeaway of global normative contestation à la Fukuyama (1989), but rather the solidification of a global order based on universalistic claims (such as the treaty-based institutionalisation of universal human rights) with a conflicting Westphalian element of state sovereignty and non-interference in domestic affairs. The Westphalian element allows for the inclusion of countries featuring a non-liberal domestic polity within the institutions of the Liberal International Order (Ikenberry, 2018), while allowing for ambiguity and tension among the applicable rules (Carpenter, 2022).[3]

The debate on the crisis of the Liberal International Order amid the rise of China has been the object of academic discussion for at least two decades (Acharya, 2018; Bo, 2018; Buzan, 2010; Duncombe & Dunne, 2018; Friedberg, 2005; Glaser, 2011; Ikenberry, 2008, 2018; Mearsheimer, 2006, 2019; Zheng, 2005). The way China has conducted its diplomatic activity at various levels of global governance and within the designated bodies has led observers to portray this emerging international actor either as a rule-breaker or as a rule-shaper—hinting at times at its willingness to become a rule-maker. Whether or not China's growing assertiveness will result in a reshaping of the rules of the existing order or the establishment of a new one—possibly following a hegemonic war—is the main open question (Ikenberry, 2018).

This debate is reflected in the field of global Internet governance. The existing multistakeholder governance model is liberal-informed, inasmuch as it is private-led and founded by the US, and China has posed as a critic of it in favour of a multilateral/intergovernmental mechanism since its very beginning (Flonk et al., 2020; Negro, 2020). However, China's attitude has changed over time as illustrated in this book.

To contextualise the debate on China and Internet governance, one needs first to look at the broader question of China's rise and it's positioning vis-à-vis the Liberal International Order. At the systemic level, part of the broader debate on China's rise and the decline of the Liberal International Order focuses on the likelihood of a hegemonic war and the replacement of the existing order with a China-led one. The Chinese academic, political, and diplomatic communities have always stressed the peacefulness of China's rise. Famously elaborated by Zheng Bijian (2005), a senior Chinese International Relations scholar and politician, the concept of 'peaceful rise' has quickly entered the 'Western' debate. It was however in the same year that Friedberg (2005) first warned that China's rise was likely to lead to a hegemonic war with the US. This view was soon echoed by Mearsheimer (2006), who dubbed China's rise as necessarily 'unpeaceful'. He finds in the security dilemma posed by the

---

[3] See for example: the inviolability of state sovereignty versus states' treaty-based obligations to monitor each others' human rights records, both being principles enshrined in the Charter of the United Nations (Walker, 2020).

anarchical nature of state-to-state relations, whereby no state can be reassured over others' intentions, the reason for US's and China's quests for regional (as a proxy for global) hegemony to end in war. The challenge for China's international image as a rising power was acknowledged by its domestic elite, to the extent that the expression 'peaceful rise' was changed to 'peaceful development' in the Chinese Communist Party's (CCP) official policy to render it less threatening to a foreign audience (Kissinger, 2011).

While widespread, the 'China threat theory' is not accepted by the whole Western academic community, especially in its most extreme and deterministic fashion as expressed in Mearsheimer's (2006) so-called 'offensive realism'. On the contrary, in an optimist liberal reading, Ikenberry (2008, 2011, 2018) stresses the resilience of the Liberal International Order in accommodating the assertiveness of newly emerged powers. If China is allowed to grow powerful in the existing order, the argument goes, it will have no incentive to disrupt and replace it. Since the Liberal International Order allowed China to become the second most economically powerful country in the world by accepting it within its institutions and organisations, such as the World Trade Organisation, China is set to become a member of the international order and see no need to confront the US militarily. It might, in his view, pose as a revisionist on specific elements of the international order, but not as an order-maker.

It would, however, be a blunt simplification to assume that the whole 'China's rise debate' debate runs along a realism-liberalism dichotomy. Whereas Mearsheimer (2006, 2019) and Ikenberry (2008, 2011, 2018) are the two ends of the spectrum, other scholars fall in between, maintaining that structural elements of the international system do play a role in pushing the US and China towards competition and confrontation (Glaser, 2011; Wang, 2011). Nonetheless, the rational management of the confrontation by the two countries' elites can avoid armed conflicts in his view. Mearsheimer's (2001) offensive realism foresees the 'tragedy of great power politics', a scenario in which tension between existing and rising powers are doomed to escalate to armed conflicts and culminate in a hegemonic war. While acknowledging the centrality of the systemic level of analysis, Glaser (2011) adds the element of individual/group reasoning in the analysis, reaching the deeply different conclusion that hegemonic war can be avoided if elites act rationally.

In the Chinese scholarship, the non-deterministic line is followed by Wang Jisi (2011), who maintains that:

> [i]f the international community appears not to understand China's aspirations [and needs], the Chinese people may ask themselves why China should be bound by rules that were essentially established by the Western powers. China can rightfully be expected to take on more international responsibilities. But then the international community should take on the responsibility of helping the world's largest member support itself.

In Wang's (2011) account, the capacity of state leaders to communicate and acknowledge each other's intentions and needs can prevent a hegemonic war. This interactionist approach appears dominant in Chinese IR literature (Y. Qin, 2012; Yan, 2014), although theoretical understandings differ. Indeed, at the time of writing tension is growing internationally and the leaderships of competing countries seem less and less willing to communicate and trust one another, yielding the emergence of blocks and spheres of influence (Ikenberry, 2024).

The debate on China's adaptation and contestation to the Liberal International Order (Ikenberry, 2018; Wang, 2011), rather than its existential threat, is complicated by the emergence of private-based governance and regime complexity. Private-based governance encompasses technical standard-making venues as well as sectors of market and economic governance where such actors as companies or civil society enjoy actorness and can influence decision-making (Zürn, 2018). In turn, regime complexity defines a governance ecosystem whereby one macro-topic is addressed by an indefinite number of fora, more or less global in scope, which are loosely interdependent and at times partially overlapping in scope and membership (Nye, 2014).

Regime complexity and private-based governance are two intertwined concepts as the former creates venues for a multitude of public and private actors to participate in policymaking, whereas the latter fosters the creation of overlapping regimes whereby a variety of actors addresses more or less overlapping topics of interest (Gómez-Mera, 2016; Kawabata, 2020; Westwinter, 2021).

In this view, this book does not focus on the debates on the (real or presumed) existential threat of China to the Liberal International Order, but rather on the normative challenge that China (and its domestic stakeholders) pose to the Liberal International Order in terms of influence in policymaking and of the reshaping of the existing rules and norms of liberal-informed global governance. This is addressed by observing multistakeholder, private-based global Internet governance in selected venues as an example of a public–private governance regime complex where several stakeholders enjoy actorness and carry their interests along and across traditional national and geopolitical lines. This governance setting is normatively liberal in its private-led characterisation, as further illustrated in the next subsection.

1.3 Internet Governance, Chinese Stakeholders, and the Liberal Order

When it comes to Internet governance, its multistakeholder characterisation is epitomical of the Liberal International Order in its free-market tenet (Palladino & Santaniello, 2021). Conversely, Internet governance models based on state sovereignty have historically been promoted by emerging and contesting authoritarian states (Flonk et al., 2020). In this view, challenges to the normative order (Kettemann, 2020) of the Internet from non-liberal actors in hegemonic competition with the US can be read within the broader debate on the future of the Liberal International Order. Nonetheless, increasing calls for increased state sovereignty over the realm of Internet governance and platform regulation are also emerging in liberal democracies, from liberal and non-liberal political actors alike (Haggart et al., 2021). Within the debate on the future of the Liberal International Order, the rise of China has been discussed for two decades and from the mid-2010s onwards the geopolitical competition between the US and China has become strongly focused on technological leadership—leading to forms of protectionism and reciprocal sanctions (Ciuriak, 2019)—thus fostering debates on the return of the state in Internet governance and the rise of digital sovereignty (Creemers, 2020; Haggart et al., 2021). Indeed, the term "digital sovereignty" itself is a contested one as, at the time of writing, it has not been defined in the policy field. Furthermore, its meaning partially overlaps with that of similar terms such as Internet sovereignty, which was elaborated in China and is built upon previous concepts such as "information sovereignty" (Cong & Thumfart, 2022; Gong, 2005; Jiang, 2010). The origin of these terms in China is discussed in further detail in Chapter 3.

Observing Chinese norm entrepreneurship in the regime complex for Internet governance through a variety of qualitative methods allows one to qualify and interpret the extent and impact of Chinese stakeholders' contestation of Internet governance norms. In this study, the author observes the processes of normative contestation, but also adaptation, to the existing norms, Chinese stakeholders conduct within the Internet governance regime complex. While the regime complex entails hundreds of norm-making actors and venues (Radu, 2019), this book looks at three key fora: the Internet Corporation for Assigned Names and Numbers (ICANN), the Internet Engineering Task Force (IETF), and the Third Generation Partnership Project (3GPP). These three bodies deal with key technical and eminently political aspects of Internet governance: the management of critical Internet resources, including unique identifiers such as IP (Internet Protocol) addresses (ICANN); the making of Internet standards, including the aforementioned critical resources (IETF); and the making of mobile connectivity standards such as the fifth-generation telephony technology (5G) (3GPP). These allow one to look at normative contestation at the core of the Internet infrastructure (DeNardis & Musiani, 2016), while also looking at the development of a strongly politicised technology such as 5G, which may influence the functioning of the Internet's basic standards in the near future (ten Oever, 2022).

Coherently with the multistakeholder characteristics of the Internet governance regime complex, this book analyses not only the actions of China and Chinese governmental actors but also those of Chinese non-state stakeholders.[4] While the unknowns on governmental control of private actors are manifold when looking at China, this book makes no prior assumption on the extent to which such control holds (Galloway & He, 2014; Wen, 2020). Instead, it observes the behaviour of companies and other stakeholders within ICANN, IETF, and 3GPP and includes the views of several groups of stakeholders through interviews. In particular, this book incorporates opinions from the technical community, that is,

---

[4] The definition of non-state stakeholders can be contentious within China. As better illustrated in Chapter 2 and throughout the book, doubts exist about how strong the Communist Party's control is on private companies (Becker et al., 2024). Furthermore, a formally Marxist-Leninist state apparatus does not feature a public-private distinction (Kruger, 2021). Nonetheless, China's shift towards free market since the 1980s yielded the rise of private capitals and companies whose interest can conflict with the Party line (Negro, 2020). This is illustrated empirically throughout the book.

those people involved in standard-making on a daily basis. Such experts possess technical knowledge otherwise inaccessible to social scientists, which provides them with a privileged view on political topics and allows them to reach qualitatively different conclusions on similar questions compared to policy experts. Furthermore, their role in the making of such technology is of utmost political salience given the politicisation of the issue in question. Incorporating their views in this research provides a basis for nuanced interpretations often missed in International Relations literature (Hornsby & Parshotam, 2018; Tanczer et al., 2018).

Whether China is contributing to centralising governance in the hands of states and to fragmenting the Internet is an open question in the literature. What will the "Internet of the future" look like if standard-making and resources distribution moves into the hands of state-centric agencies? (How) will seamless cross-border communication work across *splinternets*? Conversely, should Internet fragmentation not take place, and should authoritarian powers like China increasingly accept multistakeholderism and the existing Internet architecture, what will the existing liberal-informed Internet governance mechanisms look like in the near future?

This research has implications for all these matters. In turn, the debates addressed in the forthcoming chapters touch directly upon the debate on the rise of China in the Liberal International Order. While findings on Internet governance are not directly transferable to the whole of the order, this research suggests that there are facets of it that create incentives and conditions for actors to adapt to existing normative orders other than challenging them (Ikenberry, 2018; Wang, 2011).

1.4　In This Book

Multistakeholderism in Internet governance has been subjected to criticism and contestation since the establishment of ICANN in 1998. The liberal characterisation of the multistakeholder mechanisms of Internet governance emerges normatively in its openness to private stakeholders' participation and limited state role (Palladino & Santaniello, 2021; Scholte, 2017), coherently with the idea of transnationality in global governance surged to prominence in the 1990s (Rosenau, 1992). The extent to which such openness is a rhetorical artifice hiding power dynamics has been debated through time (Cath, 2021; Palladino & Santaniello, 2021). As a matter of fact, the special role played by the

US Department of Commerce (DoC) through its contractual position vis-à-vis ICANN has been one of the main points of contention until the contract's conclusion in 2016 (Mueller, 2017). In that context, the ICANN-centred multistakeholder governance model was contested by emerging authoritarian powers, chiefly Russia and China, who sought to push forward a state-based model (Flonk et al., 2020; Glen, 2014). The sovereigntist stances in Internet governance contributed to a growing debate over the risk of Internet fragmentation (Hoffmann et al., 2020), with normative contestation remaining an ongoing subject (Negro, 2020). In academia and oftentimes among practitioners, criticisms levelled against multistakeholderism involve its being strongly private-driven and therefore dominated by business interests (Cath, 2021; Palladino & Santaniello, 2021).

This book will dive deeper into such debates. In particular, this book observes the influence of Chinese actors, that is, China's government and Chinese non-state Internet stakeholders, on the norms of Global Internet Governance. This addresses a topic of increasing policy importance amid growing tension and competition between the US and China in the technology sector, while addressing the scholarly debates on Internet fragmentation and digital sovereignty, that is, the return of states in Internet governance (Haggart et al., 2021; Mueller, 2017).

In short, this research contributes to two major debates in the global Internet governance literature: (i) multistakeholderism and the role of governments in global Internet governance (Palladino & Santaniello, 2021); and (ii) alignment and fragmentation of the Internet (Mueller, 2017). More broadly, by addressing these two debates, this book sheds light on the decades-old debate on the future of the Liberal International Order and the question of digital sovereignty.

The first debate concerns relations among stakeholder groups in global Internet governance and the future of the multistakeholder system; the second debate focuses instead on whether the global Internet is here to stay or will yield regional and national 'splinternets'—that is, whether China is creating a separate national Internet, or instead controlling online information flows domestically through regulations while participating in and shaping the rules of the global Internet. This has implications for the realm of Internet governance strictly conceived as the management of the Internet's critical resources (Mueller, 2017; Mueller & Badiei, 2020; Raymond & DeNardis, 2015), but also for the realm of standard-making (Harcourt et al., 2020; ten Oever, 2022).

Together, these two debates feed into the emerging literature on digital sovereignty, with the return of state in Internet governance and the establishment of state-led control on the Internet architecture as two main features (Haggart et al., 2021; Musiani, 2022).

While these debates are often framed dichotomously, this research rejects the most dualistic views and tries to elaborate a nuanced interpretation of Chinese actors' role in Internet governance, acknowledging ambiguities in normative acceptance and contestation. As anticipated, contestation of the Liberal International Order comes not only from emerging state powers and their national actors but also from inside the 'core' of the Liberal Order itself (Börzel & Zürn, 2021; Deudney & Ikenberry, 2018). This is explored throughout the next chapter. In the same way, criticism of multistakeholderism and private-based governance is not purely from emerging non-liberal powers, but also from Western allies and Western scholars (Belli, 2015; Cath, 2021; Santaniello, 2021). Nonetheless, while acknowledging it, this book's focus will be on contestation from emerging actors, that is, China's state- and non-state stakeholders.

Through this analysis, this book contributes to the broader debate on China's rise and its challenge to the Liberal International Order. In particular, it looks at Internet governance as a peculiar largely private-based governance mechanism, whereby a number of public and private stakeholders enjoy actorness in policymaking in a myriad of loosely coupled regime settings, thus blurring the lines of what is often identified as 'national strategy' (Nye, 2014).

1.5 What This Book Is Not About…

Internet governance is often used as a catch-all term including any digital-related policy. As is more deeply discussed in the next chapter, its conceptual borders are blurred. This book addresses infrastructural matters, namely the standardisation of Internet infrastructure at the IETF, the distribution of critical Internet resources (or the distribution of unique identifiers) at ICANN, and the standardisation of the mobile connectivity infrastructure at 3GPP, which constitutes an Internet-based service as well as an infrastructure that grants access to the Internet—though not fitting the Internet standards category strictly speaking (more about it in the next chapter).

This book, however, does not address platform governance, cybersecurity, or China's domestic Internet governance system. The latter's evolution is discussed in Chapter 3 to facilitate a more nuanced understanding of the complexity of China's domestic ecosystem and the relationship between the Chinese government and China's domestic private actors. However, this book is rooted mainly in International Relations as a discipline and therefore addresses the role and impact of Chinese public and private stakeholders in global Internet governance. Likewise, platform governance and cybersecurity are occasionally touched upon as they intersect with infrastructural matters. Nonetheless, they do not constitute the core matter of this book.

The next subsection illustrates the book structure to guide the reader through the volume.

1.6 Book Structure

Chapter 2 delves deeper into the existing literature and policy debates introduced in the introduction. To begin with, this chapter provides a critical discussion of Internet governance debates on Internet fragmentation and multistakeholder governance (in general and around Chinese stakeholders' engagement) in the context of growing debates on digital sovereignty. Then, the chapter presents theoretical and methodological notes on regime complexity and norm entrepreneurship, which drive the author's interpretation of his findings.

Chapter 3 analyses the transformation of China's domestic digital policies in the last thirty years. This is to provide context to China's and Chinese stakeholders' engagement with global Internet governance, which is the core topic of this book. The chapter's objective is to show that domestically China is not a monolithic whole but features a number of actors with partially overlapping but often contrasting interests.

Chapter 4 provides qualitative empirical evidence on Chinese stakeholders' engagement in the governance (standardisation and distribution) of critical Internet resources. Based on document analysis and interviews, this chapter brings a twofold contribution. First, it shows how Chinese engagement in this subset has transformed in time and how, instead, it features continuity in certain aspects. Second, implications for Internet fragmentation and the future of multistakeholder Internet governance. Based on empirical findings, this chapter argues that Chinese stakeholders have progressively integrated into the functioning of Internet standardisation at the IETF and resource distribution at ICANN. The chapter concludes that the more Chinese stakeholders have become capable of influencing decision-making within the IETF and ICANN, the more they have accepted their norms and functioning mechanisms.

Similarly to the previously described chapter, Chapter 5 provides qualitative empirical evidence on Chinese stakeholders' engagement in mobile connectivity infrastructure standardisation. Based on document analysis and interviews, this chapter brings a twofold contribution. First, it shows how Chinese engagement in this second subset has transformed over time and how it also features continuity in certain aspects. Second, it discusses implications for Internet fragmentation and the future of multistakeholder Internet governance in a sector that deeply influences Internet politics. Based on qualitative findings from interviews and documents, the chapter finds that in mobile connectivity standardisation, much like in critical Internet resources governance, Chinese stakeholders have progressively integrated themselves into the functioning of the existing mechanisms and reached a dominant position on par with historically dominant European actors.

Chapter 6 discusses the empirical findings illustrated in the previous chapters in the light of regime complexity and norm entrepreneurship literature. It draws conclusions on Chinese stakeholders' engagement in Internet governance and its implications. This chapter brings three conclusions. First, Chinese stakeholders have progressively engaged in multistakeholder Internet governance. The more they become powerful, the more they can influence decision-making. The more they can influence decision-making, the lower their interest in replacing the existing governance mechanisms. Second, Chinese stakeholders are not pushing for Internet fragmentation. The more Chinese industries grow, the more they become interested in a globally unified Internet infrastructure as this allows them to market the same devices all over the world. To foster societal control, the Chinese government is resorting to regulatory control rather than Internet fragmentation at the infrastructure level. Third and final, as global Internet and multistakeholder Internet governance are byproducts of the liberal international order, these findings show that Chinese stakeholders are interested in participating in the order and influencing its normativity from within rather than engaging in the making of a new order.

Finally, the conclusions draw the closing remarks on the research illustrated in the book. This book is followed by two appendices, Appendix A expands on the research methods adopted in this research, while

Appendix B presents a sample interview questionnaire used during data collection.

REFERENCES

Acharya, A. (2018). *The End of American World Order* (2nd ed.). Polity Press.
Alcaro, R. (2018). The Liberal Order and its Contestations. A Conceptual Framework. *the International Spectator, 53*(1), 1–10.
Bauman, Z., Bigo, D., Esteves, P., Guild, E., Jabri, V., Lyon, D., & Walker, R. B. (2014). After Snowden: Rethinking the Impact of Surveillance. *International Political Sociology, 8*(2), 121–144.
Becker, C., ten Oever, N., & Nanni, R. (2024). Interrogating the Standardisation of Surveillance in 5G amid US-China Competition. *Information, Communication and Society, 0*(0).
Beisheim, M., & Simon, N. (2018). Multistakeholder Partnerships for the SDGs: Actors' Views on UN Metagovernance. *Global Governance: A Review of Multilateralism and International Organizations, 24*(4), 497–515.
Belli, L. (2015). A Heterostakeholder Cooperation for Sustainable Internet Policymaking. *Internet Policy Review, 4*(2), 1–21.
Bo, P. (2018). China, Global Governance, and Hegemony: Neo-gramscian Perspective in the World Order. *Journal of China and International Relations, 6*(1), 48–72.
Börzel, T. A., & Zürn, M. (2021). Contestations of the Liberal International Order: From Liberal Multilateralism to Postnational Liberalism. *International Organization, 75*(2), 282–305.
Buzan, B. (2010). China in International Society: Is 'Peaceful Rise' Possible? *The Chinese Journal of International Politics, 3*(1), 5–36.
Carpenter, T. G. (2022). Ukraine: A War to Save the Rules-Based International Order? *Policy Commons.* https://policycommons.net/artifacts/3087845/ukraine/3888663/ (January 19, 2024).
Carr, M. (2015). Power Plays in Global Internet Governance. *Millennium: Journal of International Studies, 43*(2), 640–659.
Cath, C. (2021). The Technology We Choose to Create: Human Rights Advocacy in the Internet Engineering Task Force. *Telecommunications Policy, 45*(6). https://doi.org/10.1016/j.telpol.2021.102144.
Ciuriak, D. (2019). The US-China Trade War: Technological Roots and WTO Responses. *Global Solutions Journal, 4*, 130–135.
Clapham, A. (2022). Non-State Actors. In D. Moeckli, S. Shah & S. Sivakumaran (Eds.), *International Human Rights Law* (3rd ed.). Oxford University Press.
Cong, W., & Thumfart, J. (2022). A Chinese Precursor to the Digital Sovereignty Debate: Digital Anti-colonialism and Authoritarianism from the Post-Cold war era to the Tunis Agenda. *Global Studies Quarterly, 2*(4), 1–13.

Creemers, R. (2020). China's Conception of Cyber Sovereignty: Rhetoric and Realization. In D. Broeders & B. Van den Berg (Eds.), *Governing Cyberspace. Behavior, Power, and Diplomacy*. Rowman and Littlefield.

DeNardis, L., & Musiani, F. (2016). Governance by Infrastructure. In F. Musiani, D. Cogburn, L. DeNardis & N. S. Levinson (Eds.), *The Turn to Infrastructure in Internet Governance*. Palgrave Macmillan.

Deudney, D., & Ikenberry, G. J. (2018, July). The Resilient Order. *Foreign Affairs*. https://www.foreignaffairs.com/articles/world/2018-06-14/liberal-world (March 23, 2020).

Duncombe, C., & Dunne, T. (2018). After liberal world order. *International Affairs, 94*(1), 25–42.

Flonk, D., Jachtenfuchs, M., & Obendiek, A. S. (2020). Authority Conflicts in Internet Governance: Liberals vs. Sovereigntists? *Global Constitutionalism, 9*(2): 364–386.

Friedberg, A. L. (2005). The Future of U.S.-China Relations: Is Conflict Inevitable? *International Security, 30*(2): 7–45.

Fukuyama, F. (1989). The End of History? *The National Interest, 16*, 3–18.

Galloway, T., & He, B. (2014). "China and Technical Global Internet Governance: Beijing's Approach to Multi-Stakeholder Governance within ICANN, WSIS and the IGF", *China: An International Journal, 12*(3), 72–93.

Glaser, C. (2011). Will China's Rise Lead to War? Why Realism Does Not Mean Pessimism. *Foreign Affairs, 90*(2), 80–91.

Glen, C. M. (2014). Internet Governance: Territorializing Cyberspace? *Politics and Policy, 42*(5), 635–657.

Gómez-Mera, L. (2016). Regime Complexity and Global Governance: The Case of Trafficking in Persons. *European Journal of International Relations, 22*(3), 566–595.

Gong, W. (2005). Information Sovereignty Reviewed. *Intercultural. Communication Studies, 14*(1), 119–135.

Haggart, B., Scholte, J. A., & Tusikov, N. (2021). Introduction. Return of the State? In B. Haggart, N. Tusikov & J. A. Scholte (Eds.), *Power and Authority in Internet Governance. Return of the State?* Routledge.

Harcourt, A., Christou, G., & Simpson, S. (2020). *Global Standard Setting in Internet Governance*. Oxford University Press.

Hinds, J., Williams, E. J., & Joinson, A. N. (2020). "It wouldn't happen to me": Privacy Concerns and Perspectives Following the Cambridge Analytica Scandal. *International Journal of Human-Computer Studies, 143*, 102498.

Hoffmann, S., Lazanski, D., & Taylor, E. (2020). Standardising the Splinternet: How China's Technical Standards Could Fragment the Internet. *Journal of Cyber Policy, 5*(2), 239–264.

Hornsby, D. J., & Parshotam, A. (2018). Science Diplomacy, Epistemic Communities, and Practice in Sub-Saharan Africa. *Global Policy, 9*, 29–34.

Ikenberry, G. J. (2008). The Rise of China and the Future of the West - Can the Liberal System Survive? *Foreign Affairs, 87*(1), 23–37.
Ikenberry, G. J. (2011). *Liberal Leviathan: The Origins, Crisis, and Transformation of the American World Order.* Princeton University Press.
Ikenberry, G. J. (2018). The End of Liberal International Order? *International Affairs, 94*(1), 7–23.
Ikenberry, G. J. (2024). Three Worlds: The West, East and South and the Competition to Shape Global Order. *International Affairs, 100*(1), 121–138.
Jiang, M. (2010). Authoritarian Informationalism: China's Approach to Internet Sovereignty. *SAIS Review of International Affairs, 30*(2), 71–90.
Kawabata, T. (2020). Private Governance Schemes for Green Bond Standard: Influence on Public Authorities' Policy Making. *Green Finance, 2*(1), 35–54.
Kettemann, M. C. (2020). *The Normative Order of the Internet.* Oxford University Press.
Kissinger, H. (2011). *On China.* Penguin Books.
Kruger, G. (2021). *Strategic Subversion: From Terrorists to Superpowers, How State and Non-State Actors Undermine One Another.* AuthorHouse.
Lubin, D. (2023, December 15). Collapsing foreign direct investment might not be all bad for China's economy. *Chatham House.* https://www.chathamhouse.org/2023/12/collapsing-foreign-direct-investment-might-not-be-all-bad-chinas-economy (January 19, 2024).
Mearsheimer, J. J. (2001). *The Tragedy of Great Power Politics.* WW Norton & Company.
Mearsheimer, J. J. (2006). China's Unpeaceful Rise. *Current History, 105*(690), 160–162.
Mearsheimer, J. J. (2019). Bound to Fail: The Rise and Fall of the Liberal International Order. *International Security, 43*(4), 7–50.
Morozov, E. (2011). *The Net Delusion: How not to Liberate the World.* New Penguin.
Mueller, M. L. (2017). *Will the Internet Fragment? Sovereignty, Globalization, and Cyberspace.* Polity Press.
Mueller, M. L., & Badiei, F. (2020). Inventing Internet Governance: The Historical Trajectory of the Phenomenon and the Field. In L. DeNardis, D. Cogburn, N. Levinson & F. Musiani (Eds.), *Researching Internet Governance: Methods, Frameworks, Futures.* MIT Press.
Murgia, M., & Gross, A. (2020, March 27). Inside China's Controversial Mission to Reinvent the Internet. *Financial Times.* https://www.ft.com/content/ba94c2bc-6e27-11ea-9bca-bf503995cd6f (October 22, 2020).
Musiani, F. (2013). Network Architecture as Internet Governance. *Internet Policy Review, 2*(4), 1–9.

Musiani, F. (2022). Infrastructuring Digital Sovereignty: A Research Agenda for an Infrastructure-based Sociology of Digital Self-determination Practices. *Information, Communication & Society, 25*(6), 785–800.

Negro, G. (2020). A History of Chinese Global Internet Governance and its Relations with ITU and ICANN. *Chinese Journal of Communication, 13*(1), 104–121.

Nye, J. S. (2014). The Regime Complex for Managing Global Cyber Activities. *Global Commission on Internet Governance Paper Series, 1*. http://www.cigionline.org/publications/regime-complex-managingglobal-cyber-activities (July 25, 2019).

Palladino, N., & Santaniello, M. (2021). *Legitimacy, Power, and Inequalities in the Multistakeholder Internet Governance*. Palgrave Macmillan.

Parsi, V. E. (2021). *The Wrecking of the Liberal World Order*. Palgrave Macmillan.

Poggetti, L. (2021, January 20). *EU-China Mappings: Interactions between the EU and China on Key Issues*. Mercator Institute for China Studies. https://merics.org/de/kurzanalyse/eu-china-mappings-interactions-between-eu-and-china-key-issues (July 13, 2021).

Qin, Y. (2012). *A Relational Theory of World Politics*. Cambridge University Press.

Radu, R. (2019). *Negotiating Internet Governance*. Oxford University Press.

Raymond, M., & DeNardis, L. (2015). Multistakeholderism: Anatomy of an Inchoate Global Institution. *International Theory, 7*(3), 572–616.

Rosenau, J. N. (1992). Governance, Order, and Change in World Politics. In J. N. Rosenau & E. Czempiel (Eds.), *Governance without Government: Order and Change in World Politics*. Cambridge University Press.

Santaniello, M. (2021). From Governance Denial to State Regulation: A Controversy-based Typology of Internet Governance Models. In B. Haggart, N. Tusikov & J. A. Scholte (Eds.), *Power and Authority in Internet Governance. Return of the State?* Routledge.

Scholte, J. A. (2017). Complex Hegemony. The IANA Transition In Global Internet Governance. *Giganet: Global Internet Governance Academic Network, Annual Symposium*.

Segal, A. (2016). *The Hacked World Order: How Nations Fight, Trade, Maneuver, and Manipulate in the Digital Age*. PublicAffairs.

Segal, A. (2018, August 13). When China Rules the Web: Technology in Service of the State. *Foreign Affairs*. https://www.foreignaffairs.com/articles/china/2018-08-13/when-china-rules-web (November 10, 2020).

Sharp, H., & Kolkman, O. (2020, April 24). Discussion Paper: An Analysis of the 'New IP' proposal to the ITU-T. *Internet Society*. https://www.internetsociety.org/resources/doc/2020/discussion-paper-an-analysis-of-the-new-ip-proposal-to-the-itu-t/#:~:text=%20Key%20Elements%20of%20the%20proposed%20%E2%80%9CNew%20IP%E2%80%9D,transport%20architectures.%20C83%20and%20its%20associated...%20More%20 (October 22, 2020).

Tanczer, L. M., Brass, I., & Carr, M. (2018). CSIRTs and Global Cybersecurity: How Technical Experts Support Science Diplomacy. *Global Policy*, 9(3), 60–66.
ten Oever, N. (2022). 5G and the Notion of Network Ideology, or: The Limitations of Sociotechnical Imaginaries. *Telecommunications Policy*, 102442.
Walker, N. (2020). The sovereignty surplus. *International Journal of Constitutional Law*, 18(2), 370–428.
Wang, J. (2011, February 20). China's Search for a Grand Strategy. *Foreign Affairs*. https://www.foreignaffairs.com/articles/china/2011-02-20/chinas-search-grand-strategy (April 9, 2020).
Wen, Y. (2020). *The Huawei Model*. University of Illinois Press.
Westwinter, O. (2021). Transnational Public-private Governance Initiatives in World Politics: Introducing a New Dataset. *The Review of International Organizations*, 16(1), 137–174.
Wolfsfeld, G., Segev, E., & Sheafer, T. (2013). Social Media and the Arab Spring: Politics Comes First. *The International Journal of Press/politics*, 18(2), 115–137.
Yan, X. (2014). From Keeping a Low Profile to Striving for Achievement. *The Chinese Journal of International Politics*, 7(2), 153–184.
Zheng, B. (2005). China's 'Peaceful Rise' to Great- Power Status. In D. Shambaugh (Ed.), (2016). *The China Reader* (6th ed.). Oxford University Press.
Zürn, M. (2018). *A Theory of Global Governance. Authority, Legitimacy, and Contestation*. Oxford University Press.

CHAPTER 2

China, Internet Governance, and the Liberal International Order

2.1 INTRODUCTION

This chapter expands on the points raised in the introduction. The question of Chinese stakeholders' relation with and influence in the existing multistakeholder Internet governance mechanisms, as well as their impact (if any) on Internet fragmentation, are discussed and critically situated in literature in this chapter, before moving to the empirical analysis.

The next section places China's contestation of and adaptation to global governance norms in the broader debate on China's rise and the future of the Liberal International Order. Section 2.3 follows by discussing what Internet governance entails and its relevance for International Relations. Section 2.4 addresses the question of multistakeholderism in Internet governance, while Sect. 2.5 discusses Internet fragmentation: its meaning and implications. Both the latter sections situate China and Chinese stakeholders in these debates, stressing the non-monolithic nature of these two (sets of) actors in their actions in the global Internet governance realm. Overall, Sects. 2.3 through 2.5 expand on the topics introduced in Chapter 1. Section 2.6 provides an illustration of the functioning of the Internet governance organisations and fora in which Chinese stakeholders' actions are analysed. This section is detailed and potentially daunting to a reader who has no familiarity with Internet governance. Nonetheless, it is important to familiarise with the functioning of these bodies to fully comprehend the analysis conducted

© The Author(s), under exclusive license to Springer Nature
Singapore Pte Ltd. 2024
R. Nanni, *Rising China and Internet Governance*,
https://doi.org/10.1007/978-981-97-0357-9_2

in this book. To this end, this section should be considered as a "map" or reference for the reader to refer back to if (and when!) it becomes complicated to understand the collocation of the bodies under discussion within the organisations and fora under analysis. Moving forward, Sect. 2.7 presents a theoretical and methodological note on the research illustrated in this book, which is then complemented by Appendices A and B. Finally, Sect. 2.8 draws conclusions.

2.2 China's Rise, the Liberal International Order, and Contestation in Global Governance

The debate on the crisis of the Liberal International Order has been the object of academic discussion for at least two decades (Acharya, 2018; Duncombe & Dunne, 2018; Ikenberry, 2018; Mearsheimer, 2019). Contextually, the power shift towards Asia and the supposed beginning of the 'Asian Century' have been core matters of discussion in the literature (Abramowitz & Bosworth, 2006; Phillips, 2013), driven by the debate on China's rise (Bo, 2018; Ikenberry, 2008; Mearsheimer, 2006; Zheng, 2005). The way China has conducted its diplomatic activity at various levels of global governance and within the designated bodies has led observers to portray this emerging international actor either as a rule-breaker or as a rule-shaper—hinting at times at its willingness to become a rule-maker. Whether or not China's growing assertiveness will result in a reshaping of the rules of the existing order or to the establishment of a new one—possibly following a hegemonic war—is the main open question (Mearsheimer, 2019).

This debate is reflected in the field of global Internet governance. As introduced above, the existing multistakeholder governance model is a liberal-informed one and China has posed as a critic of it in favour of a multilateral/intergovernmental model (Flonk et al., 2020; Negro, 2020).

To contextualise the debate on China and Internet governance, it is necessary to look at the broader question of China's rise and its positioning vis-à-vis the Liberal International Order. Recalling from the introduction, the Liberal Order was established at the end of World War II in the wake of US global hegemony, and expanded globally after the Cold War (Parsi, 2021). Normatively, it entails contrasting values, such as state sovereignty and universal human rights, but also a free-market tenet that provides ground for private-based transnational governance

(Rosenau, 1992; Scholte, 2017). The questions around Chinese stakeholders' engagement in Internet governance fit the debate on China's adaptation and contestation to the Liberal International Order (Ikenberry, 2018), rather than posing an existential threat to the latter. Indeed, the latter question has been raised powerfully in the aftermath of the Covid-19 pandemic and the Russian aggression on Ukraine and the field is now undergoing a number of shifts in theoretical perspectives and research targets (Ikenberry, 2024). The debate is further complicated by the emergence of private-based governance and regime complexity, which has been particularly strong since the 1990s (Rosenau, 1992). Private-based governance encompasses technical standard-making venues as well as sectors of market and economic governance where such actors as companies or civil society enjoy actorness and can influence decision-making (Zürn, 2018). In turn, regime complexity defines a governance ecosystem whereby one macro-topic is addressed by an indefinite number of fora, more or less global in scope, which are loosely interdependent and at times partially overlapping in scope and membership (Nye, 2014).

As anticipated, regime complexity and private-based governance are two intertwined concepts (Gómez-Mera, 2016; Kawabata, 2020; Westwinter, 2021). In this context, this book focuses on the normative challenge that China and Chinese stakeholders pose to the Liberal International Order in terms of influence in policies and in terms of reshaping the existing rules and norms of liberal-informed global governance. This is done by observing multistakeholder, private-based global Internet governance in selected venues as an example of a public–private governance regime-complex cutting across traditional national and geopolitical lines.

2.3 GLOBAL INTERNET GOVERNANCE: WHAT IT ENTAILS AND WHY IT MATTERS

The history of Internet governance as we know it in the twenty-first century is deeply entrenched with the development of Liberal International Order and the tensions and challenges therein. A starting point can be identified with the 1994–1998 so-called 'DNS war', whereby the first backlash between states supporting a multilateral system of governance and states supporting a multistakeholder one for Critical Internet Resources (CIRs) took place. At this stage, multilateralists were already pushing for a UN-based supervision of CIRs, pointing at the International Telecommunication Union (ITU) as the legitimate body

(Palladino & Santaniello, 2021). However, the US authorities and epistemic communities promoted the establishment of a multistakeholder mechanism whereby CIRs management was to be conducted (mainly) by private actors, with governments maintaining a pure consultative role. This system was formalised in ICANN. Despite the role of governments being relegated to the consultative Governmental Advisory Committee (GAC), the US retained a privileged role as ICANN was founded as a private not-for-profit organisation incorporated in Californian law. The US government also retained a special connection through the so-called 'IANA contract',[1] which formalised the supervision of the US Department of Commerce over IANA (Mueller, 2017).

While this solidified the passage of the Internet to the civilian realm from the military Arpanet project, in line with the process of commercialisation already launched through the establishment of the World Wide Web, it did not encompass its emancipation from the US government. In this view, the establishment of ICANN in this form epitomised the global expansion of the Liberal International Order in its free-market tenet and a restatement of US hegemony in the so-called 'unipolar decade'. In the realm of Internet governance specifically, the establishment of ICANN formalised the concept of multistakeholderism as a governance principle for the Internet, although it was still contested (Palladino & Santaniello, 2021).

However, the new mechanism fitted within an ensemble of existing venues for standardisation and critical Internet resources governance. For example, the IETF preceded ICANN and was founded in 1986. Its standard-making activity nowadays is mainly industry-led. While the IETF makes standards for the Internet to function, the World Wide Web Consortium (W3C) was founded in 1994 to set the standards for the Web as we know it, whereas the much-older Institute of Electrical and Electronics Engineers (IEEE) sets connectivity standards such as Wi-Fi. Work in W3C and IEEE is industry-based, much like in 3GPP, the main body responsible for the elaboration of mobile connectivity standards from the third generation (3G) onwards since 1998 (Nye, 2014).

In other words, the 1990s signalled the emergence of a globalised, strongly private-based regime complex for the management and development of the Internet and Internet-enabled technologies. Within this,

---

[1] IANA: Internet Assigned Numbers Authority.

ICANN came to be central in the management of CIRs, epitomising the multistakeholder management of the Internet by private and—to a lower extent—public actors. Table 2.1 summarises the historical evolution of Internet governance illustrated in this section.

In more historical and technical detail, the management of CIRs takes the name of 'IANA stewardship'. The IANA functions, conducted by ICANN, entail three core elements: IPs and AS (Autonomous System) numbers distribution; Domain Name System (DNS) root zone management; and management of the protocol parameters (Hill, 2016; Mueller & Kuerbis, 2014; Scholte, 2017). An IP is a unique numerical identifier for network-connected devices; an AS number is "a globally unique identifier that defines a group of one or more IP prefixes

Table 2.1 Key moments in Internet governance history for China

Year	Event	Consequences
1983	TCP/IP is established	Creation of essential Internet protocols
1986	The IETF is founded	Formalisation of an Internet standards body
1998	ICANN is founded	Formalisation of multistakeholderism
2001	Beijing clashes with ICANN over Taiwan	Chinese government temporarily stops participating in ICANN
2003–2005	The UN World Summit on the Information Society (WSIS)	Confirmation of multistakeholder governance
2006–2009	ICANN–Beijing–Taipei relations are normalised	Beijing progressively returns to ICANN activities
2012	The UN World Conference on International Telecommunications	Apparent start of a "digital Cold war"
2013	Beijing hosts an ICANN meeting	Apex of the ICANN–Beijing normalisation
2013	The PRISM scandal	The US special role in ICANN lost legitimacy
2014	Cyberspace Administration of China (CAC) head endorses multistakeholderism	Part of the ICANN–Beijing normalisation
2014–2016	The IANA stewardship transition	The US renounces its special role in ICANN amid pressure (e.g. Netmundial)
2020	China's great rectification campaign	Part of the "return of state" process

run by one or more network operators that maintain a single, clearly-defined routing policy" (African Network Information Centre, 2020, hereafter AFRINIC); the DNS is a hierarchical system of servers and databases that translates domain names into IPs; the protocol parameters involve such global technical operational standards that allow Internet-connected devices to exchange data: these include the Transmission Control Protocol (TCP) and Hypertext Transfer Protocol (HTTP) (Scholte, 2017).[2]

The establishment of ICANN to oversee the IANA functions concluded the so-called 'DNS war' in favour of multistakeholderism, although the qualifications illustrated above apply regarding the US' role (Mueller, 2017). Point B of the memorandum of understanding that preceded the IANA contract and recognised ICANN's role in the IANA functions reads: "[b]efore making a transition to private sector DNS management, the DOC requires assurances that the private sector has the capability and resources to assume the important responsibilities related to the technical management of the DNS" (ICANN, 1999). Importantly, while the MoU made strict reference to DNS management, the IANA contract referred to the whole of the IANA functions (Mueller, 2017; Scholte, 2017).

It must be underlined for the sake of completeness that ICANN's role in the IANA functions is one of supervision rather than direct management: for example, ICANN allocates IPs to the Regional Internet Registries (RIRs),[3] which in turn distribute them to final users. As for the DNS management, ICANN establishes TLDs, but the sale of domain names to end users is done by the so-called 'contracted parties' known as

---

[2] TCP allows "data [to be] transferred with an end-to-end reliability from the source host to the destination host". TCP/IP is also referred to as the 'Internet Protocol Suite', that is, the series of fundamental protocols (which includes, but is not limited to, TCP and IP) allowing device identification and data exchange through the Internet to work the way it does; HTTP "is used in communication between the web pages and web servers. It allows users to download pages and connect to servers located in different parts of the globe" (ICANN, 2011).

[3] "A Regional Internet Registry (RIR) is a not-for-profit international organisation that deals with the allocation of Internet Protocol (IP) address space (IPv4 and IPv6) and the Autonomous System numbers within a geographical region". IPv4 and IPv6 refer to the two versions of IPs currently in use, IPv6 being the newest generation. While technically incompatible, the two versions have been bridged through protocols allowing devices using one IP version to communicate with those using the other (ICANN, 2021).

registries and registrars (acting on behalf of the former), both of which act based on a contract with ICANN.

In historical terms, the establishment of ICANN signposts a passage from Internet governance by the technical community to multistakeholder Internet governance. While before ICANN, the IANA activities were conducted by Jon Postel and the IETF was a niche body of technical experts, with the foundation of ICANN, a variety of stakeholders gained an institutionalised role in Internet governance (Palladino & Santaniello, 2021). Through time, the IETF itself saw its participation expanding, with a strong presence of corporate actors (Belli, 2015). In other words, while the Internet prior to the 1990s was mainly governed by the US government and mainly US-based epistemic communities, from 1998, the largely private-based multistakeholder ecosystem centred on ICANN took form. Within the debate on digital sovereignty, the return of state in Internet governance, and the future of multistakeholderism, this signals that governmental presence in private-based Internet governance has historically never completely faded away, reminding one of the Internet's military (thus state-centric) origins (Ten Oever, 2022).

In the wake of ICANN's foundation, around the beginning of the twenty-first century, China posed as a staunch multilateralist, as opposed to the multistakeholder system epitomised by ICANN (Cai, 2018a; Mueller, 2017). The ITU-centred system envisaged by multilateralists would have been largely based on a one-state-one-vote system, with non-state stakeholders in marginal positions. Currently, the ITU itself has incorporated multistakeholder consensus-based decision-making procedures. However, when it comes to regulatory decisions or decisions on which consensus cannot be built, it is the state representatives who decide by majority votes (Glen, 2014).

In turn, the multistakeholder model headed by ICANN grants governments a merely consultative role in the IANA functions (Mueller, 2017), whereas the basic Internet protocols and standards are elaborated at the IETF, a private- and consensus-based engineering body. While governments are not formally excluded from IETF work, its main contributors are engineers from tech multinationals (Arkko, 2023; Belli, 2015; IETF, 2020), although its consensus-based decision-making process limits the influence these major actors can have (Harcourt et al., 2020).

At the beginning of the twenty-first century, China's main reason for discontent vis-à-vis ICANN was the latter's recognition of Taiwan as a member of the GAC (Y. Liu, 2012). This led to China's government's suspension of participation in ICANN's meetings and GAC activities. The extent to which this 'boycott' was actually in place is debated (Creemers, 2020), but this is better observed in the forthcoming chapters. What matters at this stage is that the Chinese government held a critical position against ICANN amid the Taiwan question. Adding to this, China and other countries from the developing world criticised ICANN amid its formal relation to the US DOC (Glen, 2014; Hurel & Rocha, 2018; ICANN, 1999; Mueller, 2017).

However, between 2003 and 2005, the two rounds of the World Summit on the Information Society (WSIS—a UN-sponsored global multistakeholder forum) did not conclude with a phase out of the ICANN-centred governance model. WSIS resulted instead in the adoption of the so-called 'Tunis Agenda' and the establishment of the multistakeholder policy forum known as the 'Internet Governance Forum' (IGF) (ITU, 2005). Most importantly, the Tunis Agenda recognised multistakeholderism as a guiding principle of global Internet governance as provided by the Working Group on Internet Governance (WGIG) in its working definition of the term (WGIG, 2005). Such working definition consolidated the existing multistakeholder governance mechanism by stipulating that:

> Internet governance is the development and application by Governments, the private sector and civil society, in their respective roles, of shared principles, norms, rules, decision-making procedures, and programmes that shape the evolution and use of the Internet. (WGIG, 2005, 4)

The Tunis Agenda seemingly strengthened the global acceptance of multistakeholderism as a governance principle for the Internet: in particular, following the WSIS process the Chinese government progressively normalised relations with ICANN between 2006 and 2009 (Creemers, 2020). Furthermore, literature recognises China's acceptance that ICANN was there to stay (Galloway & He, 2014; Mueller, 2017; Negro, 2020). Nonetheless, the World Conference on International Telecommunications of 2012 (WCIT-12) was interpreted as a reawakening of the multilateralist–multistakeholderist divide. Held by the ITU to discuss and approve a revised version of the International Telecommunication Regulations (ITRs),[4] it concluded with a bloc of countries led by the US rejecting them by maintaining that the new rules would allow too strong a governmental intervention in the communication sectors (Schackleford & Craig, 2014). This led many to dub WCIT-12 as the 'Internet Yalta' (Klimburg, 2013), although this is disagreed upon by the global Internet governance scholarly community (Mueller, 2013).

At the time of writing, the importance of WCIT-12 and its meaning for both the ITU and the multistakeholder model are being reconsidered. Namely, the new ITRs became inapplicable due to the lack of support by the most economically powerful countries, while no institutional split or transfer of competence in Internet governance emerged (Winseck, 2020). However, it remains in the literature as a moment in which major normative tension in governance was experienced and perceived (Palladino & Santaniello, 2021).

The following year, the PRISM scandal hit the US, with Edward Snowden's revelations tarnishing the US' reputation and casting further doubts on the legitimacy of its exceptional role in Internet governance. This is recognised as one of the elements that triggered the launch of the so-called 'IANA stewardship transition' by the second Obama administration, which made ICANN independent of the US government in 2016, thus eliminating one of the main points of criticism against the organisation (Mueller, 2017). While the US government had repeatedly promised to end the IANA contract, this process was postponed time and time again. Many in the literature maintain that the PRISM scandal tarnished the US' reputation and exposed its vast surveillance power to a point that the transition could no longer be delayed (Mueller, 2014; Palladino & Santaniello, 2021). As far as China is concerned, however, Negro (2020) stresses China's ambivalence in its participation in both the ITU and ICANN is still visible. While the latter has become increasingly accepted and participated in by Chinese stakeholders, Chinese presence and influence in the ITU keeps growing. According to Negro (2020), this means that China's challenge to the ICANN-based Internet governance system is still there but must not be given a dichotomous reading. In fact,

---

[4] ITRs "serve as the binding global treaty designed to facilitate international interconnection and interoperability of information and communication services" (ITU, 2020a).

at the same time, high-ranking Chinese politicians and functionaries have endorsed ICANN and the multistakeholder principle.

In line with these findings, the post-IANA stewardship transition debate on China and multistakeholderism has become more nuanced. A degree of ambiguity is recognised by many and the duality of the early 2000s debate has faded (Mueller, 2017; Negro, 2020; Shen, 2016). Meanwhile, Chinese scholarship on the topic has become more prominent internationally, both from China-based Chinese scholars and from Chinese scholars abroad.

As for the issue at stake, ambiguity in China's stance towards multistakeholderism emerges from Chinese literature too. The role of Chinese private actors is extensively analysed by Shen (2016), who maintains that China has become more participatory and influential in technical standardisation activities through its private actors' presence in multistakeholder fora. She also contributes to contextualising this in the broader Chinese foreign policy strategy, which currently runs under the label of 'Belt and Road Initiative' (BRI) or 'One Belt One Road' (OBOR) (一带一路, yidai yilu) (Shen, 2018). On the other hand, Cai (2018a) acknowledges the role of Chinese private actors in multistakeholder governance, but maintains the Chinese government is central. In her words, "[b]oth the multilateralism and multi-stakeholder approaches recognize the role of different actors in global cyber governance; their major difference lies in the positioning of those actors, particularly in who is to play a dominant role" (Cai, 2018a, 59). She underlines that China supports state centrality in Internet governance and defines this approach as "multilateral pluralism based on cybersovereignty" (Cai, 2018b, 647).

Whether and to what extent Chinese private actors are state-controlled is an open question and casts doubts on the future of multistakeholderism inasmuch as formally private entities may serve to enhance state influence in multistakeholder governance. This is an overarching question in the fields of CIRs as well as mobile Internet technology standards.

This takes the discussion to the second subset of this research's analysis. Attempts to study China's policies in mobile Internet technologies standardisation processes are very few at the academic level, despite 5G having drawn attention in politics and the media. Both Zhong (2019) and Pupillo (2019), on the journalism and the think tank sides respectively, helped to shed light on the complicated and non-transparent relationship between the two. To be sure, the growth in strength of Chinese private actors has pushed China into further acceptance of the multi-stakeholder system, where its domestic companies play a major role in standardisation processes (Shen, 2016). Nonetheless, this does not allow one to discard forms of state control on private companies. Kim et al. (2020) observe China's 5G standardisation policies through the lenses of techno-nationalism. To them, techno-nationalism "commonly features when developing countries start to drive technological catch-up and economic development" (Kim et al., 2020, 3) and entails state empowerment, growth orientation, and global connection. Through these lenses, Kim et al. (2020) see patterns of alliance between government, telco, and operators (whether public or private) in an effort to create domestic technology and reduce import-dependence, while contributing to global standardisation as 'first movers' rather than 'catch-uppers'.

Through a different theoretical lens, Tang (2020) reaffirms this view of government policy (which includes funds and research and development coordination) supporting the progressive 'going out', that is, growth and expansion in the global market, of Chinese tech companies. This view is stressed by Y. Gong (2019), who underlines governmental recognition of the need to push international standardisation to achieve comparative advantage. Further Chinese literature on the topic is often concentrated on the policy implications of Huawei's condition amid the US–China trade competition (Ma, 2020), while others observed Chinese tech companies' internationalisation and relative growth until achieving a leading role in 5G standardisation. In this, literature finds in inter-sector research and development the source of such capacity, but the role of political relations remains unaddressed (Tang, 2020).

In other words, the question of political control over private companies remains unanswered and scholars within China and the West, different political situations notwithstanding, have developed heterogeneous views. What emerges from Chinese and non-Chinese literature on Chinese engagement with standardisation is a strong government role, at least in policy coordination. Whether this translates simply as more engagement in multistakeholder governance (Shen, 2016), a form of 'open' or 'repressive' multilateralism (Glen, 2014), or similarly 'multilateral pluralism based on cybersovereignty' (Cai, 2018b) is open to debate. The boundaries between coordination, influence, and control remain blurred amid the authoritarian characteristics of the Chinese government (Jia & Winseck, 2018; M. Jiang, 2012; Pupillo, 2019; Segal, 2018; Zhong, 2019).

Overall, it can be observed that the multistakeholder conception of Internet governance differed from a multilateralist understanding deeply enough as to yield normative confrontation (Flonk et al., 2020), although this has transformed and partially faded throughout the first two decades of the twenty-first century, at least as far as China is concerned (Negro, 2020). While states remain undeniably a central actor in the international order, multi-actor understandings of IR need to be adopted when observing such fields as global Internet governance where private actors can exert extensive power (Keohane & Victor, 2011; Nye, 2014).

To summarise and conclude, debates on the Chinese influence on the future of multistakeholderism and Internet fragmentation are deeply intertwined with the future of the Liberal International Order. There is disagreement in the literature on the extent to which China's government is in control of non-state stakeholders' choices and actions. However, it must be underlined that companies and state policies towards the multistakeholder governance system differ. While the Chinese government boycotted ICANN amid Taiwan's presence in the Governmental Advisory Committee, commercial stakeholders were still participating in ICANN— although the overall Chinese participation in ICANN was limited in its initial stage (Creemers, 2020; Negro, 2020). While this cannot say much about the relationship of control—whether real or presumed—between Chinese stakeholders and the party-state, it provides a nuanced view on actors' behaviour and the need for a theorisation that accounts for everyone's actorness while taking power relations into account. Furthermore, what emerges from the literature is that the relationship between Chinese actors and the existing global Internet governance system needs a non-dualistic, nuanced reading that has only recently started emerging. To this, a multi-actor approach needs to be adopted, along with understandings of such concepts as 'state-influence' and 'fragmentation' that encompass their multifaceted nature. This brief introduction to the questions at stake provides an explanatory overview of the techno-political dynamics at stake behind the most technical caveats of global Internet governance.

2.4 The Question of Multistakeholderism: What Is at Stake for the Liberal Order

A takeaway of Sect. 2.3 of this chapter is that multistakeholder Internet governance, as well as the concept of one, open universal Internet are deeply entrenched with liberalism and constitute a facet of the Liberal International Order. After all, the 'multistakeholderist vs. multilateralist' contestation illustrated in the previous section and summarised in Table 2.2 is one of 'liberals vs. sovereigntists' (Flonk et al., 2020).

As anticipated, the debate has developed lately in a less dichotomous fashion (Negro, 2020), with criticism levelled against multistakeholderism from within the Western liberal world. For instance, Santaniello (2021) pinpoints that the 2018 speech by French President Macron at the Internet Governance Forum portrays a shift towards a more state-interventionist stance in Western democracies, one that falls within the broader spectrum of digital sovereignty practices. From a different perspective, Cath (2021) finds obstacles in human rights advocacy in technical standard-making at the IETF due to longstanding conceptions of technological neutrality. While this falls outside the scope of this book, it is important to stress the heterogeneity of Western approaches to multistakeholderism and the non-dichotomous nature of the 'liberal vs. sovereigntist', or 'multistakeholderist vs. multilateralist' debate.

A further criticism levelled against multistakeholderism is that it is often unbalanced in favour of powerful corporate actors, thus constituting a fully fledged form of private governance mechanism in its neoliberal

Table 2.2 'Multistakeholder' and 'multilateral' Internet governance in sum

	Multistakeholderism (private-based governance)	*Multilateralism (state-based governance)*
Type of actors and their roles	*Private actors*: make (most) decisions; *Public actors*: mostly in consultative roles	*Private actors*: consultative; *Public actors*: make majority-vote decisions
Political connotation	Liberal	Sovereigntist
Governance fora	ICANN, IETF, IGF, 3GPP, W3C, others	Most UN fora (ITU), other state-based orgs

sense, rather than a strongly private-led but mixed public–private setting. While this is debated, it connects directly to the fact that around 80% of IETF participants were from tech multinationals by 2015 (Belli, 2015). Observing authoritative figures, Cisco, Huawei, Ericsson, Google, Nokia, and Juniper are the main yearly contributors to the IETF's work in terms of Requests for Comments (RFCs)—that is, IETF's technical documents including anything from networking protocols down to meeting notes (IETF, 2020)—published in 2022 (Arkko, 2023). In other words, influence in the making of Internet standards and their management is strongly skewed in favour of industry, which adds to business actors' formal role in policymaking in ICANN's Supporting Organisations (SOs) (Palladino & Santaniello, 2021; Scholte, 2017).

The overwhelming role of multinationals in the establishment of the Internet's basic protocols is evident. To be sure, technologists formally participate in the IETF's work in personal capacity. Furthermore, decision-making is based on rough consensus, where dissenting opinions are considered but do not constitute a veto. This entails that a meaningful open opposition to a proposed standard can be influential, no matter how powerful the proponent. Nonetheless, virtually every participant is sponsored by an entity and works on its behalf. As the wealthiest entities are also those who can pool the deepest (in terms of technical knowledge) and broadest (in terms of human resources) expertise, tech multinationals represent the leading actors in the IETF (Belli, 2015). To be sure, numbers are not necessarily symptomatic of influence, as companies like Amazon do not participate in the IETF but can influence standard-making by choosing which standards to adopt. Nonetheless, big techs' size and their capacity to participate and pool expertise make them capable of creating and establishing standards that are more likely to become widespread in the industry (Harcourt et al., 2020).

Furthermore, prior to the IANA stewardship transition that took place in 2016, there was broad criticism against ICANN amid its ties to the US DOC as mentioned above (Carr, 2015; Mueller, 2017; Negro, 2020). Despite the transition, criticism has not faded, as ICANN still constitutes a private entity incorporated in Californian law. However, following Snowden's revelations and the PRISM scandal, which triggered the IANA stewardship transition, criticism against ICANN's current form and ties awakened in the liberal field as well.

Despite this, Mueller (2017) finds the IANA stewardship transition rid ICANN of one of the most outstanding arguments against its roles.

Furthermore, Scholte (2017) observes that the community of individuals participating in ICANN, including Chinese ones almost independently of their stakeholder affiliation, widely sees ICANN as a legitimate actor in the role it conducts in global Internet governance. This, of course, does not mitigate criticism from the broader community of people involved in Internet governance at large. Most everyday users of the Internet, for example, are not aware of the existence of ICANN and its role, despite the pervasiveness of the Internet in most individuals' life (Jongen & Scholte, 2021). Nevertheless, these findings and China's ambiguity in its relationship to ICANN and the ITU (Negro, 2020) cast a multifaceted light on the challenges faced by the multistakeholder (that is, liberal-informed) global Internet governance system by such actors as the Chinese government.

In brief, contradiction in multistakeholderism is found inasmuch as it entails a role for governments, companies, and civil society at least (WGIG, 2005), but in practice there is overlap with the concept of private-based governance owing to the heavy presence of so-called 'big techs' (Belli, 2015; Palladino & Santaniello, 2021; Santaniello, 2021). As anticipated in the previous sections of this chapter, this creates tensions between the concepts of private-based governance and public–private governance.

Debates notwithstanding, this book focuses on the increasing role of states in the existing Internet governance complex and the potential shift to multilateralism under the push of a non-liberal power, that is, China. The terms 'multistakeholderism' and 'private-based governance' will be used interchangeably, as derivatives of liberalism and the Liberal International Order in their free-market form. However, a preference for the term 'multistakeholderism' must be expressed due to its all-encompassing meaning when referring to the public and private actors involved in Internet governance, despite the pre-eminence of the latter in decision-making. In turn, multilateralism is conceptualised as opposed to multistakeholderism as a governance model as it is most often promoted by non-liberal powers—as per Table 2.2.

While multilateralism is intrinsic in the Westphalian characteristics of the Liberal International Order (Deudney & Ikenberry, 2018), in the context of Internet governance, it is conceived as a sovereigntist alternative to the liberal-informed ICANN-centred multistakeholder model (Flonk et al., 2020). The normative divide between multistakeholderism and multilateralism can also be observed in the characteristics of the IETF and the ITU as standardisation venues. Not only in the private-based vs. state-based nature of the two bodies: to be precise, the ITU seeks consensual decisions among industry participants and uses state representatives' majority vote only in case of major impasses or when regulatory aspects are at stake (Glen, 2014). However, in the ITU governments have a permanent and decisional representation and ITU standards (recommendations) are approved by member states. While their implementation is not mandatory, recommendations can be incorporated in national laws as standards *de jure* (ITU, 2021). In contrast, the IETF is private- and consensus-based as described above. Finally, the ITU is historically specialised in telecommunication in a stricter sense (that is, telephony), a technology whose infrastructure is built on a different 'philosophy' than the Internet's, as better discussed below.

Furthermore, telecommunication and Internet infrastructures work in different ways: while the Internet has been built on a building-block approach, where new specifications are created using the existing ones in previously unexpected ways, telephony works on fully determined infrastructures. Moreover, the Internet infrastructure is a 'dumb pipe' used by intelligent endpoints (devices) to connect to each other. Conversely, telephones are dumb devices, and the interconnection work is done by the infrastructure. While this is a simplified illustration of the functioning of the two types of infrastructure, also considering their historical and growing interconnection in the functioning (ten Oever, 2022), it is a useful benchmark to gauge the security implications of the two types of infrastructure. For example, while surveillance in telephony can be easily done by controlling the infrastructure, Internet surveillance requires control on the endpoints. Furthermore, this characteristic of the Internet makes it less easy to disrupt. After all, the founding idea of the Internet was to have a distributed communication infrastructure in the Cold War era that could not easily be disrupted in case of military emergency (Leiner et al., 1997).

A line of thinking similar to that applied to the IETF is applicable to 3GPP, which constitutes this research's focus for the mobile Internet technology standards subsets.

To begin with, 3GPP does not possess legal personality, but is constituted by seven national and regional Standards Development Organisations (SDOs) with mixed private and public participation, as illustrated in detail later in this chapter. Through membership to these, organisations can formally participate by sending their affiliates to Technical Specification Groups' work (3GPP, 2020). As Pohlmann et al. (2020) show, 3GPP, while participated in by both private and public entities, is strongly private-driven. Huawei, Ericsson, Nokia, Samsung, and Qualcomm are among the main proponents of 5G standardisation proposals—which roughly translates as major (prospective) patent owners. To be sure, state-owned enterprises such as the Chinese manufacturer ZTE are also present, along with technical public entities. Yet, the four aforementioned Chinese, European, and US companies are the leaders in the standard-making process and are private actors responding to IPR and market needs. State–company relations notwithstanding, 3GPP work is private-based and business-oriented. Decisions are made based on consensus, with voting as a last resort (3GPP, 2020). For the sake of completeness, it must be understood that 3GPP is not the only standardiser of new generations of mobile Internet technologies. Besides, there are ad hoc bodies that have been working alongside 3GPP in elaborating 5G-based technologies as 5G developed (Blanco et al., 2017). However, mobile connectivity work was initiated in 3GPP and from 3G to 5G the most globally influential standards have been elaborated in this venue. This qualifies it as the most influential standard-making forum in this sector (ITU, 2020b; Ten Oever, 2022).

The final specifications for a mobile connectivity generation emerged from intra-3GPP interactions are then referred to the ITU Radiocommunication Sector (ITU-R), which analyses and accepts or rejects them based on the requirements it made explicit before the launch of the standardisation activity. In the case of 5G, such requirements were specified in 'International Mobile Telecommunications 2020' (IMT-2020) (ITU, 2020b).

To put it briefly, 3GPP fits the business-led, private-based governance ecosystem illustrated above. Membership is mixed, with contributors from companies as well as public bodies such as academia. However, criticisms similar to those raised against the IETF related to a few network manufacturers' leading position in the standardisation process can be raised.

In this case, too, such criticism is mitigated by the consensus-based decision-making process, which means that meaningful opposition by minor actors can influence decision-making. After all, big actors have an interest in having their own standards adopted universally and gain in terms of royalties as well as scale economies. Standards scalability is therefore a central factor, which shapes standardisation activities as a coordination game (DeNardis, 2014).

A major difference with the IETF's way of working must be underlined. Whereas the latter adopts the building-block approach illustrated above, 3GPP makes technical solutions for fully determined architecture as that is the way telephony historically works. While it is true that new generations of mobile connectivity can work on top of previous generations' infrastructure in their non-standalone (NSA) version, the final deployment is always that of a new architecture for every generation (Blanco et al., 2017; Dahlman et al., 2016). Furthermore, final specifications need to be submitted to the ITU for approval as standards.

To conclude, multistakeholderism is a governance mechanism where power is unbalanced, although stakeholders participate nominally on equal footing and in different roles. While public and private actors are involved, the decision-making process is strongly private-driven. As per Table 2.2, its connotation is liberal and has emerged in the 1990s with the globalisation of the Liberal International Order in its free-market aspects.

2.5 INTERNET FRAGMENTATION: A CHALLENGE TO THE LIBERAL ORDER IN ITS GLOBAL REACH?

To begin a discussion on the second topic of this book, namely Internet fragmentation, a mapping of the basic Internet architecture needs to be made. The Internet architecture is acceptedly divided into four layers according to the so-called TCP/IP model summarised in Table 2.3. Numbered from one to four from the lowest level to the level 'closest' to the user, the TCP/IP four layers are: (i) the network access layer (also known as 'link layer' or 'network interface layer'); (ii) the Internet layer (or 'network layer'); (iii) the transport layer; and (iv) the application layer (Russell, 2013).

Table 2.3 The TCP/IP model (Harcourt et al., 2020; Russell, 2013)

Nr	Layer name	Protocols (examples)
4	Application	HTTP/DNS/SMTP/FTP
3	Transport	TCP/UDP/QUIC
2	Internet	IP
1	Network access	Wi-Fi/Ethernet/5G

As summarised in Table 2.3, the network access layer provides interface to the networking hardware, such as the ethernet and gateways; the Internet layer is a group of internetworking specification, with the IP as the most important one; the transport layer provides reliable end-to-end transmission of the datagrams (packages) transferred from an IP address to another. Two of the most important protocols at this layer are TCP and UDP (User Datagram Protocol); finally, the application layer provides direct service to users, including FTP (File Transfer Protocol) and SMTP (Simple Mail Transfer Protocol) (ICANN, 2011).

To be sure, the taxonomy of technical layers has been subjected to debate (DeNardis, 2016). The IETF, for example, adopts the TCP/IP model, while the Open Systems Interconnection (OSI) features a seven-layer stratification (physical, data link, network, transport, session, presentation, and application layers) (DeNardis, 2016). However, OSI was superseded by the TCP/IP model, which constitutes now the basis upon which the basic working protocols of the Internet are elaborated at the IETF (Russell, 2013; Socolofsky & Kale, 1991).

Debates on Internet fragmentation do not always adopt a strictly technical perspective. On the contrary, political, economic, and regulatory considerations are made. A rapid Google Scholar search for 'Internet fragmentation' delivers about 493,000 results. A few irrelevant results notwithstanding, the first ten articles approach the issue from technical, regulatory, commercial, media, and political perspectives. More strictly technical, political, and economic articles emerge if the search is restricted to the 2016–2023 timespan, which suggests the term has been narrowed down and clarified in time. Examples of this are the pieces of work published by Mueller (2017), DeNardis (2016), and Drake et al. (2016) discussed below, all of which provide detailed—albeit diverse—definitions of "Internet fragmentation". Nonetheless, the risk of the term 'fragmentation' being used as a catchphrase is high.

To begin with, a 'Future of the Internet Initiative' White Paper for the World Economic Forum (WEF) identified three types of fragmentation: technical, governmental, and commercial. Technical fragmentation entails "conditions in the underlying infrastructure that impede the ability of systems to fully interoperate and exchange data packets and of the Internet to function consistently at all endpoints"; governmental fragmentation takes place in the presence of "[g]overnment policies and actions that constrain or prevent certain uses of the Internet to create, distribute, or access information resources"; finally, commercial fragmentation consists of "[b]usiness practices that constrain or prevent certain uses of the Internet to create, distribute, or access information resources" (Drake et al., 2016, 4). Of course, the three ideal-types of fragmentation can intersect. For example, government policies can create market incentives for companies to push towards the creation of incompatible technical standards that will be adopted by law and to which every ISP or service provider operating in the country must adapt. This is a hypothetical (and possibly extreme) example, but it is explanatory of potential intersections among the three ideal-types.

Other definitions of fragmentation based on commercial or regulatory considerations can be found. For example, the principle of 'net neutrality', albeit falling outside the scope of this book, is held to have prevented many commercial forms of fragmentation, as it entails ISPs not being allowed to selectively restrict content delivery (Kourandi et al., 2015). Furthermore, DeNardis (2016) brings clarity to the fragmentation debate by pinpointing that, historically, the Internet is not a unified whole. It is in fact a 'network of networks', most of which are privately managed and interoperable only through the adoption of common protocols. She identifies four overlapping conceptual categories: physical infrastructure; logical resources (such as IP addresses and other protocols); application and content layer; and legal layer (cutting across the previous three). By assessing the status of fragmentation in the four conceptual categories, DeNardis (2016) sheds light on the many-fold nature of the factors that may yield fragmentation. Digital literacy, accessibility (for example, connectivity or digital divide), language (most people consume contents in their local language solely), and other social elements create non-communicating 'bubbles' of users without formal fragmenting elements being in place at the regulatory, commercial, or other levels.

Nonetheless, Mueller (2017) criticises most definitions of fragmentation as too broad and distinguishes between 'alignment' and 'fragmentation'. To Mueller (2017), 'fragmentation' can only refer to the creation of a technically separate Internet, whereas every other regulatory limitation to or control of information fluxes within a country is to be dubbed as alignment to domestic legislation. In short, when states like China censor Internet contents and platforms or browsers (such as Google, Facebook, WhatsApp) they 'align' the Internet to national regulation, rather than fragmenting it. As a matter of fact, the DNS used in China is the IANA-established one and the Chinese Internet infrastructure continues to operate through TCP/IP (Mueller, 2020). The mere use of a Virtual Private Network (VPN) allows one to overcome the restrictions imposed by the so-called 'Great Firewall of China', allowing full access to Internet contents available abroad—although restrictions are growing vis-à-vis this practice in China (Li, 2023). This allows Chinese companies not to lose the network benefits, that is, the scale economies provided by being in a technically unified Internet: technically separate *splinternets* would force international device manufacturers to produce devices with different specifications for different markets in order to operate on technically separate 'internets' (Mueller, 2017).

What emerges from this debate in the literature is the deeply political nature of the concept of fragmentation. For example, despite 'commercial fragmentation' existing as a definition (Drake et al., 2016), few would accuse Netflix of fragmenting the Internet because it makes certain content available in certain countries and not in others. This is simply attributed to a system of incentives and constraints (economic, regulatory, IPR-related, etc.) within which the company makes microeconomic decisions. Nonetheless, fears of fragmentation are bigger when powerful state actors are involved (Hoffmann et al., 2020), even though with a VPN it is (technically) simpler to overcome China's 'Great Firewall' than Netflix's restrictions. Arguably, this is because many in the literature implicitly recognise that potential fragmentation from powerful state actors with deeply different political values and identities could undermine the ideological basis of the existing Internet governance model (Segal, 2016). To conclude, for fragmentation to take place there needs to be a political purpose followed by a technical split within the infrastructure such that devices connected to different networks cannot intercommunicate due to the adoption of incompatible identifiers.

In this sense, Internet fragmentation would challenge the global spread of the Liberal International Order. As established in the introduction of this chapter, the Internet and its multistakeholder governance epitomise the US' hegemony during the so-called 'unipolar decade'. If one conceives the Internet as a global network of networks allowing users to exchange data seamlessly between network-connected devices anywhere such connectivity is provided, hampering such exchange hits at the core of the Liberal Order in its global spatial dimension.

2.6 A Few Notes on Policy- and Standard-Making Functioning

Having identified the importance of Internet fragmentation and the future of multistakeholderism for the Liberal International Order, one needs to observe the detail of the functioning of Internet governance fora to make sense of the several venues for policymaking and influence that the regime complex opens up to a variety of public and private actors. Therefore, this section offers a panoramic of the functioning of the three fora analysed in this book, namely ICANN, IETF, and 3GPP.

2.6.1 Internet Corporation for Assigned Names and Numbers

To begin with, ICANN is a private not-for-profit entity registered in California. As in any private organisation, decisions are made by the Board of Directors. The Board of Directors consists of sixteen voting members and four non-voting liaisons. The organisation is then composed of Advisory Committees (ACs) and Supporting Organisations (SOs). The former represents a specific stakeholder group's interest and formulate broad advice for the Board, while the latter elaborates policy subject to Board adoption. SOs representatives appoint the Board members. The only AC with a voting member in the Board is the At-Large Advisory Committee (ALAC), which represents users. Other ACs, such as GAC, play a purely consultative role and appoint non-voting liaisons to the Board. While consultative, ACs can have a formal role in decision-making. For example, GAC consensus advice can be rejected with a 60% majority vote of the Board, which then must provide a reason (ICANN, 2019).

SOs instead play a more formal role. Rather than advice, they produce policy through consensus or super-majorities (depending on internal rules) which passes to the Board for discussion and approval.

To summarise, while the Board has a final say on ICANN's decisions, several actors are involved in policy making, whether with an advisory or policymaking role.

2.6.2 Internet Engineering Task Force

The IETF was founded in 1986 in a rather informal fashion. Currently, it has an administration, and it is part of the Internet Society, headquartered in Virginia (US) (Camarillo & Livingood, 2020). Participation in the IETF is formally on a voluntary basis, but registration fees, travel costs (meetings are held thrice a year in different continents for a week), and the high expertise needed to participate proficiently in working groups makes it necessary for most participants to be sponsored. Furthermore, the importance IETF-made standards have for the basic functioning of the Internet makes it a venue big technology companies want to have influence in. Therefore, IETF rules request participants to disclose potential conflicts of interest (Belli, 2015).

IETF work is conducted by rough consensus, that is, dissenting opinions are noted but do not constitute veto, whereas significant opposition, albeit small, means consensus on a document has not been reached. IETF work is divided into areas: Application and Real-Time; General; Internet; Operations and Management; Routing; Security; and Transport. Each area is composed of working groups (WGs), conducting work in face-to-face meetings and remotely through their open mailing list. WGs' work is based on Internet Drafts (IDs) and RFCs. The latter contain anything from research notes to technical standards, while the former are temporary documents constituting informal, available to all but not quotable, informational notes on the work conducted by or proposed to a group on a given specification.

Once a specification is agreed upon and reaches standard status through the aforementioned consensual decision-making, it is listed as 'Internet Standard' on the Official Internet Protocol Standards of the IETF's RFC Editor (RFC Editor, 2021). For a specification to become Internet Standard there is not only a need for consensus in the competent WG, but also a period of trial and general acceptance by the Internet community (Bradner, 1996).

IETF standards are voluntary industry standards and have no *de jure* enforceability (Bradner, 1996). This also makes it challenging to identify de facto Internet standards, as several proposed standards not yet recognised as fully fledged Internet standards are actually fully deployed (Harcourt et al., 2020).

2.6.3 Third Generation Partnership Project

Finally, 3GPP works differently from the aforementioned bodies. Founded in 1998 to establish the new 3G technology upon initiative of the European Telecommunications Standards Institute (ETSI), the main European telecommunication standards development organisation

(SDO), it now involves seven SDOs covering the main economies of Europe, North America, and Asia. This includes the China Communications Standards Association (CCSA, 中国通信标准化协会, zhongguo tongxin biaojunhua xiehui). The country or region label simply refers to where the SDO is established, but not necessarily to membership, as in some cases membership is open to any entity operating in the SDOs' territorial scope independently of its country of origin. For example, Huawei is a member of ETSI (ETSI, 2020a).

Most SDOs, including ETSI, are public–private in membership (including Board membership) and operate with a mix of private and public funds. For instance, ETSI was established as a private entity by the European Conference of Postal and Telecommunications Administrations (CEPT) upon input from the European Commission in 1988 (ETSI, 2020b). Similarly, CCSA has public–private membership, but works under the supervision of the Ministry of Industry and Information Technology (MIIT, 工业和信息化部, gongye he xinxihua bu) and the Standardization Administration of China (SAC, 国家标准化管理委员会, guojia biaojunhua guanli weiyuanhui), that is, a ministry and a public regulatory authority (CCSA, 2020).

Procedures in 3GPP work are instead similar to the IETF, in a way. There are three Technical Specification Groups (TSGs): Radio Access Network (RAN), Core Technology (CT), and Service and System Aspects (SA). Each of these is subdivided into working groups (WGs). Technical specifications are discussed, elaborated, and approved on the basis of 'absence of significant opposition', a principle similar to the IETF's rough consensus. Conversely to the IETF, participants here need to be affiliated to an entity member to one of the seven SDOs composing 3GPP (3GPP, 2020).

Once specifications for a new generation of mobile connectivity standards (such as 5G) are approved within 3GPP, they need to undergo ITU scrutiny. New generations of mobile Internet standards are elaborated based on guidelines released in advance by the ITU Radiocommunication Sector (ITU-R). International Mobile Telecommunications 2020 (IMT-2020) contains ITU's requirements for 5G specifications, while 4G requirements were contained in IMT-Advanced. The correspondence between generations and the relevant ITU document is not as straightforward, especially as each 'G' label is first and foremost a commercial one. For example, 4G is generally held to encompass three different but related mobile technologies: Long-Term Evolution (LTE), LTE-Advanced, and

LTE-Advanced Pro (ITU Development Sector 2021, hereafter ITU-D). What matters in this section is that specifications are made in accordance with ITU initial requirements, and it is then up to the ITU Radiocommunications Sector (ITU-R) to select the proposed standards that meet requirements and can be recognised as, for example, 5G (Guttman, 2018; ITU, 2021). After this technical process, the proposed specification is recognised as a recommendation (standard) and formally approved by ITU member states' vote (3GPP, 2020).

It is worth recalling that this has juridical implications: being a UN agency, ITU standards (recommendations) can be incorporated in states' law and become standards *de jure*. Furthermore, once a standard is recognised by the ITU, it is recognised as international independently of its geographical spread in terms of implementation. When China deployed a home-grown 3G standard (known as TD-SCDMA) incompatible with those implemented in the EU and the US, the latter claimed at the World Trade Organisation (WTO) that China was setting up technical barriers to trade. However, the case was dropped as deploying an ITU-recognised standard cannot be deemed a barrier, independently of its geographical spread. This is to stress that the ITU recognises as mobile telecommunications standard any set of specification coherent with its initial requirements, independently of the final number of approved standards and of their interoperability (Stewart et al., 2011).[5]

2.6.4 One Final Remark

This short outline of ICANN, IETF, and 3GPP functioning is not a complete account. However, it is essential to provide a first glance of how decision-making works and how power can be distributed within each venue.

The private nature of these venues, as well as their complex conformation that allows different actors to interact in different subsections, create channels of influence for a variety of actors whose impact will be explored according to the methods and theoretical approaches illustrated in the next chapter.

---

[5] At the user level, when China deployed TD-SCDMA, devices produced for the Chinese market would not be able to connect to 3G in Europe and vice-versa. However, the Chinese government allowed the smallest domestic operator, China Unicom, to deploy the 'European' standard. A user with a phone produced for the European market could thus only connect to 3G in China by choosing China Unicom as provider.

2.7 A Short Note on Theory and Methods

This book addresses two subsets of Internet governance: *(i) critical Internet resources (CIRs) governance at ICANN and standardisation at the IETF, and (ii) mobile Internet standard-making at 3GPP.* Coherently, this book refers to literature on regime complexity and norm entrepreneurship to fit the multistakeholderism and fragmentation debates within the broader questions illustrated above. Regime complexity helps to make sense of the functioning of the Internet governance ecosystem: an ensemble of loosely interrelated bodies with no hierarchies among them, where participants from a variety of sectors contribute to decision-making (Alter & Raustiala, 2018; Nye, 2014). In the Internet governance regime complex, Chinese stakeholders act as norm entrepreneurs in shaping and negotiating new norms, but also in adapting to the existing ones to maximise their influence in the standardisation and resource distribution process (Nanni, 2021; Radu et al., 2021). Overall, these streams of literature help to fit the fragmentation and multistakeholderism debate into the broader field of (liberal-informed) global governance studies and, consequently, into the debate on the future of the Liberal International Order (Jongen & Scholte, 2021). This is done with a view on the debate on digital sovereignty and the consequent "return of the state" in Internet governance (Haggart et al., 2021).

On this basis, the author conducted content analysis on documents produced by these three bodies. First, GAC meeting transcripts and communiqués have been analysed for the period relating to the IANA stewardship transition to observe the Chinese government's engagement with ICANN. Second, RFCs from three IETF working groups have been analysed to observe the impact of Chinese companies in Internet standardisation. Two timespans have been considered: 2007–2008 and 2018–2019 to observe how engagement and influence evolved throughout this time. In 2007, signs of early Chinese engagement emerged, while in 2018 the US–China trade competition peaked with the arrest of Huawei's Chief Financial Officer in Canada. Finally, 3GPP Releases (that is, the documents containing technical specification aimed at becoming global standards) related to 4G and 5G are analysed.

Furthermore, twenty-nine interviews were conducted to explore the rationale of the transformations in China's and Chinese stakeholders' engagement in Internet governance. Representatives from six stakeholder communities were interviewed: government, international organisations, businesses, civil society, academia, and technologists. While several Internet stakeholder taxonomies exist (all with their own merits and limits), the one adopted here was found to be the most encompassing (Diplofoundation, 2015). Representatives of Chinese and non-Chinese entities have been interviewed for each stakeholder community, except for government and civil society where the author could not find Chinese participants willing to participate. This may be due to the highly sensitive nature of the topic at stake and the authoritarian character of the Chinese government.

Finally, to situate China's and Chinese stakeholders' engagement in global Internet governance within a broader framework of China's domestic transformation, the author conducted a qualitative document analysis of Chinese policy documents and legislations, which is illustrated and discussed in Chapter 3. Policy documents and official reports were translated in English by the author, while for accurate legal translation the author relied upon the Stanford University-led project DigiChina (2023). English translations are always accompanied by the original text in Chinese.

Ethical issues arose when conducting interviews. In interviews, questions of anonymity have been addressed by not naming any participant in the text and agreeing on an ad hoc basis what to quote and how. An exception was made for one interview participant who explicitly requested to be quoted by full name owing to his public role at the time of the events under analysis.

Having interviewed people from the West and from China, different degrees of sensitivity arose when asking the same questions, as some respondents are nationals of democratic states while others are from autocratic ones.

Throughout the interview process, it was generally easier for the author to access Western stakeholders for interviews than their Chinese counterparts. Arguably, this is due to the autocratic characteristics of the Chinese government, but also to matters of positionality. As the researcher is a white European in a time of strong East–West geopolitical divide on the subject matter in question, subconscious assumptions on the interviewer's position may have emerged, thus forcing the author to make extra effort in building rapport with interview participants. This also connects to matters of 'digital orientalism' (Mayer, 2020), which is the tendency of Western observers to see China's cybersphere and digital policies in direct counter-position to an ideal view of what Western liberal cybersphere and digital policies (should) look like. Such bias may have subconsciously been perpetuated by the author when building rapport to interview participants.

When conducting documents analysis in Chinese, meaning could be lost in translation. While the author has a mastery of Chinese, they are not a native speaker. For this reason, the author relied upon an authoritative source such as DigiChina for legal translation, where misinterpretations of single words can carry broad implications.

2.8 Conclusion

Internet governance is a broad field, and its borders are still debated (Hofmann et al., 2017; Mueller & Badiei, 2020). The question of states' growing role in Internet governance is one that is gaining prominence in the literature (Haggart et al., 2021), with a clearly proactive role having been adopted by states in such fields as data localisation and protection (J. Liu, 2020). However, such dynamics may not be equally spread all over each domain of Internet governance. Some such domains may display a stronger path dependence and provide an incentive for emerging stakeholders to adapt to the existing normative framework and procedures, while some will see more widespread attempts to change norms and power distribution among stakeholders.

As the field is broad, this book focuses on debates on two tenets of Internet governance on the technical side, namely the making, distribution, and governance of critical Internet resources and standard-making in mobile Internet connectivity.

Similar considerations apply to China and the role of its domestic stakeholder, as this book seeks to counter the idea of a monolithic China where private companies are a mere extension of the state apparatus. This research therefore explores Chinese stakeholders' process of contestation, adaptation, and adoption of norms around three relevant venues for the two aforementioned governance subsets: ICANN, IETF, and 3GPP. Observing such venues allows one to address normative questions at the core of Internet governance and topics of central geopolitical importance such as the mobile connectivity infrastructure, with implications for the Liberal Order in its free-market tenet.

To make justice to the ambiguities and complexities in the field, this book sheds light on the drivers, role, and impact of Chinese stakeholders in and towards Internet governance and standardisation processes within the aforementioned three bodies, contributing to broader debates on multistakeholderism and Internet fragmentation. This is done through a regime-theoretic approach and the use of a combination of qualitative methods as illustrated in deeper detail in Appendix A. Through these lenses, this work sheds new light on the impact of China's rise on the Liberal International Order.

REFERENCES

3rd Generation Partnership Project. (2020, October 15). 3GPP. *A Global Initiative.* https://www.3gpp.org/.

Abramowitz, M., & Bosworth, S. (2006). America Confronts the Asian Century. *Current History, 105*(690), 147–152.

Acharya, A. (2018). *The End of American World Order* (2nd ed). Polity Press.

African Network Information Centre. (2020). *Autonomous System Number (ASN) from AFRINIC.* https://afrinic.net/asn (October 19, 2020).

Alter, K. J., & Raustiala, K. (2018). The Rise of International Regime Complexity. *Annual Review of Law and Social Science, 14*(1), 329–349.

Arkko, J. (2023). Distribution of Authors per Companies. *IETF Statistics.* https://www.arkko.com/tools/allstats/companydistr.html (July 21, 2023).

Belli, L. (2015). A Heterostakeholder Cooperation for Sustainable Internet Policymaking. *Internet Policy Review, 4*(2), 1–21.

Blanco, B., Fajardo, J. O., Giannoulakis, I., Kafetzakis, E., Peng, S., Pérez-Romero, J., Trajkovska, I., Khodashenas, P. S., Goratti, L., Paolino, M., Sfakianakis, E., Liberal, F., & Xilouris, G. (2017). Technology Pillars in the Architecture of Future 5G Mobile Networks: NFV, MEC and SDN. *Computer Standards and Interfaces, 54*(4), 216–228.

Bo, P. (2018). China, Global Governance, and Hegemony: Neo-Gramscian Perspective in the World Order. *Journal of China and International Relations, 6*(1), 48–72.

Bradner, S. (1996). RFC 2026: The Internet Standards Process - Revision 3. *IETF Datatracker.* https://datatracker.ietf.org/doc/html/rfc2026 (May 28, 2021).

Cai, C. (2018a). Global Cyber Governance. China's Contribution and Approach. *China Quarterly of International Strategic Studies, 4*(1), 55–76.

Cai, C. (2018b). China and Global Cyber Governance: Main Principles and Debates. *Asian Perspectives, 42*(4), 647–662.

Camarillo, G., & Livingood, J. (2020). RFC 8712: The IETF-ISOC Relationship. *IETF Datatracker*. https://datatracker.ietf.org/doc/html/rfc8712 (May 28, 2021).
Carr, M. (2015). Power Plays in Global Internet Governance. *Millennium: Journal of International Studies, 43*(2), 640–659.
Cath, C. (2021). The Technology we Choose to Create: Human Rights Advocacy in the Internet Engineering Task Force. *Telecommunications Policy, 45*(6). https://doi.org/10.1016/j.telpol.2021.102144
China Communications Standards Association. (2020). *CCSA Organisational Structure*. http://www.ccsa.org.cn/orgnization?title=%E7%BB%84%E7%BB%87%E6%9E%B6%E6%9E%84 (November 11, 2020). [中国通信标准化协会2020. 中国通信标准化协会组织机构].
Creemers, R. (2020). China's Conception of Cyber Sovereignty: Rhetoric and Realization. In D. Broeders & B. Van den Berg (Eds.), *Governing Cyberspace. Behavior, Power, and Diplomacy*. Rowman and Littlefield.
Dahlman, E., Parkvall, S., & Sköld, J. (2016). *4G, LTE-Advanced Pro and the Road to 5G* (3rd ed.) Elsevier.
DeNardis, L. (2014). *The Global War for Internet Governance*. Yale University Press.
DeNardis, L. (2016). One Internet: An Evidentiary Basis for Policy Making on Internet Universality and Fragmentation. In Global Commission on Internet Governance (Ed.), *A Universal Internet in a Bordered World. Research on Fragmentation, Openness and Interoperability*. CIGI and Chatham House.
Deudney, D., & Ikenberry, G. J. (2018, July). The Resilient Order. *Foreign Affairs*. https://www.foreignaffairs.com/articles/world/2018-06-14/liberal-world (March 23, 2020).
Digichina. (2023). *Digichina. A Project of the Program on Geopolitics, Technology, and Governance at the Stanford Cyber Policy Center*. https://digichina.stanford.edu/ (August 18, 2023).
DiploFoundation. (2015). *Multistakeholderism in IGF language*. http://www.diplomacy.edu/IGFLanguage/multistakeholderism (November 25, 2020).
Drake, W. J., Cerf, V. G., & Kleinwächter, W. (2016). *Internet Fragmentation: An Overview*. World Economic Forum.
Duncombe, C., & Dunne, T. (2018). After Liberal World Order. *International Affairs, 94*(1), 25–42.
European Telecommunications Standards Institute. (2020a). *3GPP*. https://www.etsi.org/committee/1418-3gpp (November 11, 2020).
European Telecommunications Standards Institute. (2020b). *Our Structure*. https://www.etsi.org/about/our-structure (November 11, 2020).
Flonk, D., Jachtenfuchs, M., & Obendiek, A. S. (2020). Authority Conflicts in Internet governance: Liberals vs. Sovereigntists? *Global Constitutionalism, 9*(2), 364–386.

Galloway, T., & He, B. (2014). China and Technical Global Internet Governance: Beijing's Approach to Multi-stakeholder Governance within ICANN, WSIS and the IGF. *China: An International Journal, 12*(3), 72–93.

Glen, C. M. (2014). Internet Governance: Territorializing Cyberspace? *Politics and Policy, 42*(5), 635–657.

Gómez-Mera, L. (2016). Regime Complexity and Global Governance: The Case of Trafficking in Persons. *European Journal of International Relations, 22*(3), 566–595.

Gong, Y. (2019). Standardisation Boosts National Governance Systems and Governance Capabilities. A Basic Analysis of the Modernisation Drive. *16th Chinese Standardisation Forum Paper Collection*, 11–249. http://www.chinacas.org/u/cms/www/201910/30142846q7r0.pdf (October 20, 2020). [龚月芳 2019. "标准化助推国家治理体系与治理能力. 现代化建设浅析". 第16届中国标准化论坛论文集, 11–249].

Guttman, E. (2018). 5G Standardisation in 3GPP. *International Telecommunication Union*. https://www.itu.int/en/ITU-T/Workshops-and-Seminars/201807/Documents/3_Erik_Guttman.pdf (May 28, 2021).

Haggart, B., Scholte, J. A., & Tusikov, N. (2021). Introduction. Return of the State? In B. Haggart, N. Tusikov & J. A. Scholte (Eds.), *Power and Authority in Internet Governance. Return of the State?* Routledge.

Harcourt, A., Christou, G., & Simpson, S. (2020). *Global Standard Setting in Internet Governance*. Oxford University Press.

Hill, R. (2016). Internet Governance, Multi-stakeholder Models, and the IANA Transition: Shining Example or Dark Side? *Journal of Cyber Policy, 1*(2), 176–197.

Hoffmann, S., Lazanski, D., & Taylor, E. (2020). Standardising the Splinternet: How China's Technical Standards could Fragment the Internet. *Journal of Cyber Policy, 5*(2), 239–264.

Hofmann, J., Katzenback, C., & Gollatz, K. (2017). Between Coordination and Regulation: Finding the Governance in Internet Governance. *New Media and Society, 19*(9), 1406–1423.

Hurel, L. M., & Rocha, M. S. (2018). Brazil, China and Internet Governance: Mapping Divergence and Convergence. *Journal of China and International Relations*, Special issue, 98–115.

Ikenberry, G. J. (2008). The Rise of China and the Future of the West - Can the Liberal System Survive? *Foreign Affairs, 87*(1), 23–37.

Ikenberry, G. J. (2018). The End of Liberal International Order? *International Affairs, 94*(1), 7–23.

Ikenberry, G. J. (2024). Three Worlds: The West, East and South and the Competition to Shape Global Order. *International Affairs, 100*(1), 121–138.

International Telecommunication Union. (2005). Tunis Agenda for the Information Society. WSIS-05/TUNIS/DOC/6(Rev.1)-E. https://www.itu.int/net/wsis/docs2/tunis/off/6rev1.html (December 18, 2019).
International Telecommunication Union. (2020a). International Telecommunication Regulations. https://www.itu.int/en/wcit-12/Pages/itrs.aspx (October 20, 2020).
International Telecommunication Union. (2020b). *ITU Towards 'IMT for 2020 and Beyond'*. https://www.itu.int/en/ITU-R/study-groups/rsg5/rwp5d/imt-2020/Pages/default.aspx (October 15, 2020).
International Telecommunication Union. (2021, March 15). New ITU Standards Optimize Transport Networks Support for IMT-2020/5G. *ITUNews*. https://www.itu.int/en/myitu/News/2021/03/15/12/36/New-ITU-standards-optimize-transport-networks-support-for-5G (May 28, 2021).
ITU Development Sector. (2021). Mobile Communications. *International Telecommunication Union*. https://www.itu.int/ITU-D/tech/MobileCommunications/IMT_INTRODUCING/IMT_2G3G4G.html (May 28, 2021).
Internet Corporation for Assigned Names and Numbers. (1999). *Memorandum of Understanding between the U.S. Department of Commerce and Internet Corporation for Assigned Names and Numbers*. https://www.icann.org/resources/unthemed-pages/icann-mou-1998-11-25-en (July 22, 2020).
Internet Corporation for Assigned Names and Numbers. (2011). *ICANNWiki*. https://icannwiki.org/ (October 30, 2020).
Internet Corporation for Assigned Names and Numbers. (2019, November 2018). *Bylaws for Internet Corporation for Assigned Names and Numbers. A California Nonprofit Public-Benefit Corporation*. https://www.icann.org/resources/pages/governance/bylaws-en (May 27, 2021).
Internet Corporation for Assigned Names and Numbers (2021, January 2019). *Regional Internet Registry*. https://icannwiki.org/Regional_Internet_Registry (April 8, 2024).
Internet Engineering Task Force. (2020). *Internet Standards*. https://ietf.org/standards/ (February 5, 2020).
Jia, L., & Winseck, D. (2018). The Political Economy of Chinese Internet Companies: Financialization, Concentration, and Capitalization. *International Communication Gazette, 80*(1), 30–59.
Jiang, M. (2012). Internet Companies in China. Dancing between the Party Line and the Bottom Line. *AsieVision, 47*.
Jongen, H., & Scholte, J. A. (2021). Legitimacy in Multistakeholder Global Governance at ICANN. *Global Governance, 27*(2), 298–324.
Kawabata, T. (2020). Private Governance Schemes for Green Bond Standard: Influence on Public Authorities' Policy Making. *Green Finance, 2*(1), 35–54.
Keohane, R. O., & Victor, D. G. (2011). The Regime Complex for Climate Change. *Perspectives on Politics, 9*(1), 7–23.

Kim, M., Lee, H., & Kwak, J. (2020). The Changing Patterns of China's International Standardization in ICT under Techno-nationalism: A Reflection through 5G Standardization. *International Journal of Information Management, 54*, 1–8.

Klimburg, A. (2013). The Internet Yalta. *Center for a New American Security.*

Kourandi, F., Krämer, J., & Valletti, T. (2015). Net Neutrality, Exclusivity Contracts, and Internet Fragmentation. *Information Systems Research, 26*(2), 320–338.

Leiner, B. M., Cerf, V. G., Clark, D. D., Kahn, R. E., Kleinrock, L., Lynch, D. C., Postel, J., Roberts, L. G., & Wolff, S. (1997). Brief History of the Internet. *Internet Society.* https://www.internetsociety.org/internet/history-internet/brief-history-internet/ (May 20, 2021).

Li, G. (2023). Internet Censorship in China. A Functioning Digital Panopticon. In N. Talmacs & A. Y. Peng (Eds.), *Communications in Contemporary China. Orchestrating Thinking.* Routledge.

Liu, J. (2020). China's Data Localization. *Chinese Journal of Communication, 13*(1), 84–103.

Liu, Y. (2012). The Rise of China and Global Internet Governance. *China Media Research, 8*(2), 46–55.

Ma, S. (2020). Political Risk Analysis of Huawei's International Expansion in the Context of US-China Competition. *Journal of Contemporary Asia-Pacific, 13*(1): 4–29. [马骊2020. 中美竞争背景下华为5G国际拓展的政治风险分析. 当代亚太, 13年第1期: 第4–29页]

Mayer, M. (2020). China's Authoritarian Internet and Digital Orientalism. In D. Feldner (Ed.), *Redesigning Organizations. Concepts for the Connected Society.* Springer.

Mearsheimer, J. J. (2006). China's Unpeaceful Rise. *Current History, 105*(690), 160–162.

Mearsheimer, J. J. (2019). Bound to Fail: The Rise and Fall of the Liberal International Order. *International Security, 43*(4), 7–50.

Mueller, M. L. (2013). Are We in a Digital Cold War? *GigaNet: The Global Governance of the Internet: Intergovernmentalism, Multistakeholderism and Networks.* http://citeseerx.ist.psu.edu/viewdoc/download?doi=10.1.1.363.2569&rep=rep1&type=pdf (July 18, 2019).

Mueller, M. (2014). Detaching Internet Governance from the State: Globalizing the IANA. *Georgetown Journal of International Affairs*, 35–44.

Mueller, M. L. (2017). *Will the Internet Fragment? Sovereignty, Globalization, and Cyberspace.* Polity Press.

Mueller, M. L. (2020, February 26). The Knake-Mueller Wager: Will China Form an Alternate DNS Root? *Internet Governance Project.* https://www.internetgovernance.org/2020/02/26/the-knake-mueller-wager-will-china-form-an-alternate-dns-root/ (October 10, 2021).

Mueller, M. L., & Badiei, F. (2020). Inventing Internet Governance: The Historical Trajectory of the Phenomenon and the Field. In L. DeNardis, D. Cogburn, N. Levinson & F. Musiani (Eds.), *Researching Internet Governance: Methods, Frameworks, Futures*. MIT Press.

Mueller, M., & Kuerbis, B. (2014, March 3). Roadmap for globalizing IANA: Four principles and a proposal for reform. *Internet Governance Project*. https://tinyurl.com/3peddzah (October 12, 2023).

Nanni, R. (2021). The 'China' Question in Mobile Internet Standard-making: Insights from Expert Interviews. *Telecommunications Policy, 45*(6), 1–12.

Negro, G. (2020). A History of Chinese Global Internet Governance and its Relations with ITU and ICANN. *Chinese Journal of Communication, 13*(1), 104–121.

Nye, J. S. (2014). The Regime Complex for Managing Global Cyber Activities. *Global Commission on Internet Governance Paper Series, 1*. http://www.cigionline.org/publications/regime-complex-managingglobal-cyber-activities (July 25, 2019).

Palladino, N., & Santaniello, M. (2021). *Legitimacy, Power, and Inequalities in the Multistakeholder Internet Governance*. Palgrave Macmillan.

Parsi, V. E. (2021). *The Wrecking of the Liberal World Order*. Springer Nature.

Phillips, A. (2013). A Dangerous Synergy: Energy Securitization, Great Power Rivalry and Strategic Stability in the Asian Century. *The Pacific Review, 26*(1), 17–38.

Pohlmann, T., Blind, K., & Hess, P. (2020). *Fact Finding Study on Patents Declared to the 5G Standard*. IPLytics and Technische Universitaet Berlin.

Pupillo, L. (2019, June 21). 5G and National Security. CEPS. https://www.ceps.eu/5g-and-nationalsecurity/ (October 20, 2020).

Radu, R., Kettemann, M. C., Meyer, T., & Shahin, J. (2021). Normfare: Norm Entrepreneurship in Internet Governance. *Telecommunications Policy, 45*(6), 1–7.

RFC Editor. (2021). *Official Internet Protocol Standards*. https://tinyurl.com/3x22kre4 (May 28, 2021).

Rosenau, J. N. (1992). Governance, Order, and Change in World Politics. In J. N. Rosenau & E. Czempiel (Eds.), *Governance without Government: Order and Change in World Politics*. Cambridge University Press.

Russell, A. L. (2013, July 30). OSI: The Internet That Wasn't. *IEEE Spectrum*. https://spectrum.ieee.org/tech-history/cyberspace/osi-the-internet-that-wasnt (November 27, 2020).

Santaniello, M. (2021). From Governance Denial to State Regulation: A Controversy-Based Typology of Internet Governance Models. In B. Haggart, N. Tusikov & J. A. Scholte (Eds.), *Power and Authority in Internet Governance. Return of the State?*. Routledge.

Schackleford, S., & Craig, A. (2014). Beyond the New 'Digital Divide': Analyzing the Evolving Role of National Governments in Internet Governance and Enhancing Cybersecurity. *Stanford Journal of International Law*, *50*(119), 1–65.

Scholte, J. A. (2017). Complex Hegemony. The IANA Transition in Global Internet Governance. *GigaNet: Global Internet Governance Academic Network, Annual Symposium*.

Segal, A. (2016). *The Hacked World Order: How Nations Fight, Trade, Maneuver, and Manipulate in the Digital Age*. PublicAffairs.

Segal, A. (2018, August 13). When China Rules the Web: Technology in Service of the State. *Foreign Affairs*. https://www.foreignaffairs.com/articles/china/2018-08-13/when-china-rules-web (November 10, 2020).

Shen, H. (2016). China and Global Internet Governance: Toward an Alternative Analytical Framework. *Chinese Journal of Communication*, *9*(3), 304–324.

Shen, H. (2018). Building a Digital Silk Road? Situating the Internet in China's Belt and Road Initiative. *International Journal of Communication*, *12*, 2683–2701.

Socolofsky, T., & Kale, C. (1991). RFC 1180: A TCP/IP Tutorial. *IETF Datatracker*. https://datatracker.ietf.org/doc/html/rfc1180#page-2 (May 14, 2021).

Stewart, J., Shen, X., Wang, C., & Graham, I. (2011). From 3G to 4G: Standards and the Development of Mobile Broadband in China. *Technology Analysis and Strategic Management*, *23*(7), 773–788.

Tang, M. (2020). From 'Bringing-in' to 'Going-out': Transnationalizing China's Internet Capital Through State Policies. *Chinese Journal of Communication*, *13*(1), 27–46.

Ten Oever, N. (2022). 5G and the Notion of Network Ideology, or: the Limitations of Sociotechnical Imaginaries. *Telecommunications Policy*, 102442.

Westwinter, O. (2021). Transnational Public-private Governance Initiatives in World Politics: Introducing a New Dataset. *The Review of International Organizations*, *16*(1), 137–174.

Winseck, D. (2020). Is the International Telecommunication Union Still Relevant in 'the Internet Age?' Lessons From the 2012 World Conference on International Telecommunications (WCIT). In G. Balbi & A. Fickers (Eds.), *History of the International Telecommunication Union*. De Gruyter.

Working Group on Internet Governance. (2005). *Report of the Working Group on Internet Governance*. 05.41622.

Zheng, B. (2005). China's 'Peaceful Rise' to Great- Power Status. In D. Shambaugh (Ed.), *The China Reader* (6th ed.) Oxford University Press.

Zhong, R. (2019, April 25). Who Owns Huawei? The Company Tried to Explain. It Got Complicated. *New York Times*. https://www.nytimes.com/2019/04/25/technology/who-owns-huawei.html (October 20, 2020).

Zürn, M. (2018). *A Theory of Global Governance. Authority, Legitimacy, and Contestation*. Oxford University Press.

CHAPTER 3

Situating Chinese Engagement in Internet Governance: China's Domestic Digital Policy Reviewed

3.1 Introduction

China's and Chinese companies' positioning vis-à-vis Internet and telecommunications standards and resource management has not developed in a vacuum. This chapter provides a historical overview and contextualisation of China's domestic digital policies to complement the analysis conducted in the forthcoming chapters on Chinese stakeholders' engagement with global Internet governance. While this book is concentrated on Chinese engagement with Internet governance at the global level, an analytical overview of China's domestic digital ecosystem is necessary to gauge its complexity and discard simplistic views depicting China, its government, and its companies as a monolithic whole controlled by the Chinese Communist Party (Brandt & Thun, 2021; Breslin, 2012; Shen, 2016).

To begin with, contrary to common belief spread in most Western media, governmental support to tech companies in China has not been constant, and rather has varied from sector to sector (Mueller & Farhat, 2022; Shen, 2022; Wen, 2020). Chinese technology champions have enjoyed state financial and policy support as well as enduring times of clash against governmental policies and exclusion from their own domestic market (de Kloet et al., 2019; Tang, 2020). In the early 2000s, Huawei became an international company amid China's domestic infrastructure market saturation, but later was identified as a national champion and received financial support (Barbieri et al., 2013; Hensmans & Liu, 2020; Wen, 2020). Likewise, in the platform economy, companies such as Tencent and Alibaba grew thanks to governmental laissez-faire and the economic protectionist effects of the so-called "Great Firewall of China" (a subset of a larger policy project known as "Golden Shield Project", 金盾工程, jindun gongcheng), which contributed to keeping Silicon Valley competitors out of the Chinese market especially after 2009, with the exclusion of Facebook and Twitter (Creemers, 2022; Plantin & De Seta, 2019). However, Chinese platform companies have endured a regulatory crackdown since 2020 known as "Great Rectification" that is still ongoing at the time of writing (Shen, 2022; Zhong, 2021). It must be stressed that different companies in different sectors had different relations with the Chinese government in different moments in history and there is no single trend applicable to the whole "tech sector" in its broadest definition. Furthermore, prior to governmental interventions banning US-based platform services, nascent Chinese platform companies faced harsh competition from Western equivalents that had already established a presence in the Chinese territory and only later did they come to enjoy state support and protection (Mueller & Farhat, 2022; Rolf & Schindler, 2023). Nonetheless, it is worth noting that WeChat was already more successful than WhatsApp prior to the latter's removal from the Chinese market, signalling Chinese users' preference for a Chinese-grown software product that was arguably better tailored around their expectations. In general, several non-Chinese software companies have failed to adapt their products to the preferences of Chinese usership (L. Cao et al., 2023; Zhang et al., 2021).

At the time of writing, China is undergoing a phase in which the government is trying to gain stronger control over domestic tech companies in the financial and platforms sectors, with the aforementioned Great Rectification campaign as its epitome. In the name of wealth redistribution (officially "Common Prosperity", 共同富裕, gongtong fuyu), the Great Rectification campaign is characterised in the tech sector by the Chinese government's attempt to strengthen its capacity to impose rules and political guidance over platform companies (Shen, 2022). Indeed, governments all over the world are currently struggling with applying domestic law to big tech multinationals often headquartered elsewhere and fiscally registered in tax havens. According to large scholarly sectors, China's operations are to be interpreted as actions to control the political implications of growing data-heavy business groups that may coalesce into power groups (A. H. Creemers, 2023; Zhang, 2022). Furthermore, groups such as Alibaba are strong in the platform economy as well as in the financial sector, where they provide and control e-payment tools and conduct important operations in financial markets in China and overseas. Therefore, the Great Rectification campaign is also to rein in a largely deregulated financial sector that has increasingly created concerns among citizens and government alike (Chorzempa & Huang, 2022). On the popular culture side, a number of celebrities have been "rectified" as the lifestyle they lived and/or promoted was not considered coherent with Party values (Creemers, 2023). Overall, the Great Rectification has cultural, financial, and power components in that it targets people and organisations conveying heterodox values, largely unregulated financial actors, as well as big tech groups whose large collection of people's everyday data (Shen & He, 2022) can help them to influence users' behaviour and (political and social) choices. All together, the campaign has contributed to the Chinese government's attempt to rein in power groups and to appease popular requests regarding increasing regulation and control over private companies' use of citizens' data (Creemers, 2023).

While the Great Rectification campaign is recent, dating back only to 2020, the terms "rectification" and "Common Prosperity" date back to Mao Zedong's time, at least in their current connotation (Teiwes, 1979). During the cultural revolution, actions of rectification targeted so-called "black" subjects (Noumoff, 1967; Teiwes, 1979), that is, individuals who were labelled as counter-revolutionaries due to their activities (present or past) and/or their family connections (such as having a landlord as an ancestor). However, in the context of China's digital policies in the 2020s the term "rectification" regards bringing the platform economy under stricter governmental rule (O. Creemers, 2023; Wang, 2022). Something similar applies to "common prosperity": the concept was introduced in 1953, in the wake of the 1949 revolution and the consolidation of the Party's power in China. According to Dunford (2022, 36), "[o]n December 12, 1953, [the concept] appeared in the headline of a People's Daily article titled 'The Path of Socialism is the Path to Common Prosperity'". While most media accounts credit Xi Jinping for the revival of the "Common Prosperity" idea in 2020 (O. Wang, 2022), its reintroduction in Chinese policy discourse actually dates back to the late 1990s. After almost two decades of market-oriented reform that led to growing inequality, the question of wealth redistribution returned gradually to the Party's agenda from 1999 onwards (Dunford, 2022). According to sectors of the literature, the eleventh five-year plan (2006–2010) already represented a shift towards a common prosperity goal (Fan, 2006), although arguably it was only in 2020 under Xi's leadership that the term was revived to a point that it became known and addressed in foreign media.

Despite the Great Rectification campaign, private capital retains influence in state policy and its own capacity to act globally: notwithstanding a narrower global market for Huawei, which has now turned towards China's domestic market for major revenues (Brown, 2021), this company is still active in international Internet standardisation and it continues to lead the 5G standardisation race along with Ericsson and Samsung (Arkko, 2023; Becker et al., 2024). After all, device and network manufacturers have not been targeted in the Common Prosperity campaign (Creemers, 2023; Nanni, 2022; Shen, 2022). This fits within a larger process of retraction of private capitals and increased presence of the state in the economy (国进民退, guojin mintui) predates Xi's leadership (Yang & Jiang, 2012), and characterises China's current domestic Internet governance ecosystem (Cai, 2018; Gao, 2022).

It is in this historico-political context that the evolution of Chinese stakeholders' engagement in global Internet governance and telecommunications standardisation has evolved. Within this context, the documents analysed here showcase how China can foster societal control domestically through the regulation of online information fluxes while remaining infrastructurally and politically integrated into the global Internet governance ecosystem.

Through academic literature and the first-hand analysis of legal and policy documents,[1] three historical phases have been identified and addressed below. First, the 1994–2008 phase was characterised by information control but large business laissez-faire, with foreign capital (first and foremost from the US) flowing into China's digital economy and

---

[1] As anticipated in Chapter 2, policy documents and texts in Chinese are translated into English by the author, while translations of legal texts are taken from DigiChina (2023). Each translated piece of text carries the indication of whether it was translated by the author or by a third source. Each piece of legislation is analysed in Chinese to ensure the original text is considered in the analysis, but it is referenced in English to ensure all readers of this book can access a version of the legal text they can read. DigiChina translations are the author's first choice as they are quite accurate and always report both the original text (in Chinese) and the English translation.

Chinese players being relegated to marginal positions even domestically (Mueller & Farhat, 2022; Wen, 2020). Second, the 2009–2016 was characterised by restrictions on platforms and web services providers, beginning with the ban on Facebook and Twitter in 2009, and the emergence of Internet sovereignty[2] (网络主权, wangluo zhuquan) as a formal policy term included in policy papers (Creemers, 2020). Third, the current phase started in 2016 and is characterised not only by information control and market restrictions, but also by growing regulations on data and strategic information assets as well as stronger governmental effort to enforce domestic law over platform companies (Shen, 2022).

3.2 Phase 1: 1994–2008. Information Control and Capital Deregulation

A large share of Internet content and information regulation in China dates back to the "Golden Projects", in particular the Golden Shield Project which started in 1998. The Golden Shield Project was established by the Jiang Zemin administration and is aimed at controlling information fluxes that could hinder domestic political equilibria. It was established in an era in which the Internet was only starting to become a constant presence in Chinese people's everyday life, with the first stable Internet connection established in 1994. However, the Golden Shield Project remains a core element of China's information- and digitalisation-related policies. The state-led crackdown on the religious group Falun Gong is often indicated as (one of) the trigger(s) of the Golden Shield Project (Negro, 2017). Simultaneously, the 1990s were characterised by economic reform to respond to the fall of international communism and the malaise that followed the 1989 protests (Shiu & Sutter, 1996). In the then-emerging digital economy environment, the 1990s were characterised by reforms of the telecommunications system and a restructuring

---

[2] The term 网络主权 (wangluo zhuquan) is alternately translated as Internet sovereignty, cyber sovereignty or network sovereignty. In this book the author preferred the term 'Internet sovereignty' as it is used in the official translation of the 2010 White Paper on the (status of the) Internet in China. In its Chinese version, the term used is 互联网主权 (hulianwang zhuquan) (Xinhua, 2010). 互联网 (hulianwang) translates more directly as "Internet", while 网络 (wangluo) can be translated as "network". The meanings, however, are largely interchangeable.

of the state administration apparatus thereof (Negro, 2017; Shen, 2022; Wen, 2020).

While these measures were also aimed at controlling information fluxes within the country (Shen, 2022), the 2000s were characterised by an open market, where US and European capital penetrated the Chinese market and allowed Chinese digital platforms to grow (Mueller & Farhat, 2022). This included relatively unregulated transactions in data (K. Creemers, 2022; Qin, 2015). Indeed, while it is generally true that the Golden Shield Project and the bans against Silicon Valley companies introduced since 2009 served a protectionist role to allow companies like Alibaba to grow (Plantin & De Seta, 2019), the early history of Chinese platforms was characterised mainly by foreign investment, state disengagement with the platform economy, and a largely unregulated flux of customers' data across the Internet (Mueller & Farhat, 2022). For example, WeChat's (微信, weixin) market dominance vis-à-vis WhatsApp within China was evident even before the latter's ban in 2017 (Negro, 2017). The foreign domination in China's domestic market was also true in the network infrastructure market, where Huawei found a saturated market and sought to internationalise between the 1990s and early 2000s (Wen, 2020), as will be discussed later in the book.

The cohabitation between censorship and an unregulated digital market followed the principles reiterated by President Hu Jintao in the 38th Collective Study Session of the Politburo of the Central Committee of the Chinese Communist Party:

> *Strengthening the construction and management of an Internet culture, fully unleashing the important role of the Internet in the socialist cultural construction of our country, will help to improve the ideological and moral, scientific, and cultural quality of the whole nation. It will help to expand the frontier of propaganda and ideological work, and help to expand the appeal and charm of the socialist spiritual civilisation. It will help enhance our country's soft power. We must vigorously develop and spread a healthy Internet culture with a positive attitude and an innovative spirit, while effectively building, using, and managing the Internet* (The Central People's Government of the People's Republic of China 2007) [translation by the author].[3]

---

[3] Original text: 加强网络文化建设和管理，充分发挥互联网在我国社会主义文化建设中的重要作用，有利于提高全民族的思想道德素质和科学文化素质，有利于扩大宣传思想工作的阵地，有利于扩大社会主义精神文明的辐射力和感染力，有利于增强我国的软实力。

In short, a strong information regulation effort was pushed forward by the Communist Party to ensure the development of the Internet would not be conducive of political instability within China. It could be argued that the 2000s corresponded to China's biggest digitalisation spur, in that a large share of the country started using digital services in their daily life also thanks to the deployment of the 3G infrastructure, that is, the first mobile connectivity service (J. Zhang & Liang, 2007). Nowadays, the vast majority of the Chinese people access the Internet through their phone rather than a computer according to the China Internet Network Information Centre (2020, 中国互联网信息中心, zhongguo hulianwang xinxi zhongxin), signalling the importance of mobile connectivity across the Chinese society.

The telecommunication market of China, like that of most other countries, is key to interpreting the dynamics of development of the national Internet economy. This is due to the constant interaction and interdependence between the telephony and the Internet infrastructures, which has transformed through decades but never faded (ten Oever, 2022). As anticipated, the 1994–2008 phase was one of reform and restructuring of the public and the relatively new private sector. Established in 1994, the then quasi-monopolist China Telecom came through the 1990s to be flanked by such carriers as China Mobile, China Unicom, China Railcom, Jitong, and China Netcom. By 2004, China Mobile, China Telecom, China Netcom, and China Unicom were the four biggest telephony service providers in China in order of revenues (Ho, 2013). In 2008, China Netcom was merged with China Unicom and the new company retained the latter's name.

The fact that, up to the present day, all of China's telephony service providers are state-owned enterprises may mislead the observer into thinking that telephony (and now mobile connectivity) is a tightly state-controlled market. On the contrary, cliques, political factions, power groups, and even different bureaucratic structures competed to gain power and influence in this sector in the 1990s and early 2000s (Negro, 2020; Wen, 2020). For example, the establishment of China Telecom in 1994 was led by the Ministry of Posts and Telecommunications, while the Ministry of Electronic Industry led the establishment of China Unicom

---

我们必须以积极的态度、创新的精神,大力发展和传播健康向上的网络文化,切实把互联网建设好、利用好、管理好。

and Jitong, which however initially retained a much more marginal position in comparison to China Telecom (Ho, 2013). While this signals competition across bureaucracies of the Chinese state apparatus, signs of dynamics across power groups also emerged in this phase, with the then-President Jiang Zemin's son, Jiang Mianheng, obtaining a leadership position in China Netcom. He did this through the Shanghai Alliance Investment Ltd., a company established by the Shanghai municipality and in which he had invested a major quota (Ho, 2013). The demise of Jiang Mianheng, with the final merger of China Netcom into China Unicom, came in the early 2000s, coincidentally at almost the same time as Jiang Zemin's end of mandate as President and Party Secretary, thus falling foul to the trap of the power dynamics that characterised Jiang Zemin's succession (Yang, 2003).

While it is important to stress the complexity and competitiveness of China's digital market and policy environment, the author does not wish to overestimate the impact of the transition between Jiang's and Hu's presidencies over the demise of Jiang Mianheng or the shifts in digital policies more at large. Indeed, both Jiang Zemin and Hu Jintao were Deng Xiaoping's protégés and continued his policies of market expansion and economic liberalisation under tight societal control (Ho, 2013; Yang, 2003). While Jiang presided over a politically stable decade, he retained Li Peng as his Prime Minister until 1998. Li Peng was Prime Minister in June 1989 and was among the most hawkish hardliners against the Tiananmen Square protesters. In a similar sign of continuity, under Hu Jintao's presidency, Jiang Zemin was president of the Central Military Commission, the politico-military head of the Chinese national defence system (Harwit, 2005; Ho, 2013; Mohanty, 2012). In the telecommunications and Internet sector, the reforms were characterised by continuity and they culminated in 2008 with the creation of the Ministry of Industry and Information Technology (MIIT), which subsumed the duties of the aforementioned Ministry of Electronics Industry and the later-born Ministry of Information Industry. The latter had in turn subsumed the roles of the Ministry of Posts and Telecommunications in 1998 (Ho, 2013; Negro, 2017; Wen, 2020). Within this institutional context, Chinese authorities sought to govern both the development of the telecommunications and Internet infrastructures and the Chinese-language web ecosystem. In 1997, the China Internet Network Information Centre (CNNIC) was founded. CNNIC manages the distribution of Chinese-language domain names as well as the distribution of domain names under the ".cn" top-level domain (Horsley & Creemers, 2023). Like its equivalents in many other countries, CNNIC responds to the national government, more specifically to the Cyberspace Administration of China (CAC, 国家互联网信息办公室, guojia hulianwang xinxi bangongshi). The CAC is China's official Internet regulator and censor, able to take legal actions and sanction Internet companies under Chinese law among other aspects. The CAC's foreign policy role has at times also been relevant. In particular, CAC director Lu Wei's speech at ICANN in 2014 has gained international attention as better discussed in the next section (Negro, 2020). Further detail on the CAC's history is elaborated in the next section.

In the realm of global Internet governance, these years of growing regulatory effort vis-à-vis the spread of online access and content correspond to China's years of stronger contestation of the US-led multistakeholder global Internet governance mechanisms. This was also accompanied by threats of infrastructural fragmentation including the establishment of a separate DNS, which however did not take place beyond the mere preemption of ICANN over the deployment of Chinese-character internationalised domain names (IDNs), as discussed in more depth in Chapter 4 (Arsène, 2015). What matters here is that the idea of capital deregulation should not push one to believe that the Chinese government's regulatory effort in this first phase was concentrated on information alone. On the contrary, the government sought to establish protectionist measures to foster Chinese companies in growing domestic technology for the telecommunications infrastructure (Cong & Thumfart, 2022). Furthermore, the Chinese government has sought to coordinate and lead domestic Internet infrastructure development-related policies since the Internet's inception (Tan et al., 1999), thus fostering a situation in which the Chinese Internet infrastructure is strongly local with very few contact points with Internet infrastructure based abroad despite retaining interoperability (Allen, 2019). This is further discussed in more depth and breadth in Chapters 4 through 6.

This notwithstanding, in this first stage (1994–2008), these measures were more scattered and uncoordinated, favouring instead the growth of private capital and the influx of foreign investment which often competed with Chinese capitals in the digital economy (Mueller & Farhat, 2022). In short, this first phase was characterised by a relatively free-flowing capital and a growingly regulated information flux.

Chapter 4 will provide further discussion about Chinese actors' approach to infrastructural aspects at the global level, within the discussion of Chinese engagement in multistakeholder Internet governance. Furthermore, Chapter 5 will present more nuance in Chinese companies' engagement with foreign markets vis-à-vis domestic market conditions as a facet of Chinese stakeholders' engagement in global Internet governance. In this chapter, these elements are illustrated for context vis-à-vis China's domestic digital policies. To this end, the next section analyses the second phase in the evolution of China's domestic digital policies.

3.3 Phase 2: 2009–2016. Information Control and Platform Bans

The second period cuts across the late phase of Hu Jintao's presidency (2003–2013) and Xi's early years as head of the State and the Party. To begin with, 2010 was a key turning point as the Information Office of the State Council of the People's Republic of China (SCIO) published the white paper on "The (status of the) Internet in China" (中国互联网状况, zhongguo hulianwang zhuangkuang) (Xinhua, 2010). Hu's policies of control on online social activities brought China's first large platform bans in 2009, when Facebook and Twitter were blocked in the country in the aftermath of riots in Xinjiang (Barry, 2022; Song et al., 2015). This was followed by Google's choice to leave mainland China—more precisely, to redirect its servers towards Hong Kong, where it remained accessible and fully available—in 2010, as it could not reach an agreement with Beijing on how much content to censor (Helft & Barboza, 2010). This represented a policy shift as Internet content was previously regulated but never to a point of banning a major platform or web service provider tout-court. The introduction of the concept of Internet sovereignty in the 2010 white paper on "The (status of the) Internet in China" signals the start of a new doctrine that anticipates stronger regulations domestically and the international debate on digital sovereignty (Creemers, 2020). The concept of Internet sovereignty is introduced as follows in the chapter titled "Protecting Internet Security":

> *The Internet sovereignty of China should be respected and protected. Citizens of the People's Republic of China and foreign citizens, legal persons and other organizations within Chinese territory have the right and freedom to use the Internet; at the same time, they must obey the laws and regulations of China*

and conscientiously protect Internet security [official translation] (Xinhua, 2010).[4]

Quite simply, this piece of text puts online behaviour and Internet-enabled activities taking place within China under the scope of Chinese law. "The right and freedom to use the Internet" is therefore limited by Chinese legal provisions, thus also the limit on using certain platform services and not others. This is framed as a security matter, as the title of the chapter clearly indicates, and sets the doctrinal basis for new forthcoming legislation regulating not only the role of platforms, but also the flux of data and information both within and outside the country.

This White Paper was published in the wake of the Facebook and Twitter bans, as well as Google's redirection of its servers towards Hong Kong (Creemers, 2020). Furthermore, the literature finds that policy debate on Internet sovereignty was coupled with a spur in the academic debate on the matter in the wake of these facts and right after Xi Jinping's election to Party Secretary (Negro, 2023). In other words, this second phase sees an increase in attention to the Internet sovereignty concept as well as an expansion of sovereignty-bound digital policies, from information control to platform bans and regulations. Contextually, as anticipated in the previous section, the CAC was founded in 2011 to establish a centralised authority in charge for managing content filtering and political control over the Web within China. More specifically, in 2011, the State Internet Information Office (SIIO) was established to replace the Bureau of Internet News Regulation, whose role was more narrowly oriented on online information control. The SIIO was then renamed CAC in 2014[5] and given larger regulatory powers beyond information control, with capacity to intervene in several realms of platform regulation including

---

[4] In this passage, the original text uses the term *hulianwang zhuquan* (互联网主权) rather than *wangluo zhuquan* (网络主权), the latter being most often found in literature and therefore also most often used throughout this book. The two terms can be conceived as synonyms and the former translates more literally as "Internet sovereignty". Alternatively, *wangluo zhuquan* can be translated as "network sovereignty", but the implied meaning does not change. Original text: 中国的互联网主权应受到尊重和维护。中华人民共和国公民及在中华人民共和国境内的外国公民、法人和其他组织在享有使用互联网权利和自由的同时，应当遵守中国法律法规、自觉维护互联网安全。

[5] Indeed, the SIIO and CAC's name in Chinese is invariant: 国家互联网信息办公室, guojia hulianwang xinxi bangongshi, which literally translates as "State Internet Information Office" (Horsley, 2022).

on (potential) data security issues (Miao & Lei, 2016). As anticipated above, the CNNIC also responds to the CAC. Like the SIIO, the CAC responds to the State Council Information Office (SCIO, 国务院新闻办公室, guowuyuan xinwen bangongshi) which is an organ of the Chinese government (SCIO, 2024). Among its most well-known active interventions in the Chinese Internet ecosystem is the 2021 crackdown on the ride-hailing application Didi, citing national and data security concerns in the context of the aforementioned Great Rectification campaign (Horsley, 2022).

China's Internet sovereignty concept pairs with that of digital sovereignty which has become prominent in the European Union, but it draws from older concepts such as Gong Wenxiang's (2005) "information sovereignty" (信息主权, xinxi zhuquan) (Cong & Thumfart, 2022; Hong & Goodnight, 2020; Jiang, 2010; Zeng et al., 2017). In short, China's ongoing and increasing regulatory effort towards digital technologies is not limited to the post-2020 crackdown, but fits a longer process of formalisation of growing state intervention in the digital economy.

When Xi Jinping took over Hu Jintao's roles in 2012 (Party Secretary) and 2013 (President of the Republic), he immediately launched the anti-corruption (反腐败, fanfubai) campaign. Indeed, corruption had grown within the Party and Chinese society across the previous two decades, amid rapid free-market reform and insufficient controls in place (Palmer, 2022). The anti-corruption campaign had an impact on how private companies could interact with state-owned enterprises (SOEs) and on the relationship between public and private capitals, as well as foreign and domestic capitals (Sun & Yuan, 2017). It also set the doctrinal basis for stronger state authorities' interventions vis-à-vis the actions of private companies. While the anti-corruption campaign falls outside the scope of this article, it is essential to stress its role in motivating state intervention in the private economy under Xi's leadership.

In conjunction with the anti-corruption campaign, Xi Jinping put the Internet not only at the core of China's domestic development, but also of its foreign relations. As early as 2014, Xi Jinping stressed the need of "making efforts to set the country to become a cyber great power" [translation by the author] (Xinhua, 2014a).[6] The term used here for

---

[6] Original text: 努力把我国建设成为网络强国.

"cyber great power" is "*wangluo qiangguo*" (网络强国). In Chinese political discourse, the term *qiangguo* strictly indicates the English term "great power" as opposed to *daguo* (大国), which is officially translated as "great country". The latter term is held to be less threatening than the former as it is used in rejection of the Western concept of "hegemony" (霸权, baquan), a linguistic ambiguity that has existed at least since 2014 in Chinese political discourse (Zappone, 2022). At times, however, the term *qiangguo* is used as describing a country that is stronger on the international stage compared to a *daguo*. For example, a 2023 People's Daily article relaunched on Qiushi titles "From a cyber great country to a cyber great power", thus signalling the latter meaning in the popular press as well as in party theory publications (People's Daily, 2023).[7] Qiushi is the Party's official public theoretical discussion outlet, therefore its commentaries carry a strong weight in identifying what is considered of high ideological importance for the Party at a given historical stage. Therefore, Xi's choice to use the term *qiangguo* to describe China's ambitions in the Internet realm is significant.[8] Under Xi, China has sought to portray itself as the promoter of an anti-hegemonic and democratic form of global Internet governance, while still participating in the existing US-founded Internet governance fora abiding by the existing rules (Cai, 2018; Nanni, 2022; Negro, 2020; Shen, 2016). China's and private Chinese stakeholders' practices in global Internet governance is addressed in Chapters 4 and 5, but the ambiguity between contestation and adaptation to international norms in Internet governance is key to interpreting China's domestic Internet (and data) governance policies. In Xi Jinping's early days, China and Chinese stakeholders became more present in global multistakeholder Internet governance fora as illustrated in the forthcoming chapters, but domestically Beijing launched the World Internet Conference (WIC, 世界互联网大会, shijie hulianwang dahui) (Hurel & Rocha, 2018). While it does not constitute a decision-making forum, its creation can arguably be read as a response to other forms of multistakeholder governance promoted at the global level such as the UN Internet Governance Forum

---

[7] Original text: 从网络大国阔步迈向网络强国.

[8] Sectors of the literature point out that the term *wangluo qiangguo* (网络强国) can mean "Internet Empower the Nation", a conception that has entered Party doctrine (Liu, 2023). In the specific document in question in this chapter, however, the term is used to indicate a "cyber great power", a terminology also recognised in Party doctrine and in literature (de la Bruyère, 2021).

(IGF) (Arsène, 2016). The policy impact of the WIC is admittedly limited, but its establishment in 2014 in the aftermath of the Snowden revelations is telling of its positioning in China's discursive effort vis-à-vis the US role in global (Internet) governance (Negro, 2020). Indeed, the final statement of the first WIC was initially meant to include a reference to respecting the Internet sovereignty of all nations and participation by heads of state came mainly from developing countries. While this was abandoned, it was later stated by the then-head of the Cyberspace Administration of China (CAC), Lu Wei, in an op-ed (Arsène, 2016), thus sending a political signal to the US-led Internet governance ecosystem. Contextually, however, Lu Wei expressed public support for multistakeholder governance mechanisms at ICANN in 2014. More specifically, he stated that the Chinese government supported CNNIC in its cooperation with ICANN and expressed optimism for the success of ICANN's reform that had just been launched in 2014 (ICANN, 2014). This translated into less confrontation between ICANN and China following the completion of the IANA stewardship transition (Negro, 2020), as better discussed in Chapter 4. On more rhetorical as well as domestic political levels, China's Ministry of Foreign Affairs adopted the *International Strategy of Cooperation on Cyberspace* in 2017, which introduced the ambiguous concept of "multi-party" governance (Xinhua, 2014b). While the Strategy repeatedly indicates multilateral venues as suitable for democratic and representative Internet governance, it follows each such statement with a reference to multi-party governance, arguably legitimising public–private (that is, multistakeholder) governance mechanisms without mentioning them explicitly (Tjahja et al., 2022; Zhu & Chen, 2022). This confirms the ambiguity found in literature between China's de facto support to multistakeholder mechanisms, which emerged from the mid-2000s onwards, and its critical position oftentimes supportive of multilateral governance venues as an alternative (Negro, 2020). The implications of these aspects are better discussed in Chapter 4.

To summarise, domestic drivers such as the anti-corruption campaign as well as a growing confrontation with the US, with Silicon Valley competitors now being excluded from the Chinese market and the US' reputation being tarnished by Snowden's revelations, characterise this second phase in China's domestic digital governance development. While no major data- or digital technology-related regulations were introduced in this phase, governmental intervention vis-à-vis (foreign) platforms increased. Furthermore, growing attention on the information fluxes and the actors who handled the information (that is, which platforms and under what rules) was growing. The spike in US–China competition that has started in 2016 (ongoing at the time of writing) is characterised by emerging technology regulation as discussed in the next section.

3.4 Phase 3: 2016–Ongoing. Internet Sovereignty and Common Prosperity

The year 2016 was a turning point in the debate on digital sovereignty (or Internet sovereignty, depending on which actors are analysed): the European Union approved the General Data Protection Regulation (GDPR), pioneering the concept of extraterritorial data protection (Pohle & Thiel, 2020); in the US, Donald Trump won the presidential elections beginning an era of open competition with China and increasing protectionism in the tech sector grounded in security concerns (ten Oever, 2022); China introduced its Cybersecurity Law (网络安全法, wangluo anquan fa), which entered into force the following year (Creemers, 2022) and highered its stake vis-à-vis the US in the technological competition amid an accelerating market tension (Poggetti, 2021). The US' positioning is explained in the literature through commercial drivers, as Chinese tech companies grew capable of competing with Silicon Valley giants (Ciuriak, 2019). Indeed, the security concerns raised by the US government have never been supported by hard technical proof (ten Oever, 2022). On the other hand, EU and Chinese reactions can be read as a result of a growing mistrust in the global digital governance environment (beyond mere CIRs governance), epitomised by the 2013 Snowden revelations over the US government's illegal espionage activities (Cai, 2018; Creemers, 2022; Pohle & Thiel, 2020).

When discussing China's capacity to exercise societal control on Internet-based activities while adopting a universally compatible infrastructure, the latest data governance legislation is a good starting point. Entering into force in 2021, the Data Security Law (DSL, 数据安全法, shuju anquan fa) and the Personal Information Protection Law (PIPL, 个人信息保护法, geren xinxi baohu fa) constitute the core of such legislation. Article 19 of the DSL states "the State is to establish and complete data transaction management systems, standardise data transaction behaviour, and cultivate a data transaction market" [translation by DigiChina].[9] In a nutshell, the DSL aims to create a mechanism of review and a set of standards for the Chinese government to retain an overview of the data that is transacted abroad and prevent unwanted transactions. This includes but is not limited to personal data, which is more explicitly protected by the PIPL. The PIPL "applies to the activities of handling the personal information of natural persons within the borders of the People's Republic of China"[10] (art. 3) [translation by DigiChina] and defines personal information as "all kinds of information, recorded by electronic or other means, related to identified or identifiable natural persons, not including information after anonymization handling" (art. 4, comma 1) [translation by DigiChina].[11] Significantly, Chinese legislation separates the concepts of personal information (个人信息, geren xinxi) protection and privacy (隐私, yinsi) protection, similarly to other jurisdictions (Creemers, 2022; Cui & Qi, 2021).

It would be overly simplistic to conclude that the DSL creates a centralised state control system overseeing data transactions between China and the wider world. Indeed, Chinese laws tend to be generic and enunciate principles, which then concretise through subsequent regulations and court jurisprudence. The DSL, for example, often features such language as "the state is to support…" [translation by DigiChina (2023)],[12] which makes the text a mere statement of intents rather than an applicable piece of legislation. By and large, DSL requirements have been made practical through the Outbound Data Transfer Security Assessment Measures. The Measures provide that (art. 4):

> Data handlers[13] providing data abroad shall, in any of the following circumstances, apply for outbound data transfer security assessment with the national cybersecurity and informatization department through their

---

[9] Original text: 国家建立健全数据交易管理制度，规范数据交易行为，培育数据交易市场.

[10] Original text: 在中华人民共和国境内处理自然人个人信息的活动，适用本.

[11] Original text: 个人信息是以电子或者其他方式记录的与已识别或可识别的自然人有关的各种信息，不包括匿名化处理后的信息.

[12] Original text: 国家支持…

[13] A "data handler" (数据处理者, shuju chulizhe) is anyone who at any point collects, uses, stores or in any way enters in possession of data. PIPL and DSL themselves do not distinguish between data processors and data controllers, a distinction which is only operated in subsequent legislation.

local provincial-level cybersecurity and informatization department: (1) Where the data handler provides important data abroad; (2) Critical information infrastructure operators and data handlers handling the personal information of over 1 million people providing personal information abroad; (3) Data handlers providing abroad the personal information of more than 100,000 people or the sensitive personal information of more than 10,000 people since January 1 of the previous year; (4) Other circumstances where the State cybersecurity and informatization department provides data export security assessment must be applied for. [translation by DigiChina][14]

In short, China is establishing a way to oversee critical data fluxes and make private actors in key economic positions (critical information infrastructure operators, for example) responsible for the data security process. These measures are also responsive to the 2017 Cybersecurity Law. On top of charging the state with establishing national cybersecurity standards, the law establishes in Article 35 that.

Critical information infrastructure operators purchasing network products and services that might impact national security shall undergo a national security review organised by the State cybersecurity and informatization departments and relevant departments of the State Council. [translation by DigiChina (2023)][15]

To this end, the "Critical Information Infrastructure Security Protection Regulations" (关键信息基础设施安全保护条例, guanjian xinxi jichu sheshi anquan baohu tiaoli) have been introduced to strengthen and concretise the provisions of the Cybersecurity Law included in Article 35. Article 2 of the Regulations read.

Critical information infrastructure as mentioned in these regulations, refers to important network infrastructure, information systems, etc., in

---

[14] Original text: 数据处理者向境外提供数据,有下列情形之一的,应当通过所在地省级网信部门向国家网信部门申报数据出境安全评估:(一)数据处理者向境外提供重要数据;(二)关键信息基础设施运营者和处理100万人以上个人信息的数据处理者向境外提供个人信息;(三)自上年1月1日起累计向境外提供10万人个人信息或者1万人敏感个人信息的数据处理者向境外提供个人信息;(四)国家网信部门规定的其他需要申报数据出境安全评估的情形。

[15] Original text: 关键信息基础设施的运营者采购网络产品和服务,可能影响国家安全的,应当通过国家网信部门会同国务院有关部门组织的国家安全审查。

important industries and sectors such as public telecommunications and information services, energy, transportation, water, finance, public services, e-government, national defense science, technology, and industry, etc., as well as where their destruction, loss of functionality, or data leakage may gravely harm national security, the national economy and people's livelihood, or the public interest. [translation by DigiChina][16]

Articles 8 and 9 then follow up by identifying as "protection work departments" those departments and sectors within the organisations identified in Article 2. The protection work departments are in charge of devising a critical information infrastructure security strategy and report mechanisms, including the elaboration of rules to identify critical information infrastructures themselves.

In short, China set up a legislative framework that imposes strong state supervision in handling sensitive resources such as data, which fits into a larger policy trend of state interventionism in critical economic sectors as well as information control across society. However, the Critical Information Infrastructure Security Protection Regulations also allocate responsibility to companies, whether private or state-owned. Once again, this showcases a domestic governance ecosystem in which private actors are co-opted into the everyday making of the governance rules rather than one in which they passively receive the rules from the state. Of course, this does not allow one to exclude state control and influence on the outcome. On the contrary, one can safely assume that the government maintains the final say on the legislation and on what is (or is not) accepted under its law. The aspects related to the autonomy of Chinese private actors vis-à-vis government policy and regulation have been addressed above and are better discussed in the forthcoming chapters. The most important aspect at this stage is the fact that rule-making and governance responsibility within the law in China involves private and public input in Internet governance, as previously found in literature (Cai, 2018; Shen, 2016). To these, one should add other regulations, such as those on algorithms and the DNS.

---

[16] Original text: 本条例所称关键信息基础设施,是指公共通信和信息服务、能源、交通、水利、金融、公共服务、电子政务、国防科技工业等重要行业和领域的,以及其他一旦遭到破坏、丧失功能或者数据泄露,可能严重危害国家安全、国计民生、公共利益的重要网络设施、信息系统等。

While China has come to accept the ICANN-established global DNS system (F. Arsène, 2015; Wang, 2006), the 2017 DNS Rules (officially known as Internet Domain Name Management Rules, 互联网域名管理办法, hulianwang yuming guanli banfa) establish a ministerial supervision system for those who want to establish a domain name root server within China (MIIT, 2017). In other words, the DNS Rules establish an element of regulatory control over infrastructure management, although the DNS in which Chinese users and operators operate remains the IANA-managed one (Arsène, 2015). DNS rules affect CNNIC's everyday activities and fit within the ambiguity of China's attempt to strengthen domestic control on the Internet and Internet-based activities versus its general trend of acceptance of and adaptation to the existing multistakeholder global Internet governance mechanisms. This is a core aspect of the discussion conducted in Chapters 4 through 7.

On the algorithm side, the Internet Information Service Algorithmic Recommendation Management Provisions (互联网信息服务算法推荐管理规定, hulianwang xinxi fuwu suanfa tuicun guanli guiding) entered into force in 2022. This piece of legislation empowers the user to choose whether or not to receive personalised recommendations when navigating the web. Furthermore, it sets a duty for recommendation algorithms providers to disclose the characteristics of their algorithm to the state. Specifically, article 24, comma 1, establishes that.

> Providers of algorithmic recommendation services with public opinion properties or having social mobilization capabilities shall, within 10 working days of providing services, report the provider's name, form of service, domain of application, algorithm type, algorithm self-assessment report, content intended to be publicized, and other such information through the Internet information service algorithm filing system, and carry out filing formalities.[17] [translation by DigiChina (2023)]

At least on paper, this creates a new form of governmental supervision over digital service providers and empowers users vis-à-vis them. This legislation is accompanied by measures on the use of deep synthesis, that is, software programmes capable of creating utterly realistic images (the

---

[17] Original text: 具有舆论属性或者社会动员能力的算法推荐服务提供者应当在提供服务之日起十个工作日内通过互联网信息服务算法备案系统填报服务提供者的名称、服务形式、应用领域、算法类型、算法自评估报告、拟公示内容等信息,履行备案手续。

so-called "deep fakes"), as well as rules on generative Artificial Intelligence. The latter is a set of software tools that allow the creation of images and sounds through simple written input. These two sets of rules are the Provisions on the Administration of Deep Synthesis Internet Information Services (2022)[18] and the Interim Measures for the Management of Generative Artificial Intelligence Services (2023).[19]

While it is early to evaluate the outcome of these regulatory developments, one can observe that they are coherent with the discursive and Party-theoretical developments identified in the two previous sections. Indeed, a *Qiushi* article dated September 2023 stressed the attention of Xi Jinping to making China a cyber great power as discussed above, which he raised "since the 18th National Congress of the Chinese Communist Party thereafter" (Qiushi, 2023). The full passage goes as follows:

> Cybersecurity is an important part of national security: without cybersecurity, there is no national security, there is no economic and social stability, and it also becomes complicated to guarantee the interests of the people at large. Since the 18th National Congress of the Communist Party of China, Party Secretary Xi Jinping has developed a number of important new concepts, ideas and strategies on network security and informatisation work based on the general trend of informatization development and the overall domestic and international situation. These form Xi Jinping's important thoughts on the concept of cyber great power. [translation by the author] (Qiushi, 2023)[20]

This excerpt is from an article published on the occasion of the 2023 National Cybersecurity Awareness Week (国家网络安全宣传周, guojia wangluo anquan xuanchuan zhou), the title of which was "Cybersecurity is for the People. Cybersecurity depends on the people" [translation by the author].[21] This article restresses the concept of cyber great power in

---

[18] English translation available at China Law Translate: https://www.chinalawtranslate.com/en/deep-synthesis/.

[19] English translation available at China Law Translate: https://www.chinalawtranslate.com/en/generative-ai-interim/.

[20] Original text: 网络安全是国家安全的重要组成部分,没有网络安全就没有国家安全,就没有经济社会稳定运行,广大人民群众利益也难以得到保障。党的十八大以来,习近平总书记从信息化发展大势和国内国际大局出发,就网络安全和信息化工作提出一系列具有开创性意义的新理念新思想新战略,形成了习近平总书记关于网络强国的重要思想。

[21] Original text: 网络安全为人民 网络安全靠人民。

connection with the importance of cybersecurity for national security and economic and societal development. In these terms, the growing regulatory effort of the Chinese government in terms of data protection, their security, and platform regulation (including new emerging technologies such as artificial intelligence) fits the broader theoretical development of the Communist Party's official line.

The implications of all the transformations that took place during the three phases identified in this chapter are discussed in the next section.

3.5 Analysis and Discussion

The combination of literature, policy documents, and texts presented above allows for the identification of the three aforementioned historical phases in China's history of digital policy. To be sure, like any other historical taxonomy it presents its own limits: to begin with, it would be overly simplistic to assume that the first phase, characterised by information control and business laissez-faire, featured absolutely no governmental attempt at influencing the private economy. While tech companies were allowed to thrive under relatively unregulated conditions and facing strong competition from foreign capitals, attempts at identifying national champions and regulating foreign capitals access to the Chinese market already existed (Leutert, 2022). This included loans from development banks to companies, mainly state-owned enterprises (Gallagher & Irwin, 2014; Lin et al., 2020). For example, telecom/Internet service providers have always been state-owned, while Huawei's first identification as a national champion took place in 1996, when the government slowly started protectionist policies to reduce foreign capitals domination in China's telecommunication infrastructure market (Melnik, 2019; Wen, 2020). Nonetheless, Huawei was pushed towards internationalisation between the 1990s and the early 2000s precisely because of China's market saturation due to the presence of foreign capitals (Wen, 2020). This also applies to the platform economy: early platform companies in China found themselves competing with their Western counterparts at a time of capital deregulation (Mueller & Farhat, 2022), but the regulatory effort of the government vis-à-vis information fluxes (beginning with the Golden Shield Project) progressively limited the capacity of US capitals to invest in China (Shen, 2022). As illustrated above, Google's exit from the Chinese market took place amidst disagreement over what content to censor for the Chinese usership.

Almost simultaneously, Facebook and Twitter were banned over information flows related to the 2009 Xinjiang disorders, thus signalling a new step in Chinese information control: one in which both information flows and platforms as a whole were targeted.

All in all, in the first phase identified in this chapter (1994–2008), China's regulatory effort was less coordinated and pervasive than it later became (Taylor, 2022), as it mainly impacted information flows. However, more coordinated effort—also featuring new regulations—emerged in the 2010s and addresses not only information flows, but also platform regulation and data flows.

In other words, the Chinese government's regulatory effort vis-à-vis the digital economy has grown throughout the three historical phases identified in this chapter, from a narrower focus on information fluxes until the early 2000s (though by no means ever strictly limited to information solely) to one of stronger attention to data, platforms, and infrastructures. The strong element of continuity in the three phases is the Chinese government's willingness to harness the Internet for economic growth and international political weight while limiting domestic political turmoil.

It goes without saying that the historical taxonomy is an ideal type and any subdivision can be debated in light of the continuities that exist from one phase to the next, as well as from one presidency to the next. Nonetheless, transformations are also visible and China created technological giants in the platform economy and in network manufacturing—the latter being the closest target of this book. As illustrated in this section, this happened through a growing and expanding regulatory effort in the digital economy that came to cover companies' behaviour, users' behaviour, as well as limiting foreign competition to allow domestic companies to grow. This, however, should not be construed as a process of overwhelming control by the Chinese government over Chinese capital. Despite recent governmental attempts to reestablish regulatory control over Chinese platform companies, capital in China still carries interests that overlap only partially with those of the government (Creemers, 2022; Shen, 2022; Wen, 2020). The implications of this in global Internet governance are better illustrated and discussed in the forthcoming chapters.

This chapter provided the basis for the analysis provided in Chapters 4 through 6. The complexity of China's state–capital relations, as well as the complex relation between China's domestic and foreign politics, must be borne in mind when analysing the engagement of Chinese stakeholders in global Internet governance.

3.6 Conclusive Remarks

China's domestic relations between state and companies in the tech sector have evolved over time, with the government constantly trying to retain control of information fluxes but acquiring an active role in the digital economy only at a later stage. The state–company relations have developed differently in different sectors of China's digital economy.

Chapters 4 through 6 will address Chinese stakeholders' positioning in global Internet governance and its transformation through time. What the present chapter highlighted is the fluidity of China's domestic digital ecosystem, which influences (though by no means determines) its positioning at the global level. Analytically, Chapter 6 brings together China's domestic development and its global positioning vis-à-vis Internet governance. The most important thing to bear in mind at this stage is that domestically China is not a monolithic whole, but a country in which different companies and different sectors of the economy entertain a different relationship with the government and where the government's policies transform in time. This is essential to observe the complexity of Chinese stakeholders' engagement in global Internet governance.

References

Allen, D. (2019, June 19). Analysis by Oracle Internet Intelligence Highlights China's Unique Approach to Connecting to the Global Internet. *Oracle Cloud Infrastructure Internet Intelligence.* https://blogs.oracle.com/intern etintelligence/analysis-by-oracle-internet-intelligence-highlights-china%e2% 80%99s-unique-approach-to-connecting-to-the-global-internet (December 18, 2019).
Arkko, J. (2023). Distribution of Authors per Companies. *IETF Statistics.* https://www.arkko.com/tools/allstats/companydistr.html (July 21, 2023).
Arsène, S. (2015). Internet Domain Names in China. Articulating Local Control with Global Connectivity. *China Perspectives, 4*, 25–34.
Arsène, S. (2016). Global Internet Governance in Chinese Academic Literature. Rebalancing a Hegemonic World Order? *China Perspectives, 2016*(2), 25–35.
Barbieri, E., Huang, M., Di Tommaso, M. R., & Lan, H. (2013). Made-in-China: High-tech National Champions of Business Excellence. *Measuring Business Excellence, 17*(2), 48–60.

Barry, E. (2022, January 18). These Are the Countries Where Twitter, Facebook and TikTok Are Banned. *Time.* https://time.com/6139988/countries-where-twitter-facebook-tiktok-banned/ (September 11, 2023).

Becker, C., ten Oever, N., & Nanni, R. (2024). Interrogating the Standardisation of Surveillance in 5G amid US-China Competition. *Information, Communication and Society, 0*(0).

Brandt, L., & Thun, E. (2021). The Great Dialectic. In X. Fu, B. McKern, J. Chen (Eds.), *The Oxford Handbook of China Innovation.* Oxford University Press.

Breslin, S. (2012). Government-industry Relations in China: A Review of the Art of the State. In A. Walter & X. Zhang (Eds.), *East Asian Capitalism: Diversity, Continuity, and Change.* Oxford University Press.

Brown, A. (2021, June 1). *Huawei's Global Troubles Spur Beijing's Push for Self-reliance.* Mercator Institute for China Studies. https://merics.org/en/short-analysis/huaweis-global-troubles-spur-beijings-push-self-reliance (June 18, 2021).

Cai, C. (2018). Global Cyber Governance. China's Contribution and Approach. *China Quarterly of International Strategic Studies, 4*(1), 55–76.

Cao, C., Meng, Q., & Zhang, H. (2023). A Longitudinal Examination of WeChat Usage Intensity, Behavioral Engagement, and Cross-cultural Adjustment among International Students in China. *Higher Education,* 1–23.

Central People's Government of the People's Republic of China. (2007, October 10). Hu Jintao: Strengthening the Construction and Management of the Internet Culture with a Spirit of Renovation. https://www.gov.cn/test/2007-10/10/content_773145.htm (July 21, 2023) [中华人民共和国中央人民政府 (2007年10月10日). 胡锦涛:以创新的精神加强网络文化建设和管理].

China Internet Network Information Centre. (2020). *The 49th Statistical Report on China's Internet Development.*

Chorzempa, M., & Huang, Y. (2022). Chinese Fintech Innovation and Regulation. *Asian Economic Policy Review, 17,* 274–292.

Ciuriak, D. (2019). The US-China Trade War: Technological Roots and WTO Responses. *Global Solutions Journal, 4,* 130–135.

Cong, W., & Thumfart, J. (2022). A Chinese Precursor to the Digital Sovereignty Debate: Digital anti-Colonialism and Authoritarianism from the post–Cold war era to the Tunis Agenda. *Global Studies Quarterly, 2*(4), 1–13.

Creemers, R. (2020). China's Conception of Cyber Sovereignty: Rhetoric and Realization. In D. Broeders & B. Van den Berg (Eds.), *Governing Cyberspace. Behavior, Power, and Diplomacy.* Rowman and Littlefield.

Creemers, R. (2022). China's Emerging Data Protection Framework. *Journal of Cybersecurity, 8*(1), 1–12.

Creemers, R. (2023). The Great Rectification: A New Paradigm for China's Online Platform Economy. *SSRN*. https://papers.ssrn.com/sol3/papers.cfm?abstract_id=4320952 (October 13, 2023).

Critical Information Infrastructure Security Protection Regulations. (2021). https://digichina.stanford.edu/work/translation-critical-information-infrastructure-security-protection-regulations-effective-sept-1-2021/ (September 28, 2023) [关键信息基础设施安全保护条例].

Cui, S., & Qi, P. (2021). The Legal Construction of Personal Information Protection and Privacy Under the Chinese Civil Code. *Computer Law & Security Review, 41*, 1–17.

Cybersecurity Law. (2017). https://digichina.stanford.edu/work/translation-cybersecurity-law-of-the-peoples-republic-of-china-effective-june-1-2017/ (August 18, 2023) [中华人民共和国网络安全法].

Data Security Law. (2021). https://digichina.stanford.edu/work/translation-data-security-law-of-the-peoples-republic-of-china/ (August, 18, 2023) [中华人民共和国数据安全法].

De Kloet, J., Poell, T., Zeng, G., & Chow, Y. (2019). The Platformization of Chinese Society: Infrastructure, Governance, and Practice. *Chinese Journal of Communication, 12*(3), 249–256.

De la Bruyère, E. (2021). The Network Great-Power Strategy. *Asia. Policy, 16*(2), 5–16.

Digichina. (2023). *Digichina. A Project of the Program on Geopolitics, Technology, and Governance at the Stanford Cyber Policy Center*. https://digichina.stanford.edu/ (August 18, 2023).

Dunford, M. (2022). The Chinese Path to Common Prosperity. *International Critical Thought, 12*(1), 35–54.

Fan, C. C. (2006). China's Eleventh Five-Year Plan (2006–2010): From 'Getting Rich First' to 'Common Prosperity.' *Eurasian Geography and Economics, 47*(6), 708–723.

Gallagher, K. P., & Irwin, A. (2014). Exporting National Champions: China's Outward Foreign Direct Investment Finance in Comparative Perspective. *China & World Economy, 22*(6), 1–21.

Gao, X. (2022). An Attractive Alternative? China's Approach to CyberGovernance and Its Implications for the Western Model. *The International Spectator, 57*(3), 15–30.

Gong, W. (2005). Information Sovereignty Reviewed. *Intercultural Communication Studies, 14*(1), 119–135.

Harwit, E. (2005). Telecommunications and the Internet in Shanghai: Political and Economic Factors Shaping the Network in a Chinese City. *Urban Studies, 42*(10), 1837–1858.

Helft, M., & Barboza, D. (2010, March 23). Google Shuts China Site in Dispute Over Censorship. *The New York Times*. https://www.nytimes.com/2010/03/23/technology/23google.html (July 13, 2023).

Hensmans, M., & Liu, G. (2020). Huawei's long march to global leadership: Joint innovation strategy from the periphery to the center. In W. Zhang, I. Alon, C. Lattemann (Eds.), *Huawei Goes Global: Volume I: Made in China for the World*. Palgrave Macmillan.

Ho, W. (2013). What Analyses of Factional Politics of China Might Miss When the Market Becomes a Political Battlefield: The Telecommunication Sector as a Case in Point. *China Review, 13*(1), 71–92. https://www.jstor.org/stable/23462229 (August 30, 2023).

Hong, Y., & Goodnight, G. T. (2020). How to Think About Cyber Sovereignty: The Case of China. *Chinese Journal of Communication, 13*(1), 8–26.

Horsley, J. (2022, August 8). Behind the Facade of China's Cyber Super-Regulator. *DigiChina*. https://digichina.stanford.edu/work/behind-the-facade-of-chinas-cyber-super-regulator/ (January 25, 2024).

Horsley, J., & Creemers, R. (2023). *The Cyberspace Administration of China. A Portrait*. In R. Creemers, S. Papagianneas & A. Knight (Eds.), *The Emergence of China's Smart State*. Rowman & Littlefield.

Hurel, L. M., & Rocha, M. S. (2018). Brazil, China and Internet Governance: Mapping Divergence and Convergence. *Journal of China and International Relations*, Special issue, 98–115.

Interim Measures for the Management of Generative Artificial Intelligence Services (2023). https://www.chinalawtranslate.com/en/generative-ai-interim/ (September 28, 2023) [生成式人工智能服务管理暂行办法]

Internet Corporation for Assigned Names and Numbers. (2014, July 23). ICANN50 in London: Lu Wei, Minister of Cyberspace Affairs Administration of China. *Youtube*. https://www.youtube.com/watch?v=qU9tfXPFPSU&ab_channel=ICANN (January 24, 2024).

Internet Information Service Algorithmic Recommendation Management Provisions. (2022). https://digichina.stanford.edu/work/translation-internet-information-service-algorithmic-recommendation-management-provisions-effective-march-1-2022/ (September 28, 2023) [互联网信息服务算法推荐管理规定]

Jiang, M. (2010). Authoritarian informationalism: China's approach to Internet sovereignty. *SAIS Review of International Affairs, 30*(2), 71–90.

Leutert, W. (2022). Sino-Japanese Engagement in the Making of China's National Champions. *New Political Economy, 27*(6), 929–943.

Lin, K. J., Lu, X., Zhang, J., & Zheng, Y. (2020). State-owned Enterprises in China: A Review of 40 years of Research and Practice. *China Journal of Accounting Research, 13*(1), 31–55.

Liu, J. (2023). Rethinking Chinese Multistakeholder Governance of Cybersecurity. In I. Johnstone, A. Sukumar & J. Trachtman (Eds.), *Building an International Cybersecurity Regime. Multistakeholder Diplomacy*. Edward Elgar.

Melnik, J. (2019). China's "National Champions": Alibaba, Tencent, and Huawei. *Association for Asian Studies*. https://www.asianstudies.org/publications/eaa/archives/chinas-national-champions-alibaba-tencent-and-huawei/ (September 4, 2023).

Miao, W., & Lei, W. (2016). Policy Review: The Cyberspace Administration of China. *Global Media and Communication, 12*(3), 337–340.

Ministry of Industry and Information Technology of the People's Republic of China. (2017). *Internet Domain Name Management Rules*. https://tinyurl.com/49bwc6fw (September 17, 2021) [中华人民共和国工业和信息化部. 2017. 互联网域名管理办法].

Mohanty, M. (2012). 'Harmonious Society': Hu Jintao's Vision and the Chinese Party Congress. *Economic and Political Weekly, 47*(50), 12–16. https://www.jstor.org/stable/41720457.

Mueller, M. L., & Farhat, K. (2022). Regulation of Platform Market Access by the United States and China: Neo-mercantilism in Digital Services. *Policy & Internet, 14*(2), 348–367.

Nanni, R. (2022). Digital Sovereignty and Internet Standards: Normative Implications of Public-private Relations among Chinese Stakeholders in the Internet Engineering Task Force. *Information, Communication & Society, 25*(16), 2342–2362.

Negro, G. (2017). *The Internet in China: From Infrastructure to a Nascent Civil Society*. Palgrave Macmillan.

Negro, G. (2020). A History of Chinese Global Internet Governance and its Relations with ITU and ICANN. *Chinese Journal of Communication, 13*(1), 104–121.

Negro, G. (2023). An Analysis the Evolution of "Network Sovereignty" and "Information Sovereignty" in China from 2005 to 2014. In M. Timoteo, B. Verri & R. Nanni (Eds.), *Quo Vadis, Sovereignty? New Conceptual and Regulatory Boundaries in the Age of Digital China*. Springer.

Noumoff, S. J. (1967). China's Cultural Revolution as a Rectification Movement. *Pacific Affairs, 40*(3/4), 221–234.

Outbound Data Transfer Security Assessment Measures. (2022). https://digichina.stanford.edu/work/translation-outbound-data-transfer-security-assessment-measures-effective-sept-1-2022/ (August 18, 2023) [数据出境安全评估办法].

Palmer, J. (2022, October 22). What the Hell Just Happened to Hu Jintao? *Foreign Policy*. https://foreignpolicy.com/2022/10/22/china-xi-jinping-hu-jintao-ccp-congress/ (August 18, 2023).

People's Daily. (2023, July 15). From a Cyber Great Country to a Cyber Great Power. *Qiushi*. http://www.qstheory.cn/qshyjx/2023-07/15/c_1129750917.htm [人民日报(2023年7月15日)从网络大国阔步迈向网络强国. 求是].

Personal Information Protection Law. (2021). https://digichina.stanford.edu/work/translation-personal-information-protection-law-of-the-peoples-republic-of-china-effective-nov-1-2021/ (August 18, 2023) [中华人民共和国个人信息保护法].

Plantin, J., & De Seta, G. (2019). WeChat as Infrastructure: The Technonationalist Shaping of Chinese Digital Platforms. *Journal of Chinese Communication*, http://eprints.lse.ac.uk/91520/1/Plantin_WeChat-as-infrastructure.pdf (November 15, 2021).

Poggetti, L. (2021, January 20). EU-China Mappings: Interactions between the EU and China on Key Issues. Mercator Institute for China Studies. https://merics.org/de/kurzanalyse/eu-china-mappings-interactions-between-eu-and-china-key-issues (July 13, 2021).

Pohle, J., & Thiel, T. (2020). Digital Sovereignty. *Internet Policy Review, 9*(4). https://doi.org/10.14763/2020.4.1532.

Provisions on the Administration of Deep Synthesis Internet Information Services (2022). https://www.chinalawtranslate.com/en/deep-synthesis/ (September 28, 2023) [互联网信息服务深度合成管理规定].

Qin, K. (2015). Discussion on a Big Data Protection Law. *Library Studies Research, 12*, 98–100 [秦珂(2015)大数据法律保护摭谈。图书馆学研究。12期,98–100页].

Qiushi. (2023, September 11). Qiushi Commentator Series: Cybersecurity is for the People. Cybersecurity Depends on the People. http://www.qstheory.cn/wp/2023-09/12/c_1129858391.htm (October 20, 2023). [求是网 (2023年09月11日) 求是网评论员:网络安全为人民 网络安全靠人民]

Rolf, S., & Schindler, S. (2023). The US–China Rivalry and the Emergence of State Platform Capitalism. *Environment and Planning A: Economy and Space, 55*(5), 1255–1280.

Shen, H. (2016). China and Global Internet Governance: Toward an Alternative Analytical Framework. *Chinese Journal of Communication, 9*(3), 304–324.

Shen, H. (2022). *Alibaba: Infrastructuring Global China*. Routledge.

Shen, H., & He, Y. (2022). The Geopolitics of Infrastructuralized Platforms: The case of Alibaba. *Information, Communication & Society, 25*(16), 2363–2380.

Shiu, G., & Sutter, D. (1996). The Political Economy of Tiananmen Square. *Rationality and Society, 8*(3), 325–342.

Song, S. Y., Faris, R., & Kelly, J. (2015). *Beyond the wall: Mapping twitter in China*. Berkman Center Research Publication no. 2015-14. https://ssrn.com/abstract=2685358 (October 13, 2023).

State Council Information Office. (2024). *About SCIO*. http://english.scio.gov. cn/aboutscio/index.htm (January 25, 2024).
Sun, Y., & Yuan, B. (2017). Does Xi Jinping's Anticorruption Campaign Improve Regime Legitimacy? *Modern China Studies, 24*(2), 16–34.
Tan, Z., Foster, W., & Goodman, S. (1999). China's State-coordinated Internet Infrastructure. *Communications of the ACM, 42*(6), 44–52.
Tang, M. (2020). From 'Bringing-in' to 'Going-out': Transnationalizing China's Internet Capital Through State Policies. *Chinese Journal of Communication, 13*(1), 27–46.
Taylor, M. (2022). *China's Digital Authoritarianism*. Palgrave Macmillan.
Teiwes, F. C. (1979). *Revival: Politics and Purges in China. Rectification and the Decline of Party Norms, 1950–65*. Routledge.
ten Oever, N. (2022). 5G and the Notion of Network Ideology, or: The Limitations of Sociotechnical Imaginaries. *Telecommunications Policy*, 102442.
Tjahja, N., Nanni, R., & Baiduk, R. (2022). Unpacking Digital Sovereignty: Strategic Narratives from China, the European Union, and Russia. *35th Annual Conference of the Italian Political Science "Democracy and its Enemies"*.
Wang, F. F. (2006). Domain names Management and Legal Protection. *International Journal of Information Management, 26*(2), 116–127.
Wang, O. (2022, October 23). China's Communist Party cements 'Common Prosperity' as core economic agenda. *South China Morning Post*. https:// www.scmp.com/news/china/politics/article/3196908/chinas-communist-party-cements-common-prosperity-core-economic-agenda (August 24, 2023).
Wen, Y. (2020). *The Huawei Model*. University of Illinois Press.
Xinhua. (2010, June 8). Full Text: White paper on the Internet in China. *China Daily*. https://www.chinadaily.com.cn/china/2010-06/08/content_9 950198.htm (July 19, 2023) [Reporting an official translation from the Information Office of the State Council]. Chinese-language text. https://www.gov. cn/govweb/zwgk/2010-06/08/content_1622866.htm (October 20, 2023).
Xinhua. (2014a, February 27). Xi Jinping: Transforming our Country from a Cyber Great Country into a Cyber Great Power. http://www.xinhuanet. com/politics/2014-02/27/c_119538788.htm (July 19, 2023) [新华网(2014年02月27日)习近平: 把我囯从网络大囯建设成为网络强囯].
Xinhua. (2014b, May 1). *International Strategy of Cooperation on Cyberspace*. http://www.xinhuanet.com//english/china/2017-03/01/c_136094371. htm (January 24, 2024).
Yang, D. L. (2003). China in 2002: Leadership Transition and the Political Economy of Governance. *Asian Survey, 43*(1), 25–40. https://www.jstor. org/stable/10.1525/as.2003.43.1.25 (August 20, 2023).
Yang, D. L., & Jiang, J. (2012). Guojin Mintui: The Global Recession and Changing State-Economy Relations in China. In D. L. Yang (Ed.), *The Global*

Recession and China's Political Economy. China in Transformation. Palgrave Macmillan. https://doi.org/10.1057/9781137070463_3.

Zappone, T. (2022). "'China is...': China's International Positioning and Self-Identity Definition in Xi Jinping's Speeches". In X. Zhang & C. Schultz (Eds.), *China's International Communication and Relationship Building.* Routledge.

Zeng, J., Stevens, T., & Chen, Y. (2017). China's Solution to Global Cyber Governance: Unpacking the Domestic Discourse of "Internet Sovereignty." *Politics & Policy, 45*(3), 432–464.

Zhang, A. H. (2022). Agility Over Stability: China's Great Reversal in Regulating the Platform Economy. *Harvard International Law Journal, 63*(2), 457–514.

Zhang, J., & Liang, X. (2007). 3G in China: Environment and Prospect. *IEEEXplore.* https://ieeexplore.ieee.org/abstract/document/4349642 (Accessed 27 April 2021).

Zhang, L., Wei, G., Xu, Z., Huang, Q., & Liu, G. (2021). The Prevalence of Smartphones and WeChat use among older Adults with Chronic Disease in a Western China. *CIN: Computers, Informatics, Nursing, 39*(1), 42–47.

Zhong, R. (2021, July 4). China Orders Didi Off App Stores in an Escalating Crackdown. *The New York Times.* https://www.nytimes.com/2021/07/04/technology/china-didi-app-removed.html (July 6, 2021).

Zhu, L., & Chen, W. (2022). Chinese Approach to International Law with Regard to Cyberspace Governance and Cyber Operation: From the Perspective of the Five Principles of Peaceful Co-existence. *Baltic Yearbook of International Law Online, 20*(1), 187–208.

CHAPTER 4

On the Normative Impact of Chinese Stakeholders in the Governance of Critical Internet Resources: A Document- and Interview-Based Analysis

4.1 INTRODUCTION

A key takeaway from observing IETF data is the great disparity in Chinese stakeholders' engagement in the IETF (Arkko, 2023). As for ICANN, a quick glance at the roles in the various advisory committees and supporting organisations shows presence but no prominence in Chinese engagement.

In the IETF, where the most essential Internet standards are made, Huawei plays a major role and minor state-owned actors such as ZTE and the two main national Internet Service Providers (ISPs), China Mobile

---

The interview findings presented in this section and related to the IETF have also been included in Nanni, R. (2022). Digital sovereignty and Internet standards: normative implications of public-private relations among Chinese stakeholders in the Internet Engineering Task Force. *Information, Communication & Society*, 25(16): 2342–2362.
The IETF document-based findings in this chapter have also been included in: Nanni, R. (2023). Whither (de)globalisation? Internet fragmentation, authoritarianism, and the future of the Liberal International Order: evidence from China. *The Pacific Review*. Online first.

© The Author(s), under exclusive license to Springer Nature Singapore Pte Ltd. 2024
R. Nanni, *Rising China and Internet Governance*,
https://doi.org/10.1007/978-981-97-0357-9_4

and China Telecom, are more peripheral: at the time of writing, Huawei is the second corporate actor by affiliate's RFC authorship, whereas affiliates from other Chinese companies feature in fewer RFCs and Internet Drafts (Arkko, 2023). In sporadic occasions, Chinese universities also feature in the work of IETF working groups (WGs). While the centrality of Chinese stakeholders is different in different WGs, Huawei is overall the second most active corporate actor in terms of RFCs published or co-published by its affiliates per year (Arkko, 2023).

Conversely, in ICANN, where critical Internet resources are managed within the framework of the IANA functions, Chinese stakeholders keep a low profile. To be sure, some Chinese actors do cover key positions. It is the case of the Alibaba-affiliated member of ICANN's Generic Names Supporting Organization (GNSO) Council and the Chinese government's representative who formerly covered the role of GAC vicechair in the wake of the IANA stewardship transition (GNSO, 2023; Negro, 2020), a process better discussed below.

Matters of Chinese engagement and impact in Internet governance are explored through interviews and documents analysis in the forthcoming sections.

In Sect. 4.2, this chapter explores the relation between public and private Chinese actors and how they are displayed in core Internet governance activities. The following section contextualises it in the framework of ICANN, whereas Sect. 4.4 sets it in the framework of the IETF. Section 4.5 analyses the implications of the aspects explored in Sects. 4.2 through 4.4, while the concluding Sect. 4.6 reconnects findings to theory.

4.2 Chinese Stakeholders' Actions at the Core of Internet Governance

Recalling from Chapter 2, a few turning points can be identified in the history of China's engagement in Internet governance since the foundation of ICANN in 1998. These can be summarised as the foundation of ICANN (1998), the WSIS process (2003–2005), WCIT-12 (2012), and the IANA stewardship transition (2014–2016) (see Table 2.1 for more detail). It is through the historical passage among these milestones that the strengthening and weakening of multilateralist quests can be observed. While the extent to which WCIT-12 has been impactful on Internet governance history is debated, it is still referred to in literature as a key moment in which the multilateralist-multistakeholderist debate re-emerged (Palladino & Santaniello, 2021).

To begin with, it can be noted that, despite constant growth of Chinese private stakeholders in the global market (Drahokoupil et al., 2017), China's governmental role has not faded away. After all, suspicions of party-political control on Chinese businesses, whether warranted or not, is a key element in the US–China trade war (Ciuriak, 2019; Pupillo, 2019). To be sure, the government is recognised to retain a strong regulatory and coordination role in China's domestic Internet market and its industrial policies influence companies' growth and development (Negro, 2017; Shen, 2016; Wen, 2020; Zhang & Liang, 2007). While the development of Internet infrastructure and policies has been strongly state-driven through political control and accountability of Internet Service Providers (ISPs) among other aspects, different layers of Chinese bureaucracy clashed throughout the 1994–1998 telecommunications market reform and after as they held different interests on the nascent Internet market. In turn, state-owned operators as well as private manufacturers displayed their own peculiar interests in the market (Negro, 2017; Zhang & Liang, 2007). While disquisitions on China's domestic dynamics fall outside the scope of this chapter, it is essential to pinpoint that, despite governmental multilateralist stances and suspicions over governmental control on private stakeholders, China cannot be considered a monolithic whole.

In the earliest stages of ICANN-based Internet governance, while China's government suspended its participation in ICANN meetings, which was gradually resumed between 2006 and 2009 (Creemers, 2020), commercial and other Chinese stakeholders kept participating in ICANN's activities. This was confirmed time and again by research participants involved in or familiar with ICANN from most parts of the world. Many participants also confirmed a dialectical relation among the Chinese government and its domestic stakeholders in this phase. In an interview with a Chinese academic, discussing the relationship between the Chinese government and Huawei, it emerged that:

> In the dialectic, the government sometimes definitely has more power, [especially during Huawei's] early development. But on the other hand, Huawei became more and more powerful. As you can notice, Huawei's international revenue at one point (around 2010) was actually higher than its revenue in domestic China. So, Huawei has to balance its position as well, it certainly doesn't want to forfeit its people in the US, in Europe. It

will try its best to make that market open to itself. So, sometimes Huawei will push back a little bit on state initiative to keep that market open.

This interview statement finds confirmation in the literature and publicly available data. Huawei's profits have increased despite the Trump administration's restrictions also thanks to the big size of China's domestic market, where it achieved a 37% share of the smartphone market in 2020 (Buchholz, 2021). However, Huawei's presence in the global network and device market has historically been high, especially compared to other major Chinese actors, such as its direct domestic competitor, the state-owned ZTE. In 2013, Huawei's market share based on declared global LTE (4G) contracts was 39%, compared to ZTE's 2%. Huawei's share at that stage was higher than Ericsson's (31%) (Pawlicki, 2017). Nevertheless, since 2017 US sanctions pushed Huawei to invert this trend, with its domestic revenues becoming higher and higher with respect to those deriving from the international market (Brown, 2021).

In short, the power relation between Chinese private actors and the Chinese government is in a constant process of transformation and redefinition. While Huawei is only one key Chinese actor, albeit an economically and politically important one, the aforementioned figures help to confirm the existence of a dialectic state-capital relation.

Aspects of such dialectic relations between the public (including government and SOEs) and private actors in China will keep emerging throughout this chapter and the forthcoming ones. As per Chapter 3, Chinese authorities have clamped down on domestic big techs starting in 2020, arguably to strengthen political control on otherwise too powerful actors. While no action against Huawei has been taken at the time of writing, sanctions have been imposed on Alibaba, who participates as a registrar in ICANN's GNSO,[1] and Didi (Zhong, 2021). This situation is still developing at the time of writing, although it seems to have reached a less intense phase compared to the 2020–2021 biennium. While the policy is mainly addressed towards platform and fintech service providers and no action has been taken against Huawei (nor any other network

---

[1] Alibaba's financial operations were targeted and the company was bound to restructure following an antitrust pronouncement. However, Alibaba's activities as a domain name registrar never came under attack (Zhang 2022).

manufacturer), this situation must be acknowledged as it affects the aforementioned trend of growing domestic reliance for Huawei and other Chinese technology companies.

4.3 Chinese Stakeholders and Multistakeholder Governance at ICANN

While full of unknowns, the dialectic among public and private actors described in the previous section must be acknowledged as it makes China's country-level stance towards multistakeholderism more nuanced and ambiguous than often depicted. However, the role of the central government remains powerful. Observations on this will be further illustrated in the forthcoming sections.

To begin with, following the establishment of the WSIS process, China accepted the consolidation of multistakeholderism. Such consolidation came from three elements that characterised the conclusion of the 2003 and 2005 rounds of WSIS. First, this UN-sponsored initiative incorporated in its final document, the Tunis Agenda, a multistakeholder definition of Internet governance as provided by WGIG (2005); second, it launched an UN-sponsored non-decisional multistakeholder process called Internet Governance Forum (IGF); third, it did not replace ICANN, which on the contrary maintained its role and characteristics, including its formal link to the US DOC at this stage (Mueller, 2017; Palladino & Santaniello, 2021).

While China's re-accession to GAC following the consolidation of multistakeholderism in the WSIS process could be read as a (partial) acknowledgement of the latter principle from China's part, observers hinted at China as a 'repressive multilateralist' following WCIT-12 (Glen, 2014). Concerns over the increasing (geo)politicisation of the Internet grew in this context, but some scholars warned against the excessive militarisation of Internet governance that could derive from framing it in terms of 'digital cold war' and cybersecurity (Mueller, 2013). True, the Chinese government was among the supporters of the new International Telecommunication Regulations (ITRs), which were ostracised by the US-led bloc as too likely to facilitate governmental intromission in telecommunication traffic and its governance. However, the approval of the new ITRs took place through majority vote rather than consensus and made the regulations inapplicable as supporting countries were too few and economically too weak (Palladino & Santaniello, 2021).

Furthermore, the forecasted geopolitical divide did not materialise in the form of a new 'Cold war' as the following year, 2013, China hosted in Beijing the biggest ICANN meeting ever recorded until then, with the Chinese government participating in it. While this was the second China-hosted ICANN meeting, the first one did not record the Chinese government's participation. Held in Shanghai in 2002, this first China-hosted ICANN meeting took place at the beginning of China's ICANN "boycott" on the recognition of Taiwan's status in the GAC. Therefore, the meeting was planned, and held, but not participated in by Chinese governmental representatives. However, Chinese non-governmental stakeholders, including the state-sponsored NGO Internet Society of China (Negro, 2017) and future ICANN Board member Qian Hualin, were present (ICANN, 2002). By the 2013 ICANN meeting in Beijing, therefore, China-ICANN relations were re-established and a process of normalisation was on the way (Negro, 2020), as better discussed below in this chapter. Therefore, no sign of a political split between two political blocs with opposed views had emerged such to characterise the use of strong terms as "digital cold war".

Furthermore, Chinese authorities coordinated with ICANN amid China's pre-emptive actions in the IDNs space. Prior to the standardisation of domain names with non-romanised characters, China sought to push for their adoption. This carries political, cultural, and economic implications (Arsène, 2015). As ICANN and the IETF tended to postpone the discussion, China ran a system of Chinese-character domain names parallel to the ICANN-supervised DNS under the supervision of the Ministry of Industry and Information Technology (Zhang, 2019). Rather than replacing the ICANN-supervised DNS, this "Chinese DNS" run alongside it. Importantly, it contained Chinese-character names only. This put ICANN and the IETF in front of a *fait accompli* and forced to open a discussion on standardising and distributing non-romanised domain names. Once this was settled, the Chinese-character namespace was subsumed into the ICANN-supervised DNS (Arsène, 2015). In short, China threatened a DNS split and used it against ICANN and the IETF, but once the issue was settled no such split took place in the long run. This shows China's willingness to retain a unified infrastructure of unique identifiers for the Internet, an aspect that is further elaborated below and constitutes one of the key arguments of this book.

What matters in this context is that the 2002 and 2013 ICANN meetings held in China show that Chinese stakeholders' engagement with

ICANN was always in place, even in times of major strain—and indeed the China-ICANN ties have grown closer and more normalised in time. The presence of state-sponsored stakeholders at the 2002 meeting despite China's government's "boycott" showcases China's will to retain links to ICANN despite diplomatic issues. In an interview with the author, Paul Twomey, ICANN's President from 2003 to 2009, confirms that dialogues between ICANN and Beijing and ICANN and Taipei were always ongoing and officials on both sides of the strait kept contacts. Indeed, this research participant maintains there never was such a thing as a full-fledged break with ICANN or boycott thereof on China's part, contrary to what is often found in literature. As recalled above, the Chinese government's leadership finally re-accessed the GAC, after agreement was found on naming Taiwan 'Chinese Taipei' (中华台北, zhonghua taibei). Furthermore, an agreement was achieved on referring to territorial entities in the Asia–Pacific region as 'economies', rather than 'states' or 'countries', to avoid sensitivities on territorial disputes (Scholte, 2017).

A similar dynamic was in place following WCIT-12 in ICANN-China relations. This time, despite militaristic claims on the future of Internet politics, the Chinese government continued in its engagement with ICANN and the multistakeholder model. After the 2013 Beijing meeting, China participated in NetMundial in 2014, the multistakeholder forum sponsored by the Brazilian government in the wake of the PRISM scandal. NetMundial represented a peculiar phenomenon: while adherent to multistakeholderism principles, it was aimed at calling for a non-US-centric form of Internet governance (Belli, 2015; Hurel & Rocha, 2018). In the same year, Lu Wei, then director of the Cyberspace Administration of China, a regulatory authority, participated in ICANN's fiftieth public meeting (ICANN50), publicly endorsing multistakeholderism in his speech.[2] While these commitments are rhetorical, research participants familiar with the process believe they resulted from and represented a deeper engagement of China with ICANN and multistakeholderism. While Lu Wei's speech and China's participation in NetMundial took place at the outset of the IANA stewardship transition, shortly after the end of the transition that took place on 30 September 2016, China's governmental representative obtained GAC's vice-presidency (Negro,

---

[2] Further information on this in Chapter 3.

2020). Arguably, the publication of the *International Strategy of Cooperation on Cyberspace* has also signalled a move towards this direction, with the introduction of such terminology as "multi-party governance" as a concept partially overlapping with multistakeholderism, albeit ambiguously so (Zhu & Chen, 2022). This can be interpreted as a signalling towards increased acceptance of and adaptation to the existing multistakeholder governance mechanisms, as showcased by Chinese stakeholders' increased engagement with ICANN and the IETF that emerged through the interviews illustrated. Discussion over the concepts included in the *Strategy* falls outside the scope of this book. On a practical level, interview participants as well as literature (Negro, 2020) find increased participation by Chinese stakeholders in the analysed Internet governance venues.

Nonetheless, this has thus far not translated into more influential Chinese policy engagement in ICANN in terms of policies tabled or supported by Chinese stakeholders within GAC. While this is difficult to quantify as GAC is a purely advisory body working on a consensual basis (Galloway & He, 2014), thematic document analysis provided insight into it.

Between ICANN 54 and ICANN 56 (autumn 2015 to summer 2016), a key moment in the IANA stewardship transition, GAC Communiqués and meeting transcripts show Chinese input in post-transition ICANN reform has been welcomed by various parts, including Latin American and European countries such as Argentina, Brazil, Norway, and France. In particular, these countries' governments opposed the so-called 'Stress Test 18' and pushed for a two-third majority of the ICANN Board vote to be needed for the latter to reject GAC Consensus Advice. Stress Test 18 was a major point of discussion for GAC during the IANA stewardship transition and the subsequent reform of ICANN Bylaws. Stress Test 18 was based on the following working hypothesis:

> Stress Test 18 is related to a scenario where ICANN's GAC would amend its operating procedures to change from consensus decisions to majority voting for advice to the ICANN Board. Since the Board must seek a mutually acceptable solution if it rejects GAC advice, concerns were raised that the ICANN Board could be forced to arbitrate among sovereign governments if they were divided in their support for the GAC advice. In addition, if the GAC lowered its decision threshold while also participating in the

Empowered Community, some stakeholders believe this could inappropriately increase government influence over ICANN. (Cross Community Working Group on Accountability 2015, hereafter CCWG-Accountability)

Based on this, the CCWG-Accountability proposed that the threshold for the Board to reject GAC Consensus Advice be 60%, which in the sixteen-voting-member ICANN Board translates as one less vote than requested by China and the other opponents of Stress Test 18.

China was particularly vocal on this topic at ICANN 54 (October 2015), when the issue was debated in a GAC meeting with the Board. Here, France tabled a question on the rationale for the Board supporting the CCWG-Accountability bylaw reform proposal based on Stress Test 18. The Board's response received the following reaction from Russia:

> We believe the conditions under which accountability is enhanced but the role of governments is diminished, that condition is not acceptable. We had been talking about it from the very beginning. And so we can't support stress test 18 and we don't think that it has a place here. (Governmental Advisory Committee, 2015, 33, hereafter GAC)

Russia's reaction was backed by China, who shared "the same viewpoint made by Argentina, Brazil, Russia, and many other countries", including France, who restressed dissatisfaction over the Board's arguments in favour of Stress Test 18 (GAC, 2015, 33–35). Despite concern being raised by governments cutting across the usual geopolitical lines, the reformed ICANN Bylaws as entered into force in October 2016, following the completion of the IANA stewardship transition, featured the 60% threshold proposed by the CCWG-Accountability.

These aspects confirm the low-profile presence of China in the GAC as reported by interview participants, which has grown to obtain formal and active roles, but has not necessarily become influential. A similarly low profile is found elsewhere in ICANN for Chinese stakeholders. In interviews it emerged that, while China's increasingly active participation in ICANN can be observed, Chinese stakeholders' activities have not become particularly prominent with regard to policymaking. According to a research participant familiar with ICANN's work, this probably results from China's more complex ecosystem and its later involvement in ICANN. Furthermore, an academic familiar with the internal work of ICANN restressed in an interview with the author specific rhetorical aspects that hint at China's growing engagement and acceptance of ICANN at the apex of the IP and DNS governance ecosystem: while China maintained a relatively low profile throughout the IANA stewardship transition, this interview participant stressed the importance of the aforementioned speech by the then-head of CAC Lu Wei at ICANN 50 in 2014 and the appointment of China's representative GAC Vicechair right after the completion of the IANA stewardship transition. While observing no major growth in terms of the strength of Chinese actors in ICANN in recent years, this participant finds that these episodes signal a growing acceptance of the forum by the ICANN-involved Chinese Internet governance community. This is further demonstrated in literature: Jongen and Scholte (2021) found that ICANN is mostly perceived as legitimate within the ICANN community and this involves Chinese participants.

Finally, it must be stressed that Chinese participation being mostly low-key does not entail inactiveness. While Chinese participation is not numerous and a group of participants finds that Chinese impact on ICANN policymaking is relatively low, in an interview an ICANN staff member stressed Lu Wei's constant activeness in informal settings during the IANA stewardship transition on behalf of the Chinese government. In this participant's words:

> In those years there was a strong diplomatic action with the Chinese government: bilateral meetings, including high-level and ministry-level ones. [...] [Lu Wei] met with the then ICANN president to stress China's interest that ICANN go on with this independence process: ending the [IANA] contract and restructuring the governance model by changing ICANN's Bylaws.

In short, this participant stresses that China's government did engage in the IANA stewardship transition and carried an influence, while not being necessarily prominent in GAC.

To conclude on this aspect, China's relationship with ICANN has surely improved throughout time, evolving from straightforward confrontation in the early 2000s to Lu Wei's endorsement of ICANN and Guo Feng's vice-presidency of GAC. To this, growing engagement on selected policy issues, such as internationalised domain names (IDNs), must be added (Zhang, 2019).

However, a degree of ambiguity in relation to ICANN and multi-stakeholderism remained. For example, Negro (2020) finds China's multilateralist challenge to ICANN has not faded away. Research participants confirm Chinese presence has grown in the ITU, as demonstrated by the appointment of Zhao Houlin as ITU Secretary (2015–2022), though replaced by a US individual (Doreen Bogdan-Martin) following the end of his mandate. In an interview with the author an ICANN staff member stresses that this is not to be read necessarily as a confrontational move towards ICANN. In a way, China is simply leveraging one forum against the other to put pressure on reform, but on the other hand, ICANN-ITU relations improved under Zhao Houlin as ICANN became a member to the ITU-D and the two started joint capacity-building initiatives. Nevertheless, initiatives such as the 'New IP' project, which is better discussed below, periodically cast ambiguities on China's stances on multistakeholderism.

Briefly, ambiguity remains, but overall Chinese stakeholders do not aim to replace a governance model that allows them to participate and 'forum-shop' to enhance their influence.

4.4 Chinese Actors and the IETF: Public–Private Relations in Standard-Making

Contrary to ICANN, the IETF allows for assumptions to be made based on publicly available quantitative data. As Arkko (2023) shows, Huawei is currently the second main contributor to the IETF in terms of RFCs yearly authored by its affiliates, right behind Cisco. However, the former does not have the latter's longstanding experience in the IETF. Instead, Huawei started featuring increasingly prominently in RFC-related figures in 2007. Meanwhile, between 2007 and 2010, Chinese nationals' participation in the IETF experienced a sharp increase in terms of number of RFCs and Internet Drafts authors, remaining relatively steady at the 2010 level for the following decade more or less (Arkko, 2023). On a clarification note, Chinese nationals' participation and Chinese companies' participation do not go hand in hand. It goes without saying that Chinese nationals may work for non-Chinese companies and Chinese companies may employ non-Chinese nationals. Notwithstanding this, the synchronism of Huawei's escalation in IETF participation and the increasing number of Chinese RFC and Internet Drafts authors is an interesting aspect.

As research participants often pointed out, initially Chinese companies participated in such technical bodies as the IETF through their Western technologists, often hired in consultant positions. This was deemed helpful in overcoming both linguistic and cultural barriers that could have posed obstacles to engineers' work. In the words of a research participant affiliated to a European manufacturer:

> At the beginning, [Chinese stakeholders] started hiring a lot of 'standardisation people' from other companies, not necessarily Chinese people, maybe Europeans, or North Americans. But once they started, they have brought in more Chinese people into the area, so in that sense that was like a stage process: getting started, bringing in people that would be recognised and were experienced, learning from them, and now they bring in more Chinese people.

Briefly, as Chinese companies' participation increased, so did the participation of Chinese engineers employed by domestic Chinese companies. Many research participants familiar with the work of the IETF, whether technologists or not, see it as symptomatic of a growing socialisation of Chinese companies and their engineers into the rules and modi operandi of the IETF and other technical bodies. A similar process was, in fact, observed in 3GPP.

Therefore, 2007 represents a turning point. While identifying the drivers of such timing is complicated, hints can be found in the business orientation of Huawei as a device and mobile network manufacturer. To begin with, by 2007 China had not rolled out 3G yet (Stewart et al., 2011; Zhang & Liang, 2007). This posed the country in a condition of backwardness compared to Europe and the US, with the then Europe-led 3GPP setting the scene for 4G standardisation already in 2008 (3GPP, 2021). While this displayed a strong role of the central government, which slowed down the process of implementation in order to protect the home-grown 3G standard, it also gave private manufacturers a push towards penetrating foreign markets. Accordingly, this is seen as one reason behind Huawei's timings in the global market (Zhang & Liang, 2007), and arguably in global standardisation fora, too. Huawei's first infrastructural contract in Europe was signed in 2005 (Huawei, 2021; Pepermans, 2016) and the beginning of its participation in the IETF was in 2007, right when the deployment of the new version of the Internet Protocol (IPv6) began stepping up and work on 4G standardisation was about to begin at 3GPP (3GPP, 2021; Internet Society, 2017; Wen, 2020). Right in the same year, Huawei deployed its first all-IP mobile network in Germany (Huawei, 2021).

To be sure, mobile Internet is not a central topic in this chapter, as it will be addressed later in this book. Nonetheless, being Huawei a network manufacturer as well as China's 'giant' within the IETF, observing developments in the mobile infrastructure and device market helps to interpret its policy choices and those of the stakeholders it relates to.

In short, in this phase both the market needs of Huawei and state policies played a role in Huawei's internationalisation. In Wen's (2020) account, Huawei's internationalisation push was both state policy and a market need. In terms of state policy, Huawei was identified as a strategic company in a 2005 national funding plans for internationalising Chinese ICT industry (Wen, 2020), while in terms of market needs the aforementioned domestic 3G impasse pushed Huawei to seek international markets along with the high domestic competition with SOEs and foreign competitors. US and European manufacturers and carriers had in fact gained a strong position in China's domestic market before Chinese companies such as Huawei and ZTE gained their current size and position (Wen, 2020; Zhang & Liang, 2007).

In other words, the historical phase between the end of the WSIS process reaffirming multistakeholderism as a governance principle in 2005 and the reawakening of the multilateralist quest in 2012 sees an increased presence of Chinese stakeholders, mainly Huawei, in the European market and in standardisation bodies like the IETF. The main drivers behind Huawei's choices appear to be market-based, as illustrated in the previous paragraph, despite important doubts remaining about the central government's effective control on domestic actors (Pupillo, 2019; Pepermans, 2016). While Chinese corporate actors were growing active in the IETF, China's government rebuilt relations with ICANN and became more participatory in GAC. Meanwhile, further Chinese stakeholders engaged in ICANN too, albeit maintaining a relatively low profile. Indeed, a governmental role in Internet policies is acknowledged by the literature and was confirmed by most research participants (Negro, 2017; Tang, 2020). Nonetheless, evidence of direct control allowing government and private companies to be treated as a monolithic whole did not emerge in conversations with technologists familiar with 3GPP and the IETF. The more Chinese companies globalise and gain a leadership role, the more the state-companies dialectic evolves (Shen, 2016), with instances of strong coordination and instances of reciprocal criticism (Shih, 2015). However, this is a rapidly evolving situation. As mentioned above, sanctions related to the technological competition between the US and China forced Huawei to redirect its efforts towards the Chinese domestic market, which after 2017 became its main source of revenues, whereas before Huawei mainly earned income overseas. The difference between the increased reliance of Huawei on China's domestic market and its decreased revenues overseas has become prominent since 2019, with the Covid-19 pandemic potentially playing a role (Brown, 2021).

Going back to Chinese stakeholders' role in the IETF, the phase following WCIT-12 and the PRISM scandal, up to the IANA stewardship transition, did not have a direct influence on the IETF according to most research participants. The mode in which IETF work is conducted remained similar. To be sure, the IANA Stewardship Transition Coordination Group (ICG) was established, followed by a working group called IANAPLAN. However, their role was mainly to ensure that the transition affected IETF work and IETF's relation to ICANN as little as possible. At the time of IANAPLAN's launch, an email communication by the working group's chair retrievable from the IETF's public mail archive stated that

> [t]he system in place today for oversight of the IETF protocol registries component of the IANA function works well. As a result, minimal change in the oversight of the IETF protocol parameters registries is preferred in all cases and no change is preferred when possible. [...] This working group is chartered solely with respect to the planning needed for the transition, and is not meant to cover other topics related to IANA. Possible improvements outside that scope will be set aside for future consideration. However, the mechanisms required to address the removal of the overarching NTIA contract may require additional documentation or agreements. The WG will identify, but not create such required agreements. (Internet Engineering Steering Group, 2014, hereafter IESG)

To summarise, while the IETF did follow the IANA stewardship transition owing to its ties to ICANN in the regime complex, the transition itself did not influence the IETF's modus operandi nor the internal relations among actors.

The difference, however, is visible in the influential role played by Chinese stakeholders in IETF work. The three IETF working groups whose RFCs are analysed in this chapter increased Chinese presence and even centrality and pre-eminence of affiliates of Chinese corporations in the working groups. Observing the RFCs authored within idr, 6man, and alto in the same timespans put forward in Chapter 2,[3] further observations can be made. Strikingly, no single RFC was co-authored by Chinese actors' affiliates in idr for the 2007–2008 timespan, but two of the four RFCs published within the same WG between 2018 and 2019 are co-authored by Huawei and Cisco affiliates, along with affiliates from smaller companies (Ginsberg et al., 2019; Previdi et al., 2019). A third RFC, authored by Arrcus and Cisco affiliates, has been reviewed by Susan Hares, among others, who at the time was the Huawei-affiliated idr chair (Bush et al., 2019). Authorship in RFCs shows growing activeness in standard-making from Huawei's part. This is not homogeneous, however. In 6man, no RFC has been authored by Chinese companies' affiliates in the given timespans. Furthermore, the 2018–2019 timespan saw only two RFCs coming from the 6man WG, one of which is a Best Current Practice (BCP) RFC. This signals a general pattern of lower engagement in 6man from the broader IETF community. Conversely, alto represents a peculiar case: dormant in terms of produced documents between mid-2018 and mid-2019, it saw three standards-track RFCs published in 2020. One of these was co-authored by affiliates from Chinese companies, namely Huawei and China Mobile, along with affiliates from Thales Deutschland, Yale University, and Nokia (Randriamasy et al., 2020). Another one was authored by affiliates of Nokia and Yale University but reviewed by Yale and Tongji universities' affiliates. Once again, cooperation among Western, including US, and Chinese actors emerges in the IETF despite East–West geopolitical divisions.

This is relevant because the then-Trump administration impeded cooperation between Chinese companies and companies doing business with the US, as well as cooperation between Chinese and US companies in strategic research and development (R&D). This led other private US-based standard-making organisations to question the handling of Chinese companies' participation, with the Institute of Electrical and Electronics Engineers (IEEE) suspending Huawei's participation in certain activities for a short while in 2019 (IEEE, 2019). Such difficulties seem not to

---

[3] Recalling from Chapter 2, the selected timespans are June 2007 to June 2008 and June 2018 to June 2019 for idr and 6man. For alto, the selected timespans are November 2008 to November 2009, June 2018 to June 2019, and January 2020 to December 2020.

have affected the IETF, where Chinese participation and co-drafting of RFCs between US and Chinese companies has continued.

Briefly, the documents' authorship suggests Chinese actors' growing centrality and presence in the functioning of the IETF. While this is not constant and equal in every WG, Chinese RFC (co)authors are present and Huawei is the second main organisational RFC contributor after Cisco on a yearly basis (Arkko, 2023), by far the most influential Chinese actor in the IETF. Many of the RFCs analysed here, as presented within the selected WGs, have not made it to official standard status yet. As described in previous chapters, the basic reference for standard-making procedure in the IETF is RFC 2026 (Bradner, 1996). It can take years before a Standard-Track RFC develops into a full-fledged Internet standard and technology can remain in use without becoming a recognised standard in full.

In other words, Chinese stakeholders participate in the IETF conscious that the need for consensus makes cooperation with industry and technologists across geopolitical lines necessary. What instead reopened the multilateralist vs. multistakeholderist divide in the current historical phase is the presentation of the so-called 'New IP' proposal to the ITU's Telecommunication Standardization Sector (ITU-T). This proposal, then renamed 'Future Vertical Communications Network' (FVCN), was put forward in late 2019 by a group of actors including the MIIT, Huawei and two ISPs (Hogewoning, 2020; Li, 2020). Beyond media concerns (Murgia & Gross, 2020), the technical proposal has been subjected to criticism on a normative and technical level (Durand, 2020; Hogewoning, 2020; Mueller, 2020; Sharp & Kolkman, 2020).

On a normative level, the question relates to the competence of the ITU and its state-based conformation in contrast to the private-based characteristics of the IETF, traditional 'home' of TCP/IP. The IETF being a private- and consensus-based decision-making body clashes normatively with the ITU's more state-centric characteristics (Flonk et al., 2020; Sharp & Kolkman, 2020). On a technical level, the proposal lacked clarity (Mueller, 2020). While this is a new topic subject to constant evolution and lack of public information, this view was confirmed in interviews with the author as late as December 2020. Richard Li (2020), one of the leading engineers behind the FVCN/New IP idea, engaged in public relations to promote and explain the rationale behind this technical project. While this helped to bring an extent of clarity, a common understanding among research participants from various backgrounds is that the New IP proposal is not meant to replace the existing IP versions, but rather to create an Internet architecture aimed at tackling specific technical problems emerging with new Internet-enabled technologies.

The final details and results of this technical initiative are beyond the scope of this book. What matters here is the debate on the nature of the Internet and the role of actors and institutions at the core of standard-making. According to an interview participant, the New IP/FVCN raises further normative questions related to the philosophy upon which the Internet has been built: one of the building blocks rather than a fully determined architecture, which instead reflects the way in which the telecom market, including mobile Internet technologies, has evolved. In other words, despite its initial name, the New IP is not a new proposed version of the Internet Protocol, at least in its current form given the available information (Durand, 2020; Mueller, 2020). Furthermore, the New IP proposal must be observed in the broader context of technical debates over the suitability of TCP/IP for new Internet of Things (IOT) technologies that need ultra-reliable connections and low latency, such as medical IOT. In this view, work on new forms of IP and non-IP networking is ongoing at the IETF and the European Telecommunications Standards Institute (ETSI), too (Petrescu, 2021).

As far as the potential replacement of TCP/IP in the near future is concerned, it must also be added that the existence of different, technically incompatible basic protocols is not new to the Internet ecosystem. The introduction of IP version 6 (IPv6) is exemplary: its elaboration started in 1995 amid concerns that IP version 4 (IPv4) would exhaust its address space (IANA, 2019). As DeNardis (2014) illustrates, IPv4 encompassed a total of 2^{32} IP addresses, that is, around 4.3 billion. Instead, IPv6 has a total of 2^{128} (undecillions) addresses. The assignment of the last addresses available in the IPv4 space by ICANN to a Regional Internet Registry (RIR) took place in 2011 (ICANN, 2020). A few years before that, the development and implementation of IPv6 was accelerated, with a strong Chinese contribution as well (Negro, 2020). Even though the complete replacement of IPv4 with full-IPv6 networks is nowhere in sight, the two IP versions have been made fully interoperable through ad hoc technical specifications (DeNardis, 2009; Zander & Wang, 2018). Users seldom know what IP version is attributed to their network-connected devices and to the devices they are interacting with.

Notwithstanding this, a number of research participants with technical, academic, and public institutional backgrounds raised normative questions related to the New IP. Two of these emerged as particularly eminent: first if this new technology is conceived for fulfilling an 'IP-like' role, it should be standardised at the IETF rather than the ITU. The former, other than being the traditional 'IP home', is a private- and consensus-based body, whereas the latter is a state- and majority-based one (see also: Sharp & Kolkman, 2020). Second, in an interview with the author, a senior technologist maintained that "there are clear indications that the New IP architecture would include controls to impede or redirect 'unwanted' traffic - as a security measure. Technical details about the design of those controls are lacking but we should be careful [to] make sure that they will not become censorship tools". Third, as mentioned above in this section, doubts were raised concerning architectural characteristics.

Notwithstanding these normative concerns, few research participants find it likely that the New IP (if implemented) will constitute an infrastructure unable to communicate with IP-enabled network-connected devices. The dominant position Huawei (and by extension China as a state) has achieved in 5G technology at the global level would suggest it is not in its interest to promote a non-interoperable basic protocol, as it would create major transaction costs on the device market: devices aimed at different markets would need to be developed to work through different protocols in different countries or areas of the world. In line with Mueller (2017), it is more beneficial for Chinese stakeholders to retain scale economies and enjoy network benefits by adopting universal standards, shaping them through IETF activity. This point of view was raised by most research participants and finds theoretical support in economic and regime-theoretic literature on transaction costs (Alter & Raustiala, 2018).

In other words, the potential for the 'New IP' to be more disruptive than IPv6, in normative terms as well as in terms of technical fragmentation, has been pinpointed by some research participants from academia, the technical community, and governmental institutions. However, the lack of technical detail as well as the interest of major Chinese stakeholders in keeping global scale economies in the device market make IP-related initiatives unlikely to technically fragment the Internet. To be sure, other normative aspects such as the choice to present a technical proposal containing 'IP' in its name to a multilateral body, as well as the unknowns around New IP's capacity to enhance online censorship, remain unaddressed.

As mentioned, the New IP/FVCN question is an ongoing one, detail lacks, and there is no guarantee it will become an implemented technology at the time of writing. What matters in this is the role this proposal plays in portraying the ambiguity of Chinese actors' engagement in multistakeholderism.

4.5 What Is at Stake?

What is at stake for the future of the Internet given the conditions discussed above in this section? A key takeaway is that China has little interest in fragmenting the Internet at the technical level. This is strengthened by Chinese stakeholders' increasing integration in the multi-stakeholder model: it would go against their self-interest to disrupt a governance architecture that allows them to grow influential on a global scale. To be sure, there may be groups within the Chinese Communist Party (CCP) or smaller private or state-owned actors with an interest in a more closed 'national' Internet. Nonetheless, with Huawei becoming a major player in 3GPP and the IETF, technical fragmentation would go against China's economic and Huawei's business interests. In literature, this resonates with Mueller (2017), who stresses the centrality of network benefits of a technically unified Internet.

While China has progressively integrated into multistakeholder governance (ambiguities notwithstanding) and is not pushing for technical fragmentation, the question of alignment is at stake. 'Alignment' refers to the process undertaken by governments to control 'what goes on' on the Internet, that is, the data and information fluxes to which citizens and organisations have access from within the territory (Mueller, 2017). In other words, a tendency exists among governments to 'align' the Internet to domestic regulation. Examples of this are not only found in China or autocratic states, but also in liberal democracies. Two important aspects emerge from this, related to aspects discussed in Chapter 2. First, fragmentation is not an 'East vs. West' question. Second, a commonly accepted threshold of what constitutes 'fragmentation' is not set (DeNardis, 2016; Drake et al., 2016; Mueller, 2017).

Analytically, it emerges from interviews that Chinese authorities are more prone to controlling the domestic Internet ecosystem at the regulatory level, while allowing for network benefits to be enjoyed at the technical one, empowering market actors to 'go global'. The Golden Shield Project, also known as the 'Great Firewall of China' and already addressed in Chapter 2, is a good example of it (Negro, 2017), as it makes sets of information inaccessible without adopting separate basic protocols for networking. What is interesting in the Golden Shield Project is its scalar implementation as China became more integrated into the global market and the world's digital economy. Launched in 1998, the project reached full capacity ten years later (Negro, 2017), that is, when China's 3G network was rolled out, granting expanded Internet access to at least a portion of the population (Stewart et al., 2011). Furthermore, it is at this stage that Huawei started enhancing its active participation in the IETF (Arkko, 2023), amid delays in domestic 3G rollout (Zhang & Liang, 2007). This was followed by the Facebook and Google bans in 2009 and 2012, respectively (Quinn, 2012). In the latter case, it was only the browsing service that was banned, while the company maintained offices in mainland China at the time of writing and redirected its servers to Hong Kong (Helft & Barboza, 2010). When China banned WhatsApp in 2017 (Haas, 2017), the development of 5G was already launched, with Huawei poised to become one of the main contributors to the global 5G specification (Pohlmann et al., 2020). In this context, Chinese companies developed alternative platforms, with WeChat playing the role of both WhatsApp and Facebook in its being a mobile and desktop app performing platform and private messaging functions—other than a set of further services such as payments.

This aspect was addressed in interviews. Research participants familiar with the Chinese Internet ecosystem pinpoint that WeChat's success in domestic China (where it is known as 微信 weixin) was already higher than WhatsApp's earlier than 2017. This suggests that, censorship notwithstanding, WeChat created a business model more successful in intercepting the taste of Chinese users. After all, Chapter 3 already stressed that measures such as the Golden Shield Project, other than having political objectives, play an economically protectionist role (Plantin & De Seta, 2019; Shen, 2022), but early Chinese platform companies grew amid foreign competition (Mueller & Farhat, 2022). While outside the scope of this book, it is worth underlining that the fragmentation of web content, rather than Internet infrastructure, based on geographical or linguistic characteristics of the users' populations can take place autonomously in cyberspace. These can be leveraged for political reasons and reinforced through acts of censorship such as those described above in this paragraph, but this does not constitute fragmentation inasmuch as content remain accessible to users elsewhere and triggers no split in the infrastructure.

A further technical element needs to be added when talking about political control on the Internet in China and its influence globally. While it is true that censorship takes place domestically through technical tools working at a higher layer than such universal standards such as TCP/IP and the DNS, which are still in place, it must be stressed that the physical Internet infrastructure of China is strongly built within China's geographical borders (Allen, 2019; Hong & Harwit, 2020). This adds to strong data localisation policies that are constantly developing (Liu, 2020).

These elements complicate the debate on fragmentation further. To what extent can a strongly censored online environment, built upon an 'almost-domestic' Internet infrastructure, be considered part of the global Internet, although it deploys the same basic standards? The author argues that keeping the infrastructure as much as possible within the country's geographical border is part of the process of control conducted on the Internet rather than a form of technical split. In fact, such platforms and services as Google and Facebook are technically accessible in China via a Virtual Private Network (VPN)—although the political consequences of it may vary. This confirms that the Chinese government sees an advantage in letting its domestic industry benefit from economies of scale and network benefits by deploying global standards for devices to function while maintaining strong control on societal activities over the Internet. Further elaboration on the meaning of fragmentation and its conceptual borders will be provided in the forthcoming chapters based on this empirical research.

To conclude, the stronger China and Chinese stakeholders have grown, the more they have become involved in the existing multistakeholder Internet governance ecosystem, as the presence of major domestic actors among the biggest competitors in the digital market, including sensitive sectors such as mobile Internet architecture, makes it disadvantageous to create technical splinters. At the same time, to cast control over what takes place in the domestic cyber-sphere, China opted for forms of information and regulatory control, while maintaining the Internet intact at the technical level. In other words, the more China grew involved in technical Internet governance at the global stage, accepting existing organisations and institutions such as the multistakeholder principle, ICANN and the

IETF, the more it strengthened control on online activities domestically: from the implementation of the Golden Shield Project, to forcing Google's services out of mainland China, to banning Twitter, Facebook, and later WhatsApp in 2017 as illustrated above.

While the author found little disagreement among research participants on Chinese stakeholders' interest not to technically split the Internet, phenomena at the societal, informational level yielded more disagreement. First and foremost, there is no agreement on what constitutes fragmentation. At the user level, many maintain the Internet was born fragmented, though not along national boundaries, as different user constituencies use different platforms and information sources. Furthermore, others maintain an extent of separation is to be expected, censorship notwithstanding, as different linguistic groups will access sources, platforms, and contents in different languages, creating separate user bases. Second, it could be argued that governmental control in terms of information and data movement is also enforced through technical tools: for example, by detecting and rerouting data packets with particular forms of encryption. However, this principle is similar to the Golden Shield's and entails no fragmentation of the basic protocols. This constitutes alignment inasmuch as it entails control of Internet-related activities through state regulation.

4.6 Conclusion

From the perspective of norm entrepreneurship, Chinese actors are maintaining a degree of ambiguity in their engagement in Internet governance which allows them to be influential in a wider variety of fora (Negro, 2020). For example, presenting the 'New IP' project at the ITU in a context of increased influence in that venue can be read as forum-shopping, that is, the practice of taking topics off the competence of a given forum and shift it to another as a technique of policy or norm negotiation (Hofmann, 2019). In regime-complex terms, while different bodies have different competences, their loose interdependence allows corporate and state actors to turn to other venues to try and push one's technology into the global standard. This increases actors' capacity for political contestation, thus allowing different actors to act as norm entrepreneurs. In the 'New IP' case, presenting a technical proposal carrying 'IP' in its name in a multilateral body that had been the protagonist of anti-ICANN contestation in the past can be read as a political signal. Notwithstanding the normative element of this, many interview participants hinted at Chinese actors' strategizing: a reason for presenting the 'New IP' proposal at the ITU is that it resembles much more a telephony infrastructure than the Internet one as illustrated above. In this case, the ITU would be an adequate standardisation forum for a technology that would not replace IP as we know it but would build a form of non-IP connectivity for IOT.

However, 'New IP' represents an ongoing project and a shifting target at the time of writing, thus not allowing strong theory-building. What matters here is the interest element behind the choice. On a more cognitivist ground, it emerges that Chinese stakeholders' interests have transformed in light not only of domestic public–private relations, but also through interaction with other actors within ICANN, the IETF, and the ITU itself. As it became apparent that ICANN was there to stay and that IETF norms and rules are rigid due to consensus being needed for standard-making, Chinese actors stepped up their participation in such venues. As illustrated above in this chapter, it is not just the consolidation of the (ICANN-centred) multistakeholder global Internet governance mechanism in the wake of WSIS that triggered Chinese actors' acceptance of such fora, but also contemporary technological innovations such as the beginning of 4G development internationally, 3G deployment in China, and an up-step in IPv6 implementation. In this process, many interview participants pinpoint Chinese actors initially hired Western technologists to participate in such fora as the IETF. As the IETF was founded in the US and was historically US- and Western-dominated, this way Chinese companies hired technologists who were already culturally and professionally aware of IETF practices. Therefore, Chinese actors (mainly companies, in this context) internalised and reproduced working practices so as to be more effective within the IETF, to the point that nowadays they participate through Chinese-born and Chinese-educated technologists who are fully fledged, effective IETF participants.

Briefly, rational interest and cognitive dynamics go hand in hand, the latter complementing the former by providing a theoretical ground for interest formation. In this, however, Chinese actors see an interest in participating and carrying weight in as many governance fora as possible, maintaining a degree of ambiguity that allows them to forum-shop (Hoffmann et al., 2020; Negro, 2020), but see interest in maintaining the existing fora in place as they can influence decision-making through the existing rules. In other words, the norm-entrepreneurial effort of Chinese stakeholders features instances of contestation through such practices as forum shopping, but also instances of adaptation to the existing normative architecture. This bases on matters of incentive and constraints at the market and political levels, but also on a learning process of socialisation through which Chinese stakeholders have familiarised with the governance processes in question and the way to influence rule- and standard-making.

Interpretively, one can see elements of continuity in China's government-led contestation against ICANN. However, the straightforward contestation experienced in the early 2000s has faded and what remains now is that form of ambiguity illustrated above. Conversely, elements of continuity are found in Chinese stakeholders' participation in ICANN, too. Even the years of China's strain and non-participation in GAC saw Chinese public, private, and state-sponsored groups and subjects participating in ICANN. In the IETF, Chinese actors became active participants in 2007, when Huawei's participation started growing until becoming the second most prominent corporate actor per RFCs published by its affiliates (Arkko, 2023). The mix of policy and market drivers (and constraints) that pushed Huawei's action in its early years in the IETF has been illustrated above in this chapter. They entail market constrictions domestically, but also an economic and political need for stronger influence in standard-making both in the Internet standard-making and telephony, with Chinese stakeholders' role in 3GPP being analysed in the next chapter.

Overall, what matters theoretically in this section is that ICANN and IETF rules and norms are rigid. Consensus (or supermajority, in many ICANN SOs cases) is needed in decision-making, which makes it difficult to influence an organisation's policies without forms of compromise. This is also due to the voluntary and scalable nature of the technologies in question. This creates forms of regime resilience, strengthened by elements of technological path dependence. In this context, Chinese stakeholders preferred to carry influence within the existing fora following existing rules rather than pushing for normative shifts. As Chinese stakeholders grew more economically powerful, they found it more advantageous to step up participation and influence decision-making in such fora as ICANN and IETF, while retaining presence and influence in the ITU, where the current Secretary General is a Chinese national at the time of writing.

Amid normative rigidity and the solidification of the ICANN-centred multistakeholder Internet governance model that followed WSIS, Chinese stakeholders adapted to the existing norms and rules of Internet governance at ICANN and the IETF rather than adapting such rules to their interest. This happened amid market and policy pushes as illustrated above and involved a learning process by Chinese stakeholders, who internalised expertise on the working culture and mechanisms of such bodies as the IETF by hiring experienced Western personnel from other companies before enhancing their participation through Chinese-born staff members educated in China and/or in the West. Chinese stakeholders' adaptation to the existing rules and norms was visible during the IANA stewardship transition, too. Rather than pushing for the outright replacement of ICANN, which would have been the expected stance given China's government's historical support for multilateralism (Flonk et al., 2020), the Chinese government played a key—albeit low-profile—role in pushing for the transition, rendering ICANN as autonomous as possible from the US government.

To be sure, some interview participants believe that the transition is still insufficient for China, which is still in a challenging position with regards to ICANN. This is also found in literature and confirmed above in light of China's ambiguity at the ITU. Nonetheless, the historical process of China's engagement in the ICANN-centred multistakeholder governance model is one of further acceptance and adaptation the more China and its domestic stakeholders grew capable of influencing decision-making.

On the 'fragmentation' side of this project's research questions, a few statements can be made. First, conceiving fragmentation as a technical split that creates two separate and non-communicable networks, this chapter shows that Chinese actors have an interest in maintaining the Internet universal. Producing different devices for different markets using different protocols to connect to the Internet hampers technological scalability and this chapter shows that convergence in standard is present elsewhere, too, not only in critical Internet resources. Chinese stakeholders maintain an interest in pursuing network benefits. To maintain political and social control on the Internet, the Chinese government opts for censorship tools acting at a higher level than basic Internet protocols, along with regulatory instruments. In other words, China engaged in a process of alignment of the Internet to domestic regulation that dates back at least to the implementation of the Golden Shield Project and allowed it to control information fluxes and promote the growth of domestic platforms alternative to the Western ones, which played both a political and economically protectionist role (Shen, 2022). This aspect of domestic regulatory alignment is addressed to a deeper extent in Chapter 6.

To summarise and conclude, the rigidity due to the need for consensus in Internet standard- and policymaking, along with the need for scale economies and network benefits, pushed Chinese stakeholders to adapt to the existing rules and increase their influence within the given institutional and normative settings. The more Chinese actors became capable of influencing ICANN and IETF work, the more they became participatory in it. At the same time, the more Chinese public- and private-owned actors became influential globally, the more the Chinese government pushed for a process of alignment domestically (Mueller, 2017). The Golden Shield Project, carrying out both a political task and a protectionist one to shield Chinese companies from Silicon Valley competition (Shen, 2022), has been enhanced to censor Facebook, Google, and then WhatsApp in three different moments as China became more prominent globally and more present in standard-making and Internet governance. This shows a process of adaptation of Chinese companies to existing norms.

To be sure, this cannot be taken to entail full normative acceptance. Ambiguities persist both in China's behaviour among ICANN, the IETF, and the ITU (Negro, 2020), and in official documents. In its 2017 International Strategy of Cooperation on Cyberspace, China expresses support for multilateral governance with multi-party (multistakeholder) participation, an important ambiguity in the formulation. At the same time, it must be stressed that this document refers to a broader scope of governance than critical Internet resources strictly speaking, and it endorses the push for ICANN reform without ever rejecting its role (Ministry of Foreign Affairs of the PRC, 2017).

Nonetheless, there is a general acceptance of the persistence of such bodies as ICANN and the IETF in their existing form and recognition of the advantage of participating in them.

References

3rd Generation Partnership Project. (2021). *LTE*. https://www.3gpp.org/technologies/keywords-acronyms/98-lte (Accessed 15 January 2021).

Allen, D. (2019, June 19). Analysis by Oracle Internet Intelligence Highlights China's Unique Approach to Connecting to the Global Internet. *Oracle Cloud Infrastructure Internet Intelligence*. https://blogs.oracle.com/internetintelligence/analysis-by-oracle-internet-intelligence-highlights-china%e2%80%99s-unique-approach-to-connecting-to-the-global-internet (Accessed 18 December 2019).

Alter, K. J., & Raustiala, K. (2018). The Rise of International Regime Complexity. *Annual Review of Law and Social Science, 14*(1), 329–349.
Arkko, J. (2023). Distribution of Authors per Companies. *IETF Statistics.* https://www.arkko.com/tools/allstats/companydistr.html (Accessed 21 July 2023).
Arsène, S. (2015). Internet Domain Names in China. Articulating Local Control with Global Connectivity. *China Perspectives, 4,* 25–34.
Belli, L. (2015). A Heterostakeholder Cooperation for Sustainable Internet Policymaking. *Internet Policy Review, 4*(2), 1–21.
Bradner, S. (1996). RFC 2026: The Internet Standards Process—Revision 3. *IETF Datatracker.* https://datatracker.ietf.org/doc/html/rfc2026 (Accessed 28 May 2021).
Brown, A. (2021, June 1). *Huawei's Global Troubles Spur Beijing's Push for Self-Reliance.* Mercator Institute for China Studies. https://merics.org/en/short-analysis/huaweis-global-troubles-spur-beijings-push-self-reliance (Accessed 18 June 2021).
Buchholz, K. (2021, April 19). Huawei Continues Steep Global Rise. *Statista.* https://www.statista.com/chart/16827/huawei-revenue-and-smartphone-market-share/ (Accessed 12 September 2023).
Bush, R., Patel, K., & Ward, D. (2019). RFC 8654. Extended Message Support for BGP. *Internet Engineering Task Force.*
Ciuriak, D. (2019). The US-China Trade War: Technological Roots and WTO Responses. *Global Solutions Journal, 4,* 130–135.
Creemers, R. (2020). China's conception of cyber sovereignty: Rhetoric and realization. In D. Broeders, & B. Van den Berg (Eds.), *Governing cyberspace. Behavior, power, and diplomacy.* Rowman and Littlefield.
Cross Community Working Group Accountability. (2015). Stress Tests. *Internet Corporation for Assigned Names and Numbers.*
DeNardis, L. (2009). *Protocol Politics: The Globalization of Internet Governance.* MIT Press.
DeNardis, L. (2014). *The Global War for Internet Governance.* Yale University Press.
DeNardis, L. (2016). One Internet: An Evidentiary Basis for Policy Making on Internet Universality and Fragmentation. In Global Commission on Internet Governance (Ed.), *A Universal Internet in a Bordered World. Research on Fragmentation, Openness and Interoperability.* CIGI and Chatham House.
Drahokoupil, J., McCaleb, A., Pawlicki, P., & Szunomár, A. (2017). Huawei in Europe: Strategic Integration of Local Capabilities in a Global Production Network. In J. Drahokoupil (Ed.), *Chinese Investment in Europe: Corporate Strategies and Labour Relations.* ETUI.
Drake, W. J., Cerf, V. G., & Kleinwächter, W. (2016). *Internet Fragmentation: An Overview.* World Economic Forum.

Durand, A. (2020, October 27). *New IP. ICANN OCTO-017.* https://www.icann.org/en/system/files/files/octo-017-27oct20-en.pdf (Accessed 26 November 2020).

Flonk, D., Jachtenfuchs, M., & Obendiek, A. S. (2020). Authority Conflicts in Internet Governance: Liberals vs. Sovereigntists? *Global Constitutionalism*, 9(2), 364–386.

Galloway, T., & He, B. (2014). China and Technical Global Internet Governance: Beijing's Approach to Multi-Stakeholder Governance within ICANN, WSIS and the IGF. *China: An International Journal*, 12(3), 72–93.

Generic Names Supporting Organization (2023, August 2). *GNSO Council.* https://gnso.icann.org/en/about/council (Accessed 18 October 2023).

Ginsberg, L., Previdi, S., Wu, Q., Tantsura, J., & Filsfils, C. (2019). RFC 8571. BGP—Link State (BGP-LS) Advertisement of IGP Traffic Engineering Performance Metric Extensions. *Internet Engineering Task Force.*

Glen, C. M. (2014). Internet Governance: Territorializing Cyberspace? *Politics and Policy*, 42(5), 635–657.

Governmental Advisory Committee. (2015, October 21). *Dublin—Board and GAC Meeting.* https://meetings.icann.org/en/constituency/governmental-advisory-committee-gac?page=4 (Accessed 6 July 2021).

Haas, B. (2017, July 19). China Blocks WhatsApp Services as Censors Tighten Grip on Internet. *The Guardian.* https://amp.theguardian.com/technology/2017/jul/19/china-blocks-whatsapp-services-as-censors-tighten-grip-on-internet (Accessed 20 September 2021).

Helft, M., & Barboza, D. (2010, March 23). Google Shuts China Site in Dispute Over Censorship. *The New York Times.* https://www.nytimes.com/2010/03/23/technology/23google.html (Accessed 13 July 2023).

Hoffmann, S., Lazanski, D., & Taylor, E. (2020). Standardising the Splinternet: How China's Technical Standards Could Fragment the Internet. *Journal of Cyber Policy*, 5(2), 239–264.

Hofmann, S. C. (2019). The Politics of Overlapping Organizations: Hostage-taking, Forum-Shopping and Brokering. *Journal of European Public Policy*, 26(6), 883–905.

Hogewoning, M. (2020, November 10). Update on WTSA-20 Preparations and New IP. *RIPE NCC.* https://labs.ripe.net/Members/marco_hogewoning/update-on-wtsa-20-preparations-and-new-ip (Accessed 26 November 2020).

Hong, Y., & Harwit, E. (2020). China's Globalizing Internet: History, Power, and Governance. *Chinese Journal of Communication*, 13(1), 1–7.

Huawei. (2021). *History.* https://www.huawei.eu/who-we-are/history (Accessed 18 January 2021).

Hurel, L. M., & Rocha, M. S. (2018). Brazil, China and Internet Governance: Mapping Divergence and Convergence. *Journal of China and International Relations* (Special issue), 98–115.

Institute of Electrical and Electronics Engineers. (2019, June 2). *IEEE Lifts Restrictions on Editorial and Peer Review Activities.* https://www.ieee.org/about/news/2019/statement-update-ieee-lifts-restrictions-on-editorial-and-peer-review-activities.html (Accessed 8 July 2021).

Internet Assigned Numbers Authority. (2019, March 1). *IPv4 Recovered Address Space.* https://www.iana.org/assignments/ipv4-recovered-address-space/ipv4-recovered-address-space.xhtml (Accessed 4 April 2022).

Internet Corporation for Assigned Names and Numbers. (2002). *ICANN Archives.* https://archive.icann.org/en/meetings/shanghai/ (Accessed 19 August 2021).

Internet Corporation for Assigned Names and Numbers. (2020). Regional Internet Registry. *ICANNWiki.* https://icannwiki.org/Regional_Internet_Registry (Accessed 17 December 2020).

Internet Engineering Steering Group. (2014, September 8). [Ianaplan] WG Action: Formed Planning for the IANA/NTIA Transition (ianaplan). *IETF Mail Archive.* https://mailarchive.ietf.org/arch/browse/ianaplan/?q=blanchet&so=date (Accessed 4 April 2022).

Internet Society. (2017, May 25). *State of IPv6 Deployment 2017.* https://www.internetsociety.org/resources/doc/2017/state-of-ipv6-deployment-2017/ (Accessed 19 July 2021).

Jongen, H., & Scholte, J. A. (2021). Legitimacy in multistakeholder global governance at ICANN. Global Governance: *A Review of Multilateralism and International Organizations, 27*(2), 298–324.

Li, R. (2020, June 2). Some Notes on 'An Analysis of the "New IP" Proposal to the ITU-T'. *Internet4Future.* https://internet4future.wordpress.com/2020/06/02/some-notes-on-an-analysis-of-the-new-ip-proposal-to-the-itu-t/ (Accessed 22 October 2020).

Liu, J. (2020). China's Data Localization. *Chinese Journal of Communication, 13*(1), 84–103.

Ministry of Foreign Affairs of the People's Republic of China. (2017). *International Strategy of Cooperation in Cyberspace.* http://www.xinhuanet.com//english/china/2017-03/01/c_136094371_5.htm (Accessed 14 July 2021).

Mueller, M. L. (2013). Are We in a Digital Cold War? *GigaNet: The Global Governance of the Internet: Intergovernmentalism, Multistakeholderism and Networks.* http://citeseerx.ist.psu.edu/viewdoc/download?doi=10.1.1.363.2569&rep=rep1&type=pdf (Accessed 18 July 2019).

Mueller, M. L. (2017). *Will the Internet Fragment? Sovereignty, Globalization, and Cyberspace.* Polity Press.

Mueller, M. L. (2020, March 30). About that Chinese 'Reinvention' of the Internet… *Internet Governance Project.* https://www.internetgovernance.org/2020/03/30/about-that-chinese-reinvention-of-the-internet/ (Accessed 22 October 2020).

Mueller, M. L., & Farhat, K. (2022). Regulation of Platform Market Access by the United States and China: Neo-Mercantilism in Digital Services. *Policy & Internet, 14*(2), 348–367.

Murgia, M., & Gross, A. (2020, March 27). Inside China's Controversial Mission to Reinvent the Internet. *Financial Times.* https://www.ft.com/content/ba9 4c2bc-6e27-11ea-9bca-bf503995cd6f (Accessed 22 October 2020).

Nanni, R. (2023). Whither (De)globalisation? Internet Fragmentation, Authoritarianism, and the Future of the Liberal International Order: Evidence from China. *The Pacific Review.* Online first.

Negro, G. (2017). *The Internet in China: From Infrastructure to a Nascent Civil Society.* Palgrave Macmillan.

Negro, G. (2020). A History of Chinese Global Internet Governance and Its Relations with ITU and ICANN. *Chinese Journal of Communication, 13*(1), 104–121.

Palladino, N., & Santaniello, M. (2021). *Legitimacy, Power, and Inequalities in the Multistakeholder Internet Governance: Analyzing IANA Transition.* Palgrave Macmillan.

Pawlicki, P. (2017). Challenger Multinationals in Telecommunications: Huawei and ZTE. In J. Drahokoupil (Ed.), *Chinese Investment in Europe: Corporate Strategies and Labour Relations.* ETUI.

Pepermans, A. (2016). The Huawei Case and What It Reveals About Europe's Trade Policy. *European Foreign Affairs Review, 21*(4), 539–557.

Petrescu, A. (2021, January 15). [6gip] IP-Related New Efforts. *IETF Mail Archive.* https://mailarchive.ietf.org/arch/browse/6gip/?gbt=1&q= IP-related%20new%20efforts (Accessed 4 April 2022).

Plantin, J., & De Seta, G. (2019). WeChat as Infrastructure: The Technonationalist Shaping of Chinese Digital Platforms. *Journal of Chinese Communication.* http://eprints.lse.ac.uk/91520/1/Plantin_WeChat-as-infrastructure. pdf (Accessed 15 November 2021).

Pohlmann, T., Blind, K., & Hess, P. (2020). *Fact Finding Study on Patents Declared to the 5G Standard.* IPLytics and Technische Universitaet Berlin.

Previdi, S., Filsfils, C., Lindem, A., Sreekantiah, A., & Gredler, H. (2019). RFC 8669. Segment Routing Prefix Segment Identifier Extensions for BGP. *Internet Engineering Task Force.*

Pupillo, L. (2019, June 21). 5G and National Security. CEPS. https://www. ceps.eu/5g-and-nationalsecurity/ (Accessed 20 October 2020).

Quinn, B. (2012, November 9). Google Services Blocked in China. *The Guardian.* https://www.theguardian.com/technology/2012/nov/09/ google-services-blocked-china-gmail (Accessed 6 July 2021).

Randriamasy, S., Yang, R. Y., Wu, Q., Deng, L., & Schwan, N. (2020). RFC 8896. Application-Layer Traffic Optimization (ALTO) Cost Calendar.

Internet Engineering Task Force. https://www.ietf.org/proceedings/91/slides/slides-91-alto-3.pdf (Accessed 4 April 2022).

Scholte, J. A. (2017). Complex Hegemony: The IANA Transition in Global Internet Governance. *GigaNet: Global Internet Governance Academic Network, Annual Symposium.*

Sharp, H., & Kolkman, O. (2020, April 24). Discussion Paper: An analysis of the 'New IP' Proposal to the ITU-T. *Internet Society.* https://www.internetsociety.org/resources/doc/2020/discussion-paper-an-analysis-of-the-new-ip-proposal-to-the-itu-t/#:~:text=%20Key%20Elements%20of%20the%20proposed%20%E2%80%9CNew%20IP%E2%80%9D,transport%20architectures.%20C83%20and%20its%20associated...%20More%20 (Accessed 22 October 2020).

Shen, H. (2016). China and Global Internet Governance: Toward an Alternative Analytical Framework. *Chinese Journal of Communication, 9*(3), 304–324.

Shen, H. (2022). *Alibaba: Infrastructuring Global China.* Routledge.

Shih, G. (2015, April 21). Exclusive—Huawei CEO Says Chinese Cybersecurity Rules Could Backfire. *Reuters.* https://in.news.yahoo.com/exclusive-huawei-ceo-says-chinese-cybersecurity-rules-could-133148214--finance.html (Accessed 16 June 2021).

Stewart, J., Shen, X., Wang, C., & Graham, I. (2011). From 3G to 4G: Standards and the Development of Mobile Broadband in China. *Technology Analysis and Strategic Management, 23*(7), 773–788.

Tang, M. (2020). From 'Bringing-in' to 'Going-out': Transnationalizing China's Internet Capital Through State Policies. *Chinese Journal of Communication, 13*(1), 27–46.

Wen, Y. (2020). *The Huawei Model: The Rise of China's Technology Giant.* University of Illinois Press.

Working Group on Internet Governance. (2005). *Report of the Working Group on Internet Governance.* 05.41622.

Zander, S., & Wang, X. (2018). Are We There Yet? IPv6 in Australia and China. *ACM Transactions on Internet Technology (TOIT), 18*(3), 1–20.

Zhang, A. H. (2022). Agility Over Stability: China's Great Reversal in Regulating the Platform Economy. *Harvard International Law Journal, 63*(2), 457–514.

Zhang, J., & Liang, X. (2007). 3G in China: Environment and Prospect. *IEEEXplore.* https://ieeexplore.ieee.org/abstract/document/4349642 (Accessed 27 April 2021).

Zhang, J. (2019, January 8). Internationalized Domain Names and Universal Acceptance: Spreading the Word in China. *Internet Corporation for Assigned Names and Numbers.* https://www.icann.org/en/blogs/details/internationalized-domain-names-and-universal-acceptance-spreading-the-word-in-china-8-1-2019-en (Accessed 26 May 2021).

Zhong, R. (2021, July 4). China Orders Didi Off App Stores in an Escalating Crackdown. *New York Times*. https://www.nytimes.com/2021/07/04/technology/china-didi-app-removed.html (Accessed 6 July 2021).

Zhu, L., & Chen, W. (2022). Chinese Approach to International Law with Regard to Cyberspace Governance and Cyber Operation: From the Perspective of the Five Principles of Peaceful Co-Existence. *Baltic Yearbook of International Law Online, 20*(1), 187–208.

CHAPTER 5

On the Normative Impact of Chinese Stakeholders in Mobile Internet Standard-Making. A Document- and Interview-Based Analysis

5.1 INTRODUCTION

The question of mobile Internet connectivity has become increasingly politicised and has reached high media coverage amid the US–China technological competition that accelerated under the Trump administration and solidified thereafter (Ciuriak, 2019). Such a hype contributed to confusion over the topic, with the outcry for the risk of Internet fragmentation (Hoffmann et al., 2020; Tayal, 2021). True, the development of 5G, the latest generation of mobile Internet connectivity, imposed new pressure on the functioning of core Internet protocols (ten Oever, 2022). By allowing increasing IoT-related connectivity, new

---

The interview findings illustrated in this chapter have also been included in shorter form in: Nanni, R. (2021). The 'China' question in mobile Internet standard-making: Insights from expert interviews. *Telecommunications Policy*, 45(6): 1–12.

The document-based findings are also included in shorter form in: Nanni, R. (2023). Whither (de)globalisation? Internet fragmentation, authoritarianism, and the future of the Liberal International Order: evidence from China. *The Pacific Review*. Online first.

problems of latency have emerged in relation to TCP/IP-based data transport, affecting critical IoT services such as those for remote surgery, requiring reliable connectivity and low-latency data transmission. This has pushed standardisation bodies and companies to work on connectivity mechanisms alternative to IP, with geopolitical conundrums attached when it comes to such things as Huawei's 'New IP' proposal illustrated in Chapter 4 (Hogewoning, 2020). Furthermore, these same developments are yielding overlaps and interdependency between telephony and Internet infrastructures inasmuch as the former are all-IP and allow Internet-based connectivity of new devices, with further implications for the configurability and security of the network according to sectors of the literature (ten Oever, 2022).

As illustrated in Chapter 2, the work of 3GPP does not fit the multistakeholder framework in a straightforward manner, although it goes along the same pattern of private-based governance of technological resources and standard-making related to scalable technologies. A main difference is that participation in 3GPP is not open to all but is connected to affiliation to a member organisation of one of the seven standards development organisations that constitute it. Furthermore, patents-based incentives are different: in 3GPP, patents have a larger impact and maximise a company's royalty gains when recognised as essential (that is, standard-essential patents, SEPs) to the making of both network infrastructure and device production (Buggenhagen & Blind, 2022).

In political terms, 5G is increasingly central in state-to-state competition amid growing restrictions against Chinese network manufacturers in the US and the EU and China's increased reliance on domestic technology. This arguably constitutes a form of market fragmentation, whereby some countries may open their domestic markets to Western or Chinese companies exclusively along geopolitical lines (Poggetti, 2021). Conversely, on the technical end, a trend towards harmonised mobile Internet standards is visible, as illustrated through interviews and standardisation documents in this chapter.

These aspects will be explored within this chapter proceeding in historical order. Sections 5.2 through 5.4 explore the drivers and dynamics of Chinese stakeholders' engagement in mobile connectivity standard-making in 3G, 4G, and 5G respectively. Section 5.5 builds on the empirical analysis in the previous sections to address the normative implications of Chinese stakeholders' transformation in their engagement with standardisation. Finally, Sect. 5.6 draws conclusions.

5.2 ROAD TO 3G: DOMESTIC CONSTRAINTS, MARKET DRIVERS, AND CHINESE STAKEHOLDERS' EARLY ENGAGEMENT IN 3GPP

A few aspects related to the market conditions in China, as well as the relationship between the Chinese state and companies, have been illustrated in Chapters 3 and 4, hinting at the connection between Chinese stakeholders' international engagement in Internet standard-making and in 3GPP. After all, the main Chinese companies in terms of contributions to standardisation in both fields are Huawei and ZTE followed by others (Arkko, 2023; Pohlmann et al., 2020), which shows mixed activities from SOEs as well as private companies when it comes to strategies and interests in the standardisation of telecommunications and Internet infrastructure.

Negro (2017) provides a powerful hint on this by stressing the strong connection between telecommunications policy and the Internet ecosystem in China, in light of the aforementioned interdependence between the two. He underlines how the four years preceding the establishment of ICANN and 3GPP constituted a major period of reform in the Chinese telecommunications market and in the layers of public bureaucracy in charge of its management, as illustrated in further detail in Chapter 3. Notwithstanding this, it is worth underlining that the central state maintained a strong political and administrative control. After all, the then Jiang Zemin presidency was adamant on both the necessity to engage in digital development and the need to govern its social implications. The same goes for Hu Jintao in the following decade. On the administrative hand, as far as mobile Internet connectivity is concerned, it was the government who granted operators the use of one mobile Internet standard or the other. On the political hand, up until nowadays Internet Service Providers (ISPs) are bound to control the information exchanged by users and are made politically accountable. To be sure, what was here dubbed 'administrative' has political as well as economic implications. Decisions on what standards to implement nationally affect the device market since incompatible standards force device manufacturers to produce devices with different technical characteristics for different national markets. This is most often read as a protectionist move (Shen, 2022; Stewart et al., 2011).

Powerful governmental role notwithstanding, public and private stakeholders, as well as different layers of the Chinese public bureaucracy (for example, ministries and authorities), held separate interests. In this view, Zhang and Liang (2007) provide an insightful reconstruction. By 2007, that is, the year before 3GPP set the basis for 4G equipment roll out in Release 8, China had not rolled out 3G nationally yet. Three different 3G standards had been approved by the ITU-R, one of which (known as TD-SCDMA[1]) was elaborated in China and was incompatible with the other two. Governmental delays have been attributed to political concerns and the need to protect China's domestic market, still strongly SOE-dominated and potentially incapable of withstanding global competition. Political concerns derived from the government's need to control the social implications of more widespread Internet access. It is worth recalling from Chapter 3 that the Golden Shield Project, as well as its 'Great Firewall of China' subset, was not fully implemented until 2008 (Negro, 2017). In this context, private device and network manufacturers like Huawei had, in Zhang and Liang's (2007) account, an incentive to penetrate foreign markets amid China's domestic 3G standby. To this, Wen (2020) adds that China's domestic market was strongly dominated by foreign manufacturers, as China relied on foreign companies before building its own 'national champions'.

Therefore, a market push for internationalisation was among the drivers of Huawei in the mid-2000s. At the same time, Wen (2020) stresses that at that stage Huawei had been identified, along with other private and state-owned enterprises, among the strategic companies for which special funds for internationalisation were allocated.

In interviews with Huawei-affiliated participants, the company's need to internationalise amid domestic competition with SOEs emerges as a topic and is corroborated by other participants not affiliated to Chinese stakeholders. This provides ground for interpreting Huawei's drive towards internationalisation from a market, other than government-led, perspective. To be sure, industrial policy played a role, but this does not necessarily point towards the extents of political control. Rather, it shows Huawei plays a strategic role in China's government's technological growth strategy. Given the latter authoritarian characteristics, the government's growing presence in business affairs within companies, and Huawei's growing dependence on China's domestic market, doubts about political control remain in place (Brown, 2021; Pupillo, 2019).

---

[1] TD-SCDMA: Time-Division Synchronous Code-Division Multiple Access.

Once again, however, this book seeks to acknowledge the complex relationship between the Chinese government and Chinese private companies, which is made of cooperation and control as well as dialectics as per Chapters 3 and 4.

In short, the timing of Huawei's first contract for network manufacturing in Europe (in 2005) and the beginning of its engagement (and rapid growth) in the IETF (from 2007) allowed to argue for the existence of a market incentive for Huawei to internationalise along with the Chinese government's existing industrial policy (Arkko, 2023; Huawei, 2021; Wen, 2020; Zhang & Liang, 2007). In interviews, some research participants do attribute Huawei's mid-2000s internationalisation spur to development in mobile technology and the device market.

These elements are telling on the development of public–private relations in China, the transformation of the dialectic between the two, and the impact this had on Chinese actors' stances in standard-making. As stated above, governmental role in China's 3G policy proved central: it was the government who dictated the schedule for 3G rollout, even at the cost of major delays, and led to the deployment of the Chinese-elaborated TD-SCDMA in an effort to protect the Chinese mobile market. In this context, private actors found an incentive to internationalise and became active network manufacturers abroad.

Briefly, in this phase, a Chinese-elaborated mobile Internet standard was coexisting with those elaborated mainly by Western actors (Stewart et al., 2011). The role of the central government was a protectionist one. However, private actors (Huawei, in particular) began their internationalisation as network manufacturers, enhancing their role in the European market and in the IETF. Stewart et al. (2011) confirm this view: while the MIIT (which in 2008 subsumed the Ministry of Information Industry, MII 信息产业部 xinxi changye bu) was a major promoter of the TD-SCDMA standard, the then major national mobile operator, China Mobile, was testing the implementation of other international standards amid scepticism over TD-SCDMA's real potential for success. Nonetheless, despite its incompatibility with the other internationally developed 3G standards, TD-SCDMA attracted foreign investments, with such companies as Nokia, Alcatel, and Ericsson participating in its elaboration along with Chinese private and state-owned enterprises. At the same time, it must be noted that the Chinese SDO (CCSA, then called CWTS) had entered 3GPP already in 1999 (CCSA, 2021). According to

Stewart et al. (2011), ZTE became the second-biggest patent holder in TD-SCDMA as it invested in it despite uncertainty.

However, it is worth mentioning that both ZTE and the sceptical China Mobile are SOEs, suggesting that, despite state ownership, a coherent 3G strategy did not emerge until 2008, when China Telecom, China's main telecom operator, was granted TD-SCDMA licence while China Mobile and China Unicom were allowed to deploy the other ITU-accepted standards. This happened in a bid to protect the domestic market and the home-grown technology TD-SCDMA while respecting WTO commitments on technological neutrality (Song et al., 2023; Stewart et al., 2011). As recalled in Chapter 2, TD-SCDMA was a 'Chinese' standard inasmuch as it was elaborated in China and deployed there. However, it was recognised as a 3G standard by ITU-R and the standardisation process saw strong cooperation between Chinese and Western companies, who saw an advantage in holding patents on different 3G technologies (Song et al., 2023; Stewart et al., 2011). China's quest for protecting its home-grown TD-SCDMA technology came amid a domestic market situation in which network manufacturing was still largely foreign-dominated, as companies such as Huawei were on the rise but still far from the size it achieved in 2010s (Wen, 2020).

Moreover, 3G deployment in China was not articulated and extended throughout the country. In this context, private manufacturers like Huawei chose a strategy of internationalisation and 'tech agnosticism', whereby they produced technologies for every market (that is, for every standard) without prominently participating in the standardisation process.

The scattered characterisation of 3G standard-making does not only affect China. US and Asian actors launched a standardisation initiative called 3GPP2 in this phase. More specifically, 3GPP2 was established by the US, Korean, Japanese, and Chinese institutional partners of 3GPP to elaborate CDMA-2000, a 3G standard separate from the mainly Europe-made UMTS, also referred to as WCDMA with reference to its radio access technology.[2]

As for this book's focus, what are the implications of these aspects for multistakeholder governance and technological (Internet) fragmentation? Briefly, government-companies relations in China are dialectic ones,

---

[2] WCDMA: Wideband Code Division Multiple Access.

albeit ones in which the government plays a powerful role, which suggests private actors have a space for manoeuvre when acting internationally in standard-making. In 3G, in particular, the role of the central government was a powerful one in that it imposed a delayed implementation schedule and regulated the distribution of licences in favour of the home-grown standard.

In this view, a Chinese academic research participant based in the US underlines that Chinese stakeholders' participation in 3G standardisation, even though not fully internationalised, can be read as a Chinese effort to build a domestic mobile Internet value chain in order to better participate in standardisation and rollout processes when it came to future generations (4G and 5G). This participant maintained it is complicated to evaluate the positive or negative impact of Chinese activity in 3G standardisation given this technology's relatively small presence within the Chinese territory. However, it is deemed to have created a domestic ecosystem enabling tech stakeholders to enhance their participation in 4G and 5G standardisation processes. This allowed Chinese stakeholders to gain capacity in the global standardisation ecosystem.

As Wen (2020) recalls, the early 2000s were years of major market reforms in China amid the country's accession to the World Trade Organisation (WTO). The market saturation in the then 2G infrastructure and the strong presence of SOEs provided a strong incentive for Huawei to internationalise amid oscillating relations with the government and other major SOEs in its sector, such as ZTE. Only towards the end of the first decade of the twenty-first century did Huawei change its position in the Chinese market. However, at that stage the 4G rush had already started.

5.3 A Change in Strategy: Drivers and Implications of China's Approach to 4G

In the run towards 4G standardisation, China's national strategy changed. According to some research participants, including telecommunication engineers familiar with the work of 3GPP, this derived from the 3G strategy's unsuccessfulness in promoting Chinese technology abroad. At this stage, it must be noted that Chinese participation is consolidating both in 3GPP and the IETF. Furthermore, between 2006 and 2009 the Chinese government suspended its boycott of ICANN's activities. While Chinese stakeholders' IETF and ICANN engagement is analysed in Chapter 4, it is worth mentioning their growing engagement in globally established governance institutions at this time in history.

However, this did not change China's protectionist attitude towards domestic-made mobile connectivity standards. Its home-grown 4G standard, known as LTE-TDD (also referred to TD-LTE),[3] was licensed in China in December 2013, while other global standards were only licensed by the Chinese government starting from 2015 (Wen, 2020). Once again, all the aforementioned standards are ITU-approved, and in compliance with the requirements set forth by ITU-R.

This time, deployment was broader and quicker than with 3G. Furthermore, the government is known to have endeavoured more proactively to promote TD-LTE in other developing countries, whereas TD-SCDMA was mainly deployed in China (Wen, 2020). According to Yu Jiang (2011), Chinese actors' newly found competitiveness is due to the path dependence that exists in mobile Internet technologies. In this account, path dependence allowed Chinese actors to plan for future generations' developments by basing on the available 3G-related knowledge. Such path dependence is also visible in 5G: the initial phase of its development foresaw the deployment of radio standards on the LTE core network. In this, while being a standard-maker gives one a short-term advantage, being a standard-taker allows one to partially free ride on the earlier standards towards the development of the new one. This, of course, needs to be followed by economic and financial conditions, as well as a favourable public system of incentives.

As for the dialectic between public and private actors mentioned above, this stage also features relevant elements. According to Wen (2020), Huawei, poised to achieve a leading position in the domestic and international mobile Internet market, launched a 'price war' on ZTE and major foreign equipment sellers in 2007, rising from a 2% share in China Telecom's CDMA[4] equipment market share to a 30% share the following year. ZTE declined from the leading position in this market (32% in 2007) to 15% the following year. While China Telecom's three other major equipment suppliers (the Western companies Alcatel, Motorola, and Nortel) suffered minor losses in percentage terms, ZTE fell by more

---

[3] LTE-TDD: Long-Term Evolution Time-Division Duplex.

[4] CDMA: Code-Division Multiple Access, a telecommunications standard mainly related to 2G and built-upon in 3G technology.

than half its 2007 percentage points. Once again, these aspects show that, despite an active governmental role in promoting home-grown technologies, relations among Chinese companies (whether state-owned or private) are not necessarily one of market sharing under state supervision. On the contrary, the Huawei-ZTE 'love-and-hate relationship', as it was dubbed by a research participant, emerges in most interviews with experts active in or familiar with 3GPP. This includes members of staff of Western companies, who observe the dynamics between Chinese private enterprises and SOEs as third parties. Nonetheless, in this dialectic, the role of the Chinese government has remained powerful. By 2008, when 3G rollout had just started in China, the State Council had licensed a three-billion US dollar plan for 4G-oriented research and development (R&D). While this does not add information on governmental control on companies' activities in global standardisation bodies, it suggests a strong stance from the government in promoting a profitable home-grown 4G technology (Ming & Ouyang, 2008; Yu, 2011).

At this stage in history, Chinese corporations such as Huawei and ZTE increased their international market share. Meanwhile, 4G development continued. After beginning work on Release 8 in 2008, by 2012 3GPP had already frozen Release 10, paving the way for the deployment of LTE-Advanced (Wannstrom, 2013).[5] The growth of Huawei and ZTE, China's two main network manufacturers, has partially been addressed in Chapter 3. As mentioned, by 2013 Huawei's share of LTE contracts worldwide competed directly with Ericsson's, while ZTE was more reliant on the domestic market (Drahokoupil et al., 2017). At this stage, around two-thirds of Huawei's global revenues were from foreign markets, only one third were domestic.

In hindsight one can see they were already on a declining trend since 2011, a tendency that now sees Huawei being strongly dependent on China's domestic market, which accounted for around two thirds of its revenues in 2020 (Brown, 2021). However, by 2013 Huawei was establishing itself as a global player, with a strong market presence in Europe, the Middle East, Latin America, and Africa, although in terms of

---

[5] The all-encompassing terms indicating generations, such as '4G', are generally catchphrases for a set of technologies each being a development on top of the previous one, improving performances. Releases 8 through 10 are fully-fledged 4G-related releases, referring to technologies called LTE, LTE-Advanced and LTE-Advanced Pro, which set the basis for 5G.

Chinese industrial policy there still was a protectionist tendency towards participating in 3GPP while developing a non-interoperable 4G standard domestically. This was a phase in which China deployed 4G at the same pace as the world's other major powers and participated in 3GPP work while also standardising its home-grown TD-LTE standard.

Observing the text of specifications related to Release 8, 3GPP's first LTE-related release, frozen in 2009, one can see the widespread participation of Huawei, whose affiliates also obtained rapporteur positions on some working items. The two other most prominent Chinese actors within Release 8-related specifications are ZTE and China Mobile, the main-featuring Chinese ISP. These companies are listed either as supporting members to a feature or work item or as rapporteurs' affiliation on work items (3GPP, 2009). Another important characteristic of Release 8 is that it aims in many points to integrate work from individual organisational partners and from 3GPP2, as well as subsuming the work of ETSI on Telecommunications and Internet converged Services and Protocols for Advanced Networking (TISPAN), a move that allows better coordination on the elaboration of specifications for New Generation Networks (NGN) (Vidal et al., 2007).

In Release 8 several specifications and features address the integration of 3GPP2-elaborated standards to allow for greater technological compatibility worldwide (3GPP, 2009). Many such integrations were supported by Chinese stakeholders, especially Huawei, hinting at an interest towards creating a 3GPP-elaborated 4G standard as broadly applicable as possible. While this could also have other drivers and objectives that fall outside the scope of this article, it is interesting to see that such patterns of behaviour of Chinese companies in Release 8 are coherent with interview findings. As anticipated, research participants pinpointed both Chinese stakeholders' growth in presence in 3GPP during the 4G standardisation phase (2008–2013, roughly) and China's increased deployment of the 3GPP-elaborated 4G standard.

Following 2013, 3GPP2 remained dormant while its members have been increasingly active in 3GPP. Pohlmann et al. (2020) find for example that South Korean actors like Samsung were the main owners of 5G-related patent families by the beginning of 2020, while Huawei was the main standard contributor in absolute terms. Furthermore, UMTS was also implemented in China, Japan, and South Korea, although it runs along other standards operated by different ISPs. It must also be underlined that Release 8-related specifications stress 3GPP's work to integrate

LTE and WiMAX technologies, a radio standard alternative to LTE in the 4G run (3GPP, 2009). This signals once again a trend towards convergence in standards, an aspect that is further illustrated below and that returns in interviews.

In short, 4G set the basis for the situation illustrated by Pohlmann et al. (2020) and summarised in Chapter 1, whereby Huawei represents one of the main standard-makers in 5G.

5.4 5G: Chinese Companies' Catch-Up in Telecommunications

A key takeaway from the previous section is that 3G and 4G paved the way for the Chinese industry to increase its strength towards a leadership position in mobile Internet standard-making while starting from a position of backwardness. Chinese companies, in particular, Huawei, reached a position of leadership in this phase, along with other international giants such as Samsung and Ericsson.

What emerges from most interviews on this topic is an increasing interest for Chinese actors to act as standard-makers at the global level instead of engaging in smaller-scale elaboration and implementation of technical standards that, despite formal ITU recognition, are conceived to become coexisting to the globally deployed ones. In terms of public policy, Huawei reinforces this view by stressing its activeness in global standard-making.

In an interview with the author, a senior Huawei-affiliated telecommunication engineer underlined that by 2020 around 14% of Huawei's capital and 50% of the company's human resources were invested in research and development (R&D). To this research participant, this strategy is aimed at enhancing the company's capacity to create and promote global standards, a fundamental element to gain a strong position in the market. Furthermore, this research participant agrees that the existence of multiple, incompatible, 3G mobile Internet standards was detrimental to the development of the global market and thus to companies'—including Huawei's—interests, which is the reason why they are now striving to elaborate a global 5G standard. Telecommunication engineers not affiliated with Huawei tend to confirm this view. Among them, engineers active within 3GPP confirm that no technical fragmentation attempt has come from China in 5G standardisation, where Huawei has been the top 5G standardisation contributor in quantitative terms, followed by Ericsson (Pohlmann et al., 2020).

In November 2020, only a few months after these interviews, these interpretations were corroborated by ITU-T's approval of two 3GPP-elaborated 5G radio interface standards. While no separate technical proposal came from China, the only locally elaborated 5G standard that met ITU-R's IMT-2020 criteria was from Telecommunications Standards Development Society India (TSDSI). At the time of writing, however, the ITU has stated that global interoperability has been reached (ITU, 2020). It must be stressed however that a few further 5G-related releases are expected to come from 3GPP at the time of writing (ten Oever, 2022), as telecommunications infrastructure generations are developed throughout the implementation phase. Furthermore, it must be specified that among the two 3GPP-promoted 5G radio interface standards recognised by the ITU, one was promoted by Chinese companies among others, albeit still within the 3GPP realm. However, this simply featured an extra IOT-related specification and is interoperable with the other one (ITU, 2020).

Observing the specifications related to Release 15, one can see engagement from part of Huawei, ZTE and the three state-owned ISPs. In the document contributions list, Huawei is often sided by HiSilicon, its fully owned chip-making division. Compared to specifications related to Release 8, there are fewer references to the integration of specifications elaborated by different bodies. Conversely, the effort visible in Release 8 to harmonise 3GPP2 and WiMAX provisions within 3GPP work seems to be replaced in Release 15 by measures to interoperate LTE and 5G infrastructure, coherently with the objective to build a non-standalone 5G connectivity in this phase, allowing 5G's New Radio to operate on top of the LTE core network. As mentioned above in this chapter, this is done in anticipation of the standalone specifications provided in Release 16. The fact that less harmonisation work was needed at this stage signals once again the trend towards harmonised mobile Internet standards that emerged in interviews, which brought about an operationally compatible 5G landscape on a global scale.

On a different note, the 5G rollout has only just begun and geopolitics is deeply entrenched with market policies (Maxigas & ten Oever, 2023). Longstanding debates in Europe about whether or not to include Huawei in the construction of core networks and in auctions for the radio spectrum are exemplary (Ciuriak, 2019; Economist, 2020; Poggetti, 2021).

Therefore, a deeper insight below the surface of public policy shows not only that Huawei is a major rule-maker in 5G standardisation, but also that there is no intention from Chinese stakeholders to elaborate a separate, incompatible national 5G standard. However, geopolitical divides remain visible within the network and device markets, as better discussed in the next section.

To summarise, the three 5G radio interface standards approved by the ITU at the end of 2020 ensure compatibility, confirming the views expressed by most interview participants throughout the research process and the aforementioned process of convergence in standards. This entails that Chinese companies' activities in mobile Internet standardisation processes grew in time and became more influential. Participation and influence grew together: as the capacity of Chinese stakeholders to influence decision-making grew, so did their interest in shaping global standards and avoiding local incompatible specifications. It goes without saying that the need for a growing company to expand its market is an essential driver of the aforementioned actions, as it emerged throughout interviews.

5.5 The Rise of China (and Chinese Industry) in Telecommunications: Normative Implications

A key finding illustrated in the previous section is that it is mainly through private actors—above all, Huawei (Pohlmann et al., 2020)—that China is becoming stronger in mobile connectivity standard-making. Research participants knowledgeable about 3GPP's work usually observe a governmental role in standards-related policymaking, but generally limited to matters of policy coordination. As it emerges in literature, governmental support and government policies do play a role in Chinese companies' 'going out' that is acknowledged in both Western and Chinese literature, although the extent to which its role is dominant is not apparent (Cai, 2018; Segal, 2018; Shen, 2016; Tang, 2020). In addition, the threshold between influence and coordination, on the one hand, and control, on the other, is blurred (Liu, 2021; Moore, 2023; Pupillo, 2019; Zhong, 2019).

Particularly relevant is the contribution of a US-based Chinese academic, who underlined in an interview with the author the dynamicity of the relationship between China's government and Chinese companies. This research participant stressed the strong role of the state in the early

2000s, when China opted for the adoption of a nationwide 3G standard incompatible with the one deployed in Europe and elaborated within 3GPP. Importantly, the image of China's inner politics emerging from this interview is not a monolithic one, although a strong, albeit evolving, state-business tie is visible:

> Probably you should view it as a longer historical process: China's participation in shaping the mobile communication standards started very early with 3G and there was a very big debate in China on whether [Chinese actors should have participated] in this game or just follow[ed] the US's or Europe's standard. So, [...] even today, you can't say [Chinese participation in 3G was] a success or failure because it has only very, very limited presence within Chinese borders, [but currently] I think almost the majority would agree that [without] China's participation in shaping this early standard, Huawei today would not be able to reach standards in 5G. In 3G, China basically built its whole production chain, so now Huawei can take advantage of this huge [value] chain to shape this technical standard.

Generally speaking, research participants knowledgeable about 3GPP could not identify instances in which forms of governmental control on Chinese companies were visible beyond matters of coordination and policy direction.

In other words, ambiguities in public–private relations persist and it is difficult to assess the normative impact of Chinese actors on multistakeholderism. On a formal level, China's engagement in 3GPP is strongly business-driven. Huawei is a private actor, whereas other state-owned enterprises such as ZTE are much less active and influential in 3GPP. However, the extent to which China's government controls companies' business processes is unknown. Nonetheless, most research participants familiar with 3GPP's work, independently of their affiliation, tend to confirm state-business ties but see governmental coordination, rather than governmental control, behind Chinese companies. In this, the Chinese state leadership remains ambiguous. For instance, China's president Xi Jinping called for efforts "to unite people from the private sector around the Communist Party of China (CPC) to better promote the healthy development of the private sector" (Buckley & Bradsher, 2020; Xinhua, 2020a, 2020b). While he did not elaborate on what this means in practical terms, practices for stricter governmental control on companies' activities have been implemented through antitrust measures following the launch of the Common Prosperity (or Great Rectification) campaign (Bush, 2021; Kong et al., 2022; Zhong, 2021). Briefly, whether and to what extent China may increase states' influence in multistakeholder Internet governance through de facto state-controlled, but formally private, actors remains an open question.

Ambiguity notwithstanding, patterns of behaviour similar to those found in the IETF emerge among Chinese actors in 3GPP. According to interview participants active within 3GPP, Chinese stakeholders went from a numerically and technologically marginal position to one of prominence under both perspectives. Besides Chinese stakeholders' quantitative prominence observed in document analysis and systematised by Pohlmann et al. (2020), interview participants underline that Chinese growth in 3GPP started with Chinese companies hiring Western consultants familiar with the forum's working culture and environment. Progressively, Chinese companies' grew their numerical presence within and across 3GPP working groups with an increasing presence of Chinese-born and Chinese-educated engineers. This follows the pattern illustrated for Chinese engagement in the IETF in Chapter 4. In the words of an interview participant formerly affiliated to a European telco and active within 3GPP,

> it is an evolving topic: the first step taken by Chinese companies was to hire American and English colleagues – even some colleagues from [my company] have been hired by Huawei, in particular, and they took on Huawei's standardisation activities. So, there was a quite big 'trading season', alternatively through consultants, to bring [to 3GPP] the company's position through people who had no linguistic barriers and were in the – so to say – 'European or American mindset' to interact in standard-making organisations, which is different from the Chinese one. From this point of view, I must say it is impressive to see [how] cultural backgrounds influence participation in standard-making organisations. [...] The second step was to [strongly increase their presence in] 3GPP, by which I mean that Huawei in particular has very sizeable delegations in working groups. I mean, if I look at the RAN plenary, which is the one I follow, where normally there are around 300 people following face-to-face meetings, Huawei has 30 to 40 people present: that is, more than 10% of the physical participants are from Huawei. ZTE has lower figures, but they are always present and there are other strong Chinese actors: I'm thinking of Oppo.

As it emerges in interviews, the growth of Chinese stakeholders in 3GPP, much like in the IETF, was a process of learning and adaptation to the body's standard-making norms. The adaptation process went along Chinese companies' market growth, especially in Huawei's case, while domestically China was launching different deployment strategies: from protectionism, with the promotion of the home-grown 3G standard TD-SCDMA, to a global stance with their participation in an industrial leadership position in a fully interoperable 5G environment. This process was also followed by a faster deployment policy at the domestic level: if 3G deployment in China was not ready until 2008, 4G and 5G deployments were synchronic with Europe and the US.

Summarising, mobile Internet connectivity has experienced a convergence in standards: three major non-interoperable 3G standards were deployed in three major markets, with CDMA-2000 being the dominant standard in the US, UMTS being dominant in the EU, and TD-SCDMA in China. Nowadays, the three 5G radio interface standards recognised by the ITU—two from 3GPP (3GPP 5G-SRIT and 3GPP 5G-RIT) and one from TSDSI (5Gi)—grant a wide extent of interoperability. In the ITU's own words, "these technologies were deemed to be sufficiently detailed to enable worldwide compatibility of operation and equipment, including roaming" (ITU, 2020). Chinese stakeholders such as Huawei are supportive and fully participatory in this trend as their global market reach requires globally scalable technological solutions. However, such convergence in standards is confronted by a growing market divide, whereby countries tend to (or are pushed to) choose between network manufacturers from Western(-leaning) countries or China. In the context of the growing US–China trade competition, many US allies within and outside the EU adopted some extent of restrictions towards Huawei and other Chinese manufacturers (Poggetti, 2021). Despite centrality in the media (Ciuriak, 2019), in terms of standardisation politics, this is a separate matter. While it can and does affect the speed and characteristics of deployment policies, it falls outside the scope of this book.

5.6 Conclusion

At the theoretical level, similar considerations can be advanced as per the analysis of critical Internet resources presented in Chapter 4.

From a regime-theoretic perspective, Chinese actors maintained an extent of ambiguity in time towards mobile connectivity standards, too.

While having accessed 3GPP at an early stage in 1999, they participated in 3GPP2 and elaborated domestic 3G and 4G standards along the other internationally recognised ones. However, such ambiguity appears to have faded with 5G development, as Chinese stakeholders became capable of contributing to global 5G specifications. Therefore, Chinese actors have grown within the existing governance complex, and transformed the balance of power within it by growing to a standard-maker position within 3GPP but have not changed its institutional rules, norms, and principles so far. Indeed, no new regimes, organisations, nor separate technical standards have been established. In several interview participants' accounts, informal rules within 3GPP and other bodies involved in the making of 5G-based technologies have transformed amid changes in the balance among different stakeholder groups. For example, the surge of the so-called 'Over the Top' (OTT) service providers is seen as a factor. However, no normative change is seen coming from a group of stakeholders on national lines. On the contrary, as illustrated above in this chapter, Chinese stakeholders have progressively become prominent within 3GPP's work and participation through a growing number of engineers who were born and educated in China, signalling a growing acceptance and familiarity with 3GPP's institutional environment.

This matter can be observed in terms of norm entrepreneurship. The findings illustrated in this chapter show that the more Chinese state- and non-state stakeholders have grown capable of influencing decision-making, the more they have accepted norms and rules and adopted them to promote their national and/or business interests. The historical perspective of their progressive engagement with the existing mobile Internet standardisation architecture is telling: from partial isolation on 3G, to a form of partial engagement on 4G, to a leadership role in 3GPP work on 5G (mostly as far as Huawei is concerned). Recalling from Chapter 4, it can be noted that this was accompanied by a contemporary shift from multilateralist stances in global Internet governance towards increased, albeit ambiguous, acceptance of multistakeholderism. As illustrated above, in the early 2000s, when separate 3G standards were deployed, China stood as a staunch multilateralist, which confirms its role as a defiant outsider to the institutional arrangement. In the run towards 2010, when 4G started being deployed, and shortly after, China alternated further engagement in the multistakeholder system (with Huawei's presence at the IETF increasing steadily since 2007) but contributed to reawakening multilateralist conundrums at WCIT in 2012 (Glen,

2014). This is also reflected in China's ambiguous stance on mobile Internet standards, as it deployed nationally both the LTE and LTE-TDD standards.

In the years preceding 2020, that is, the deployment of 5G, Chinese actors were fully engaged in 3GPP work as illustrated above and expressed increasing support for and involvement in the multistakeholder system (Mueller, 2017; Shen, 2016), especially in the wake of the IANA stewardship transition (Jongen & Scholte, 2021; Mueller, 2017). In summary, Chinese stakeholders display interest in accepting the norms and institutional architectures that allow them to participate fully and cast their power globally. As mentioned, Huawei has become the most influential actor in 5G standardisation within the European-born 3GPP without establishing or seeking to establish any alternative standardisation body but following a path of progressive involvement in and engagement with the existing governance mechanisms that followed—to a broad extent—a wider national strategy where the Chinese state played, at least, a role of financial supporter and political coordinator.

As anticipated elsewhere in this book, technologists participating first-hand in 3GPP work raised qualitatively different interpretations of Chinese stakeholders' engagement in mobile connectivity standard-making compared to policy experts. Many interview participants familiar with the work of 3GPP stressed the process of adaptation of Chinese stakeholders not only in terms of political norms applying to collective actors (governments, companies, or other organisations), but also at the individual level. Contrary to widespread media debates on technological and Internet fragmentation along geopolitical lines, Chinese stakeholders are in a process of growth within the Internet governance regime complex. As far as mobile connectivity standards are concerned, a convergence in standards from 3G to 5G is visible as illustrated in this chapter.

In conclusion, it emerges that, despite ambiguities arose over time, China and its domestic actors have become increasingly involved in the existing standardisation venues: they have increasingly acknowledged and adopted universal standards and contributed to their making. This happened through a market and policy push that provided growth incentives to Chinese actors and made them capable of influencing standard-making, but also through a learning process as illustrated above in this Chapter. Drawing from Chapters 3 and 4, one can see that this trend from Chinese stakeholders is valid both in critical Internet resources governance and in mobile Internet standard-making. This carries broader implications for China's engagement in and with the Liberal International Order, inasmuch as multistakeholder, private-based Internet governance is a facet of it as per Chapter 2.

In strictly theoretical terms, this proves the normative rigidity of the Internet governance regime complex recalled in Chapter 2: as promoting alternative standards through alternative fora proved to be economically untenable given the geographically narrow deployment of TD-SCDMA, Chinese stakeholders progressively adapted and integrated within 3GPP's work. Furthermore, this happened through patterns of competition and collaboration among Chinese actors, signalling non-overlapping interests at play among them despite common nationality.

Certainly, conclusions drawn from the field of mobile Internet standards do not allow straightforward generalisation to a systemic level. For example, scholars and policymakers are divided on the meaning of China establishing financial institutions parallel to the global ones, such as the Asian Infrastructure Investment Bank (AIIB) (Gabusi, 2019; Qian et al., 2023). Furthermore, China has certainly not transformed domestically to accept liberal norms (Economy, 2018; Taylor, 2022). While these topics go beyond the scope of this research, they are illustrated to stress that what applies to China in global Internet governance or its subsets may not be universally applicable to Chinese action in other policy fields. Furthermore, it must be re-stressed that ambiguities in the Internet governance context remain from China's part (Negro, 2020; Tai & Zhu, 2022).

Open debates notwithstanding, evidence from such a strongly politicised field as mobile Internet technology standards, which carries heavy economic and geopolitical weight, provides helpful insight into broader issues. Being the subset of Internet governance in question interrelated with great power dynamics, being technological supremacy historically linked to US hegemony (Winseck, 2020), it can be safely argued that the findings hereby presented are transferable to other fields of inquiry involving superpower dynamics, public–private power relations, issues of private authority in global governance, as well as systemic analyses on the future of the Liberal International Order. This aspect is addressed in the next chapter, on top of essential questions on Internet fragmentation, alignment, and the future of multistakeholderism.

References

3rd Generation Partnership Project. (2009). *Release 8*. https://www.3gpp.org/specifications/releases/72-release-8 (Accessed 27 August 2021).

Arkko, J. (2023). Distribution of Authors per Companies. *IETF Statistics*. https://www.arkko.com/tools/allstats/companydistr.html (Accessed 21 July 2023).

Brown, A. (2021, June 1). *Huawei's Global Troubles Spur Beijing's Push for Self-reliance*. Mercator Institute for China Studies. https://merics.org/en/short-analysis/huaweis-global-troubles-spur-beijings-push-self-reliance (Accessed 18 June 2021).

Buckley, C., & Bradsher, K. (2020, September 18). The Chinese Communist Party Pledged to Uphold Private Companies but Stressed That the Party 'Leads Everything'. *New York Times Chinese Online Edition*. https://cn.nytimes.com/asia-pacific/20200918/china-communist-private-business/?utm_source=newslist&utm_medium=email&utm_campaign=newsletter (Accessed 21 December 2020) [储百亮 and Bradsher, K. (2020). "中共承诺支持民营企业, 但强调党'领导一切'". 纽约时报中文网, 9月18号].

Buggenhagen, M., & Blind, K. (2022). Development of 5G—Identifying Organizations Active in Publishing, Patenting, and Standardization. *Telecommunications Policy, 46*(4), 102326.

Bush, N. (2021). Chinese Antitrust in the Trade War: Casualty, Refugee, Profiteer, Peacemaker. *Antitrust Law Journal, 84*(1), 209–264.

Cai, C. (2018). Global Cyber Governance. China's Contribution and Approach. *China Quarterly of International Strategic Studies, 4*(1), 55–76.

China Communications Standards Association. (2021). *The Organization Behind 5G Global Standards*. http://www.ccsa.org.cn/dqzz?desc=2538&link=2539&list=92&title=3GPP (Accessed 21 January 2021).

Ciuriak, D. (2019). The US-China Trade War: Technological Roots and WTO Responses. *Global Solutions Journal, 4*, 130–135.

Drahokoupil, J., McCaleb, A., Pawlicki, P., & Szunomár, A. (2017). Huawei in Europe: Strategic Integration of Local Capabilities in a Global Production Network. In J. Drahokoupil (Ed.), *Chinese Investment in Europe: Corporate Strategies and Labour Relations*. ETUI.

Economist, The. (2020, July 16). *America's War on Huawei Nears Its Endgame*. https://www.economist.com/briefing/2020/07/16/americas-war-on-huawei-nears-its-endgame (Accessed 30 October 2020).

Economy, E. C. (2018). China's New Revolution: The Reign of Xi Jinping. *Foreign Affairs, 97*(3), 60–74.

Gabusi, G. (2019). Global Standards in the Asian Infrastructure Investment Bank: The Contribution of the European Members. *Global Policy, 10*(4), 631–638.

Glen, C. M. (2014). Internet Governance: Territorializing Cyberspace? *Politics and Policy, 42*(5), 635–657.
Hoffmann, S., Lazanski, D., & Taylor, E. (2020). Standardising the Splinternet: How China's Technical Standards Could Fragment the Internet. *Journal of Cyber Policy, 5*(2), 239–264.
Hogewoning, M. (2020, November 10). Update on WTSA-20 Preparations and New IP. *RIPE NCC.* https://labs.ripe.net/Members/marco_hogewoning/update-on-wtsa-20-preparations-and-new-ip (Accessed 26 November 2020).
Huawei. (2021). *History.* https://www.huawei.eu/who-we-are/history (Accessed 18 January 2021).
International Telecommunication Union. (2020, November 26). *ITU Completes Evaluation for Global Affirmation of IMT-2020 Technologies.* Press Release. https://www.itu.int/en/mediacentre/Pages/pr26-2020-evaluation-global-affirmation-imt-2020-5g.aspx (Accessed 14 January 2021).
Jongen, H., & Scholte, J. A. (2021). Legitimacy in Multistakeholder Global Governance at ICANN. *Global Governance, 27*(2), 298–324.
Kong, X., Xu, J., & Zhang, Y. (2022). Industry Competition and Firm Productivity: Evidence from the Antitrust Policy in China. *Finance Research Letters, 47*(2), 1–8.
Liu, X. (2021). Chinese Multinational Enterprises Operating in Western Economies: Huawei in the US and the UK. *Journal of Contemporary China, 30*(129), 368–385.
Maxigas, & ten Oever, N. (2023). Geopolitics in the Infrastructural Ideology of 5G. *Global Media and China, 8*(3), 1–18.
Ming, S., & Ouyang, C. (2008). Beyond 3G. *Finance Magazine,* p. 4.
Moore, G. J. (2023). Huawei, Cyber-Sovereignty and Liberal Norms: China's Challenge to the West/Democracies. *Journal of Chinese Political Science, 28*(1), 151–167.
Mueller, M. L. (2017). *Will the Internet Fragment? Sovereignty, Globalization, and Cyberspace.* Polity Press.
Nanni, R. (2023). Whither (De)globalisation? Internet Fragmentation, Authoritarianism, and the Future of the Liberal International Order: Evidence from China. *The Pacific Review.* Online first.
Negro, G. (2017). *The Internet in China: From Infrastructure to a Nascent Civil Society.* Palgrave Macmillan.
Negro, G. (2020). A History of Chinese Global Internet Governance and Its Relations with ITU and ICANN. *Chinese Journal of Communication, 13*(1), 104–121.
Poggetti, L. (2021, January 20). *EU-China Mappings: Interactions between the EU and China on Key Issues.* Mercator Institute for China Studies. https://merics.org/de/kurzanalyse/eu-china-mappings-interactions-between-eu-and-china-key-issues (Accessed 13 July 2021).

Pohlmann, T., Blind, K., & Hess, P. (2020). *Fact Finding Study on Patents Declared to the 5G Standard*. IPLytics and Technische Universitaet Berlin.
Pupillo, L. (2019, June 21). *5G and National Security*. CEPS. https://www.ceps.eu/5g-and-nationalsecurity/ (Accessed 20 October 2020).
Qian, J., Vreeland, J. R., & Zhao, J. (2023). The Impact of China's AIIB on the World Bank. *International Organization, 77*(1), 217–237.
Segal, A. (2018, August 13). When China Rules the Web: Technology in Service of the State. *Foreign Affairs*. https://www.foreignaffairs.com/articles/china/2018-08-13/when-china-rules-web (Accessed 10 November 2020).
Shen, H. (2016). China and Global Internet Governance: Toward an Alternative Analytical Framework. *Chinese Journal of Communication, 9*(3), 304–324.
Shen, H. (2022). *Alibaba: Infrastructuring Global China*. Routledge.
Song, Z., Jia, M., & Yang, Z. (2023). Technical Standard Competition in the Mobile Communication Industry: A Literature Review. *The International Journal of Business Management and Technology, 7*(4), 1–11.
Stewart, J., Shen, X., Wang, C., & Graham, I. (2011). From 3G to 4G: Standards and the Development of Mobile Broadband in China. *Technology Analysis and Strategic Management, 23*(7), 773–788.
Tai, K., & Zhu, Y. Y. (2022). A Historical Explanation of Chinese Cybersovereignty. *International Relations of the Asia-Pacific, 22*(3), 469–499.
Tang, M. (2020). From 'Bringing-in' to 'Going-out': Transnationalizing China's Internet Capital Through State Policies. *Chinese Journal of Communication, 13*(1), 27–46.
Tayal, A. (2021). 5G—Industry 4.0 and Fragmentation of the Internet. *Phronesis Partners*. https://phronesis-partners.com/insights/5g-network-slicing/ (Accessed 22 July 2021).
Taylor, M. (2022). *China's Digital Authoritarianism*. Palgrave Macmillan.
ten Oever, N. (2022). 5G and the Notion of Network Ideology, or: The Limitations of Sociotechnical Imaginaries. *Telecommunications Policy, 47*, 102442.
Vidal, I., Garcia, J., Valera, F., Soto, I., & Azcorra, A. (2007). Integration of a QoS Aware End User Network Within the TISPAN NGN Solutions. *IEEEXplore*. https://doi.org/10.1109/ECUMN.2007.29 (Accessed 30 August 2021).
Wannstrom, J. (2013). LTE-Advanced. *Third Generation Partnership Project*. https://www.3gpp.org/technologies/keywords-acronyms/97-lte-advanced (Accessed 22 July 2021).
Wen, Y. (2020). *The Huawei Model: The Rise of China's Technology Giant*. University of Illinois Press.
Winseck, D. (2020). Is the International Telecommunication Union Still Relevant in 'the Internet Age?' Lessons From the 2012 World Conference on

International Telecommunications (WCIT). In G. Balbi & A. Fickers (Eds.), *History of the International Telecommunication Union*. De Gruyter.

Xinhua. (2020a, September 17). *Adhere to the 'Two Unshakables'. Bring Private Enterprises Around the Party to Better Promote the Healthy Development of the Private Economy*. http://www.xinhuanet.com/mrdx/2020-09/17/c_139375287.htm (Accessed 21 December 2020) [新华网 (2020). "坚持'两个毫不动摇'. 把民营经济人士团结在党的周围 更好推动民营经济健康发展". 9月17日].

Xinhua. (2020b, September 16). *Xi Focus: Xi Stresses Promoting Healthy Development of Private Sector*. http://www.xinhuanet.com/english/2020-09/16/c_139373545.htm (Accessed 21 December 2020).

Yu, J. (2011). From 3G to 4G: Technology Evolution and Path Dynamics in China's Mobile Telecommunication Sector. *Technology Analysis and Strategic Management, 23*(10), 1079–1093.

Zhang, J., & Liang, X. (2007). 3G in China: Environment and Prospect. *IEEEXplore*. https://ieeexplore.ieee.org/abstract/document/4349642 (Accessed 27 April 2021).

Zhong, R. (2019, April 25). Who Owns Huawei? The Company Tried to Explain: It Got Complicated. *New York Times*. https://www.nytimes.com/2019/04/25/technology/who-owns-huawei.html (Accessed 20 October 2020).

Zhong, R. (2021, July 4). China Orders Didi Off App Stores in an Escalating Crackdown. *New York Times*. https://www.nytimes.com/2021/07/04/technology/china-didi-app-removed.html (Accessed 6 July 2021).

CHAPTER 6

The Rise of China, Internet Fragmentation, and the Future of Multistakeholderism: Implications for the Liberal International Order

6.1 Introduction

This chapter draws from the analysis built in Chapters 3–5 to answer the questions at stake in this book, namely Chinese stakeholders' role vis-à-vis multistakeholder global Internet governance and China's influence on Internet fragmentation. This is done observing Chinese engagement in mobile connectivity standardisation (3GPP) and critical Internet resources standardisation and resources distribution (IETF and ICANN). Chapters 3–5 portray a complex scenario for the rise of China and Chinese public and private stakeholders. Contrary to the dualist conception of the multilateralist challenge to multistakeholderism of the early 2000s (as documented in: Flonk et al., 2020; Negro, 2020), and contrary to the dichotomous views on the future of Internet governance emerged amid the US–China technological competition (as addressed in: Ciuriak, 2019), the rise of Chinese stakeholders featured a mix of contestation of and adaptation to the existing multistakeholder Internet governance regime complex. Inasmuch as such a regime complex is a facet of Liberal International Order as illustrated in Chapter 2, these aspects have implications on the future of the order and its capacity to integrate emerging actors and withstand revisionist attempts (Ikenberry, 2018).

ICANN and the IETF feature different characteristics, and they are in turn different from 3GPP. As per Chapter 2, 3GPP does not straightforwardly fit the multistakeholder definition that is valid for ICANN. It is more similar to the IETF in its strongly private-based and technically oriented organisation. However, the IETF is formally based on individual participation, while 3GPP has formal membership through its seven partner Standards Development Organisations (SDOs) (Nanni, 2021, 2022). Furthermore, the IETF elaborates standards essential for the Internet to function. In other words, it builds the logical architecture of the Internet. 3GPP is the main standardiser of new generations of mobile Internet-based connectivity, that is, such technologies from 3G thereafter. While allowing Internet connectivity on mobile devices, these technologies entail a telephonic infrastructure. True, the infrastructural integration and interdependence between Internet and telephony has always existed, but while the former follows a building-block approach, the latter is a fully determined infrastructure. Furthermore, functionalities are different: IETF standards allow the Internet to function the way it does, while 3GPP standards allow a form of radio access to the Internet. In other words, it is another access technology at the network access layer as per Table 2.3, which is illustrated in Chapter 2 and reported here for reference.

It is essential to recapitulate aspects from Chapter 2 here to contextualise the forthcoming paragraphs. Despite such differences among the three bodies, common patterns of growing engagement of Chinese stakeholders can be found.

This chapter observes the implications of the findings outlined in the previous chapters for multistakeholderism and Internet fragmentation.

Table 2.3 The TCP/IP model (Harcourt et al., 2020; Russell, 2013)[1]

Nr.	Layer name	Protocols (examples)
4	Application	HTTP/DNS/SMTP/FTP
3	Transport	TCP/UDP/QUIC
2	Internet	IP
1	Network access	Wi-Fi/Ethernet/5G

[1] This table was illustrated in Chapter 2. It is reported here with the same number for the reader's reference.

Building on this, it addresses the consequences of such implications for the Liberal International Order.

The next section will illustrate the implications of Chinese stakeholders' involvement in 3GPP for multistakeholderism and Internet fragmentation, while Sect. 6.3 will address the same issues for the critical Internet resources. Finally, Sect. 6.4 draws conclusions connecting the two debates to the global one on China's rise and the Liberal International Order.

6.2 Chinese Actors in 3GPP: What Consequences for Multistakeholderism, Interoperability, and Internet Fragmentation?

A key takeaway from Chapter 5 is that China aims at being a 5G standard-shaper, not at creating alternative, incompatible specifications. However, this has not always been the case. To put it briefly, China adopted an incompatible, domestic-oriented 3G standard in the early 2000s, while licensing UMTS to a minor operator. When it came to 4G technologies, China adopted both the universal standard and an incompatible locally oriented one, allowing one or another operator to provide mobile Internet services using one specification or the other. Now Chinese stakeholders are one of the key standard-setters in 5G and, as it emerged from interviews and technical literature, they show no intention of elaborating local specifications incompatible with the global ones (Pohlmann et al., 2020). Both Huawei-affiliated engineers and technologists affiliated to Western companies confirmed in interviews that no tendency towards fragmenting the work of 3GPP appeared to come from Chinese stakeholders, where Huawei is currently the top 5G standardisation contributor in quantitative terms, followed by Ericsson (Pohlmann et al., 2020).

Briefly, Huawei is a major standard-maker in 5G standardisation and there is no intention from Chinese stakeholders to elaborate a separate, incompatible national 5G specification. On the contrary, they aim at being major players in 5G at the global level. However, beyond network infrastructure standardisation, questions remain open about Huawei's device- and application-level capacity to grant interoperability. The US ban on Huawei's use of Google services makes this issue increasingly relevant. To be clear, this falls partially outside this book's scope. Furthermore, academic analysis on this aspect is sparse and mostly speculative, arguably due to the novelty of the issue at stake, which emerged powerfully in 2018 with the US–China trade war. Nonetheless, a few clarifying words are worth spending.

To start with, it must be underlined that Android is an open-source operating system, which entails that the US government could only ban the use of Google's Mobile Services (GMS) core part (Sin, 2020). As Sin (2020) explains,

> [GMS] are a collection of services with special APIs (application programme interfaces) designed by Google to allow for easy adoption by third-party developers. The services mostly cover Google's cloud ecosystem, such as Google Drive and Docs, as well as YouTube and the Google Play Store. Other Google apps that fall outside this umbrella, such as Google Maps and Chrome, work perfectly fine on a Huawei device. In fact, Gmail and Google Calendar work too, but only through third-party apps such as Microsoft's Outlook.

Furthermore, with the launch of Huawei's GMS equivalent, that is, Huawei Mobile Services (HMS), and the operating system HarmonyOS, Huawei seeks to provide a fully fledged alternative to Android and the GMS's core part while allowing its users and customers to use the same services and platforms available through Google services (Doffman, 2020). For services and platforms present on GMS but still not accessible from Huawei devices, the block seems to be porous, as several mirroring systems have been made available to access them (Sin, 2020). It is worth mentioning that Huawei has sought to internalise the whole production chain of a smartphone device, from software to hardware. To complement the above, Huawei has also got its own in-house chip-making company HiSilicon. In 2023, Huawei put a smartphone on the market possessing a microprocessor technology that was believed to be unattainable for the company amid US sanctions, thus taking the US industry and policy-making world by surprise. This chip is known as Kirin 9000s and was produced by Huawei along with Semiconductor Manufacturing International Corp (SMIC), one of China's top chip manufacturers (Reuters, 2023).

To summarise, Chinese companies' activities in mobile connectivity standardisation processes grew in time and became more influential, along with their influence growing higher across the telecommunications industry (Meena & Geng, 2022). Interviews show that participation and influence grew together: as the capacity of Chinese stakeholders to influence decision-making grew, so did their interest in shaping global standards and avoiding local incompatible specifications. It goes without saying that the need for a growing company to expand its market is an essential driver of the aforementioned actions, as it emerged throughout interviews.

This can be better analysed if contextualised in the broader context of China's participation in Internet governance, illustrated in Chapter 4. To recap, Chinese authors of Internet Drafts and Requests for Comments (RFCs) at the IETF increased sharply between 2007 and 2010 amid a relative decline of the number of Western authors (IETF, 2020) and Huawei was second only to Cisco in terms of affiliated RFC and Internet Draft authors by 2020. In this, China is the second major contributing country, although it slides down to third position if contributions from EU countries' nationals are summed by 2023 (Arkko, 2023).

Based on these figures, it can be observed that Chinese actors' presence and weight is growing throughout the Internet governance regime complex at large. In other words, China has grown more powerful in 3GPP and more participatory in other Internet governance fora, too. While literature underlines China's ambiguous behaviour towards the key organisations of the multistakeholder system, namely ICANN with respect to the role of the ITU, what generally emerges through interviews is that China and Chinese stakeholders have sought to substantially increase their presence in every subset of the Internet governance regime complex.

Moving back to mobile connectivity standards, no incompatible local Chinese specifications are under elaboration according to research participants, while Huawei is the single most important contributor to 5G standardisation within 3GPP. The approval of three globally interoperable 5G radio interface standards by the ITU confirms it (ITU, 2020), notwithstanding concerns by part of the technical and business community. Importantly, no new organisation or fora has been established by China in parallel or replacing the existing ones under consideration. The convergence in standards, however, is accompanied by a fragmentation of the market along national lines (Poggetti, 2021). Despite this, standards convergence remained in trend after the 3G and 4G experiences in limited global interoperability.

As for the debate on state-centricity in mobile connectivity standard-making, it is mainly through private actors—mainly Huawei (Pohlmann et al., 2020; ten Oever, 2022)—that China is becoming stronger in mobile Internet standard-making. Research participants knowledgeable about 3GPP's work usually observe a governmental role in standards-related policymaking, but generally limited to matters of policy coordination. As underlined before in this book, governmental support and government policies do play a role in Chinese companies' 'going out' that is acknowledged in both Western and Chinese literature, although the extent to which its role is dominant is not apparent (Cai, 2018; Segal, 2018; Shen, 2016; Tang, 2020). In addition, the threshold between influence and coordination, on the one hand, and control, on the other, is blurred (Pupillo, 2019; Zhong, 2019). Interviews in Chapter 5 underlined the dynamicity of state-company relationships in China in the run from 3G to 5G development. Generally speaking, research participants knowledgeable about 3GPP could not identify instances in which forms of governmental control on Chinese companies was visible beyond matters of coordination and policy direction.

To summarise, the state-companies relations in China in the context of mobile connectivity standardisation is more difficult to qualify. China's engagement in 3GPP is strongly business-driven, as Huawei is a private actor, whereas the state-owned enterprise ZTE is much less active and influential in 3GPP. However, state-companies ties in China are still unknown. Despite all this, most research participants familiar with 3GPP's work, independently of their affiliation, tend to confirm such ties in terms of governmental coordination, rather than governmental control. In this, the Chinese state leadership remains ambiguous. For instance, Chinese authorities are currently conducting antitrust crackdowns on several big tech providers under the Maoist banner of 'common prosperity' (Dunford, 2022), which in the context of the US–China trade competition goes hand in hands with Huawei's increasing reliance on the domestic market (Brown, 2021). In other words, whether and to what extent China may increase states' influence in multistakeholder Internet governance through state-controlled, but formally private, actors remains to be seen.

To conclude, the more China's private sector and state-owned enterprises grew capable of influencing 3GPP standardisation processes, the more they integrated into the mainstream of the aforementioned process. This convergence in standards was accompanied by a fragmentation of the market, rather than the infrastructure, in the wake of the US–China trade competition, whereby a number of EU states followed the US in restricting market access to Chinese market actors (Poggetti, 2021).

6.3 Observing Multistakeholderism and Fragmentation at the Core: Chinese Actors in the IETF and ICANN

At times, the prominence of one type of actor or another can be prevalent and the power balance in multistakeholder relations is most often skewed towards more economically powerful stakeholder groups (Santaniello, 2021). Internet fragmentation has instead received a multitude of definitions. While Mueller (2017) sees it as a technical compatibility matter and leaves political forms of control to the realm of 'alignment', Drake et al. (2016) conceptualise it as a broader phenomenon that can stem from political, commercial, as well as technical actions. Further discussion on these definitions is elaborated at the end of the present chapter.

To assess the debate on China's role vis-à-vis and within multistakeholder Internet governance, one should draw from Chapter 4. The re-accession of China to GAC has a manifold explanation. The institutionalisation of multistakeholderism as a governance principle, the permanence of ICANN (Mueller, 2010), and a compromise on Taiwan's membership are all reasons for China to normalise its troubled relation to ICANN (Scholte, 2017). As observed throughout the interview process, China has grown as a nationality group within ICANN, both in terms of its government's participation in it and in terms of stakeholders' presence. However, apart from the notable presence of an Alibaba affiliate in the GNSO Council and the vicechair of GAC obtained by the Chinese representative in the wake of the IANA stewardship transition, no visible influence was brought by Chinese stakeholders.

To be sure, many interview participants find state influence has increased in Internet governance independently of China's role. China's growing influence in the ITU, along with a more globally generalised push for increased governmental role on such aspects as data protection, data localisation, and Internet and 5G infrastructures create ground for increased state presence and influence (Haggart et al., 2021), a push that comes also from Western governments (Santaniello, 2021). Despite this, Chinese stakeholders have become increasingly present and participatory in multistakeholder Internet governance at ICANN and the IETF, as per Chapter 4, and something similar happened in 3GPP as assessed in Chapter 5. This interpretation resonates with several interview participants and with previous literature findings. Arsène (2018) confirms that, despite pushes for ICANN reforms and multilateralist quests, the Chinese government chose to find a way into the ICANN-based multistakeholder governance model to be able to influence decision-making in the existing regime complex. Furthermore, she hypothesised that with the global economic growth of Chinese non-state stakeholders, participation in multistakeholder fora is more profitable for them in terms of the influence they can exert in multiple existing governance venues.

This is confirmed throughout the interview process conducted for this research. Despite ambiguities and attempts at forum-shopping (Hofmann, 2019; Negro, 2020), most research participants confirm Chinese participation in ICANN and acceptance of norms thereof has increased, as also found by Jongen and Scholte (2021). Once again, it would be simplistic to address the ensemble of Chinese stakeholders as a monolithic whole and dialectic among actors needs to be accounted for. When addressing this matter in relation to Chinese stakeholders' acceptance of the norms of ICANN-based governance, a research participant stressed that

> the so-called 'multistakeholder community' [is] a kind of transnational elite whose identity is more that of a transnational elite network than of a particular, individual national component. In other words, [...] these people are seeing each other and interacting with each other constantly, so they're not only working at the main ICANN meetings - and one should say also the Regional Internet Registries [...]. So, what I want to say is: between the ICANN meetings; the conference calls that are going sometimes weekly, sometimes – depending on the policy processes – even every couple of days... There's constant interaction among these people and they see each other over a long period of time. And so when they meet at these meetings it's all hugs and kisses and, you know, best friends... it's [as if] they worked for a supranational company, a supranational regulatory community, if you like. I wouldn't say that the representatives of China are as integrated as many of the others, but I think they are recognised, they're part of the show, they're at the cocktail parties, they are doing everything, [...] they're absorbed into all of that. I remember the head of CNNIC (at one point, during the IANA transition) got up, took the microphone and said: "well, I can't think of any better arrangement than ICANN for the oversight system". Meaning, by implication: not the ITU, ICANN is the place.

This participant went on stressing how this applies to the members of the ICANN community, that is to say those people who participate in it on a regular basis. Conversely, this does not apply outside that pool, implying that different political circles within China have different interests and points of view when it comes to participating in Internet governance and regulating the Internet. This has powerful implications when it comes to the questions of fragmentation and alignment.

To summarise, ICANN and IETF maintained their strongly private-led governance form. True, governments can carry a weight through GAC in ICANN and attempts at state influence in standard-making have been pinpointed in the media and by some research participants. Furthermore, the debate on digital sovereignty and the return of states in Internet governance is growing (Haggart et al., 2021; Santaniello, 2021). Nonetheless, ICANN and the IETF have retained their private-based functioning.

Moving to the aspect of Internet fragmentation, the term has received a myriad of definitions. This book grounds in Mueller's (2017) narrow focus on technical fragmentation, whereby a fragmented Internet is one in which separate incompatible network protocols are adopted, hampering the transfer of data between devices adopting different protocols. It is worth recalling that this technical aspect would have direct geopolitical implication inasmuch as the different incompatible standards were to be implemented along national lines, thus rendering devices produced and sold in or for one territory incommunicable with those produced and sold in or for another.

To the extent that the global, open Internet is a facet of the Liberal International Order in its global spatial dimension, technical Internet fragmentation along geopolitical lines would be a threat to it. Findings illustrated in Chapter 4 point towards a growing acceptance of multistakeholder Internet governance from Chinese stakeholders as illustrated above in this chapter. This is valid not only for Chinese stakeholders in ICANN, but also for their homologues in the IETF, where the standardisation of the essential Internet standards takes place. As illustrated in Chapter 4, Chinese stakeholders' presence and influence in the IETF has grown constantly and Huawei is currently the second most prominent organisation in terms of RFCs published by its affiliates (Arkko, 2023). This has a direct tie to the Internet fragmentation debate.

Despite concerns over fragmentation, China has not deployed standards alternative to TCP/IP nor has it adopted a separate DNS (Arsène, 2018). On the contrary, Chinese stakeholders' growing presence and acceptance of multistakeholderism proxies an increased interest in shaping the existing universal Internet standards. This holds true for the Internet's critical resources: although in the first decade of the twenty-first century concerning news came as China anticipated ICANN in deploying IDNs in parallel with the ICANN-supervised DNS, currently the former are fully part of the latter. Surely, suspicion around China's attitude towards the existing Internet architecture are longstanding and persisting, as exemplified in Chapter 4 by the debate around the launch of the New IP proposal at the ITU in 2019. However, the likelihood of this technical proposal to yield technical fragmentation has been questioned by most interview participants.

In a few words, China adopts the same numerical identifiers and transport protocols used globally as well as the same DNS. Furthermore, Chinese stakeholders have increased their participation and interest in carrying influence within global multistakeholder Internet governance fora.

Nonetheless, this contrasts with China's domestic regulatory and technical tools of online control, which Mueller (2017) dubs 'alignment' of the Internet to domestic regulation. While a deep dive into, and interpretation of, the history of Chinese media is outside the scope of a book, one must look at China's domestic dynamics for a full interpretation of Chinese stakeholders' stance within and towards multistakeholder Internet governance, as delved deeper in Chapter 3. As previously illustrated in the empirical chapters, the Chinese government played a major role—both in terms of economic incentives and forms of control—in establishing telecommunication architecture and services within the country. Since China established its first permanent connection to the Internet in 1994, state doctrine has mandated that China must harness the economic advantage of cyberspace while at the same time maintaining control on online social phenomena (Brady, 2017).

It would be overly simplistic to maintain that the Chinese government has full control on the full range of activities that individuals conduct online. On the contrary, online citizenry in China expresses a whole variety of opinions and views, although this is constrained within the boundaries of what the state does and does not allow (Jiang, 2010; Zhang et al., 2022), which have become stricter under Xi Jinping's presidency (Chen & Greitens, 2022). To different extents, the integration of China in the global cyberspace has always been balanced domestically by tools of social control. In 1998, the Golden Shield Project (also dubbed 'the Great Firewall of China' in the West) was launched. While the most salient immediate need for the government was to contrast the spread of Falun Gong, this system of regulation and technical tools for censorship was strengthened and brought fully in place in 2008 (Negro, 2017). Following this, China shut down Facebook within its territory in 2009 in the aftermath of social and political turmoil in the city of Urumqi (in the northwestern region of Xinjiang) and triggered the closure of Google's browser in 2010, as the company redirected its server to Hong Kong and only maintained a few offices and minor services within mainland China (Negro, 2017).

Cyberspace control in China does not only affect content and services availability, but also the way such contents and services are enjoyed and/or provided. In 2017, the 'Cybersecurity Law' (网络安全法, wangluo anquan fa) established provisions for data localisation, that is, the legal requirement to store sensitive data collected in China on servers and data centres based within the Chinese territory (Liu, 2020). At the time of writing, a broader data protection framework is being established, mandating different forms of data localisation based on different types of data (Nanni, 2022). 2017 was also the year when the Internet Domain Name Management Rules (互联网域名管理办法, hulianwang yuming guanli banfa) were introduced. A first key element of this law is contained in Article 9:

> For the domestic establishment of a domain name root server or domain name root server-running body, a domain name registration management body or a domain name registration service body, permission from the Ministry of Industry and Information Technology or provincial, autonomous region or municipal telecommunications management departments (hereafter jointly named telecommunications management bodies) shall be obtained. (MIIT, 2017)[2]

A second key point is found in the following article, first comma, where conditions for domain name registrants are set:

> Those applying to establish a domain name root server or domain name root server-running body, shall meet the following conditions: (1) the

---

[2] English translation retrieved from (edited by Rogier Creemers): https://chinacopyrightandmedia.wordpress.com/2016/03/25/internet-domain-name-management-rules-opinion-seeking-revision-draft/ (September 17, 2021).
Full final text of the law (original language) retrieved from: https://tinyurl.com/49bwc6fw (September 17, 2021).

domain name root server is to be set up within the borders, and shall conform to corresponding Internet development plans and the requirements of the safe and stable operation of the domain name system [...]. (MIIT, 2017)

These rules have been established along with the aforementioned Cybersecurity Law. Furthermore, they can be read in the same context as the 2010 White Paper on the (state of the) Internet in China (The State Council Information Office of the PRC, 2010, hereafter SCIO) and the International Strategy of Cooperation on Cyberspace (ISCC, 网络空间国际合作战略, wangluokongjian guoji hezuo zhanglüe) of 2017 (Xinhua, 2017). The former document is recognised as having introduced the concept of 'Internet sovereignty' in China's official governmental discourse for the first time (Creemers, 2020).

The timing of such domestic developments is telling when read in conjunction to changes in China's stance in global Internet governance. Elaborating from Chapter 3, the Golden Shield Project was completed in 2008, though constantly enhanced, right by the beginning of the deployment of 3G in China—that is, when access to the Internet among the population started spreading much further: in 2008, Chinese Internet usership reached 298 million, surpassing the US's (Flor Cruz & Seu, 2014). The concept of 'Internet sovereignty' was introduced in the same years when crackdowns on Twitter and Facebook, along with Google's withdrawal, began (2009/2010), accompanied by the launch of homegrown Chinese applications such as WeChat (微信, weixin) in 2011 (The Economist, 2016). These were also the years (2008–2012) when development of 4G at 3GPP was conducted and Chinese companies participated in them. Furthermore, after 2007 Huawei's participation in the IETF increased steeply (Arkko, 2023). Following the 2013 PRISM scandal, China pushed for ICANN reform internationally, but maintained its participation in it and the newly established Xi Jinping presidency (2012/2013) maintained continuity with its predecessors in the management of the online activities, enhancing it with a few major measures: the 2017 closure of WhatsApp in China (B. Haas, 2017), the aforementioned DNS rules, and the crackdown on domestic *big techs* that began in late 2020 with antitrust measures against Alibaba and is ongoing at the time of writing (Nanni, 2022).

Considering this, the growing dependence of China's major international companies, such as Huawei (Brown, 2021), on domestic market revenues can reinforce state control on Chinese private actors. This can impact multistakeholderism as formally private actors would de facto be tools for governmental influence in the governance mechanism. However, this cannot be established at the current stage. Instead, one can first draw conclusions in historical hindsight on the role of Chinese stakeholders in Internet fragmentation. Before concluding, this can then be connected to their role in ICANN-centred multistakeholder Internet governance as illustrated above and in Chapter 4.

To start with, it can be safely affirmed that the Chinese government has always sought to exercise strict control on the Internet and on online activities. Adding to the examples brought above, a 2019 report by the technology company Oracle stressed that China's way to connect to the global Internet is peculiar (Allen, 2019): only domestic companies interconnect in China at Internet exchange points (IXPs) and when data is transferred within the country it is routed exclusively in China, whereas in most other countries data travels from senders to recipients through links based in other countries. Conversely, almost no other country relies on China for domestic traffic according to Oracle. At the same time, this report finds that when Chinese users connect to the global Internet, traffic mostly goes through the US (Allen, 2019). The report concludes that

> China could effectively withdraw from the global public internet and maintain domestic connectivity (essentially having an intranet). This means the rest of the world could be restricted from connecting into China, and vice versa for external connections for Chinese businesses/users. Conversely, China is uniquely dependent upon the West. [Roughly] 63% of our measurements into China are coming through the United States. If that connectivity were impacted by a global event, we would expect users in China could feel a significant impact. (Allen, 2019)

In other words, China's increased control on the Internet limits content and services, with both a political and economically protectionist goal (Plantin & De Seta, 2019; Shen, 2022) and enhances the capacity of the Chinese government of potentially preventing users and content providers within China to connect to users and content providers outside China and vice-versa. Paradoxically, this creates a form of independence but also of vulnerability, as illustrated by the aforementioned report (Allen, 2019). This also depicts China's unwillingness to detach from the global Internet. While China constantly seeks to enhance its regulatory and technical control on what goes on in cyberspace, aligning it to domestic regulation (Mueller, 2017), it maintains connectivity to the global Internet and adopts the same transport and identification protocols as the rest of the world (Arsène, 2018; Mueller, 2017).

Furthermore, China never established a separate DNS. When it did, Chinese authorities ensured it would be interoperable with the ICANN-supervised one and such unconventional split only lasted until ICANN accepted to recognise Chinese actors' requests on Chinese-characters IDNs (Arsène, 2015; Negro, 2022), as illustrated in Chapter 4. Simply put, China could possess the tools and capacity to create a separate DNS root and establish standards alternative to TCP/IP for device identification and data transfer, thus establishing a technically incompatible splinternet. However, this would be costly in terms of development and establishment (Mueller, 2017, 2020) and would hamper scale economies. As a large group of interview participants familiar with IETF work maintained, companies like Huawei see no advantage in having to produce technically different devices for different markets. On the contrary, potential for technical Internet fragmentation is most likely to come from a political push rather than economic interest. However, this is currently not on the Chinese elite's radar: first, a country's capacity to influence decision-making is strongly tied to its domestic companies' capacity to influence standard-making in such venues as the IETF. Second, the latter capacity is strongly tied to a company's economic weight, which in the global digital market depends on the global reach of its production.

Regarding the question of critical Internet resources governance, it can be safely said that the increased participation and influence of Chinese stakeholders in the IETF has not enhanced the likelihood of new incompatible Internet standards being established. The need for scalability in Internet-connected technologies, along with the normative path dependence generated by the need for consensus in IETF decision-making process, create an incentive mechanism for Chinese stakeholders to adapt to and adopt existing norms (including technical protocols) on the Internet and its governance. To foster domestic control on information fluxes on the Internet, China resorted to regulatory alignment instead of technical fragmentation to avoid losing network benefits, as theorised by Mueller (2017).

The statements on multistakeholderism and Internet fragmentation illustrated in this section must be qualified by expliciting a number of unknowns. To start with, the ongoing restrictions on big techs in China, connected to Huawei's growing dependence on its domestic market, can foster governmental control on private stakeholders. This could enhance state power in private-based governance. After all, a number of research participants have shown scepticism on China's likelihood to acknowledge ICANN and accept existing architectural designs in the long run. Such interpretations stem variably from the unknowns around such technologies as the New IP/FVCN, China's dominance in multilateral fora such as the ITU, the strong control on content and data fluxes exercised by the government, and the characteristics of the architecture illustrated above. Furthermore, literature voicing this scepticism has emerged, also hinting at the possibility that Chinese government-driven technological development may bring forms of technical fragmentation. For example, Hoffmann et al. (2020) maintain that the Chinese government-driven technological development is in fact enhancing state influence in Internet governance and could result in a technical split in the worst-case scenario where such solutions were not to integrate with those promoted by other global actors. After all, the techno-nationalist lens has often been adopted in the study of Chinese technological development (Khan, 2023; Kim et al., 2020; Plantin & De Seta, 2019). While techno-nationalism has been blurred in its definition, it is yet another way of making sense of the unconstant relationship between the state and its domestic industry, which is made of competition and collaboration alike (Nanni, 2023).

Notwithstanding the aforementioned debates, convergence in standards, the unwillingness of Chinese stakeholders to establish separate DNS root and basic Internet protocols, their increased participation and influence in such fora as ICANN, IETF, and 3GPP, all paint a picture of increased integration of Chinese stakeholders in the existing governance mechanisms and acceptance of existing Internet standards. This holds despite the persistence of ambiguities in public–private relations and positioning towards multilateral fora from China's part, along with the question of alignment of the Internet to national regulation that does not encompass China alone.

6.4 Final Remarks

Overall, the research illustrated in this book and discussed in its deepest implications in this chapter shows patterns of convergence in the technical standardisation processes of technologies that enable Internet access and the Internet's functioning. This also applies in mobile connectivity, within the scope of telecommunications standardisation. Despite growing market protectionism and competition among states, the Internet continues to be made of technically interoperable networks enabling devices in different parts of the globe and connected to different networks to communicate. This shows that the drivers of global power competition and economic interests can conflict, creating a situation where governments seek to reduce interdependence with rival actors while companies seek cross-border cooperation to increase economies of scale and network benefits. This is true also within China, where a dialectic between state and capital is in place despite the Chinese government's authoritarian characterisation and its increasing attempts at influencing and—where possible—controlling companies' behaviour.

On this basis, this book rejects the idea that China is pushing towards Internet fragmentation on an infrastructural level, much as control on online activities is growing domestically. Furthermore, this research stresses Chinese stakeholders' market interest vis-à-vis a unified infrastructure and therefore a unified market, one that the Chinese government can govern but not ignore. Finally, what emerged throughout this book is Chinese stakeholders'—whether publicly owned or private—capacity to adapt to the existing normative orders, refraining from taking the risk of remaking the 'rules of the game' when they can reach a powerful and influential position by playing according to the existing ones.

These findings entail that despite a growing governmental presence in China's digital ecosystem, Chinese actors are adapting to the existing multistakeholder global Internet governance mechanisms. In other words, China's quest for Internet sovereignty, as well as other countries and block's quest for digital sovereignty (definitions notwithstanding), is not compromising the functioning of multistakeholder Internet governance at the global level, thus confirming the Internet governance regime complex's resilience.

On this ground, the next chapter draws the final conclusions and draws a few considerations for future research path.

References

Allen, D. (2019, June 19). Analysis by Oracle Internet Intelligence Highlights China's Unique Approach to Connecting to the Global Internet. *Oracle*

Cloud Infrastructure Internet Intelligence. https://blogs.oracle.com/intern etintelligence/analysis-by-oracle-internet-intelligence-highlights-china%e2% 80%99s-unique-approach-to-connecting-to-the-global-internet (Accessed 18 December 2019).
Arkko, J. (2023). Distribution of Authors per Companies. *IETF Statistics.* https://www.arkko.com/tools/allstats/companydistr.html (Accessed 21 July 2023).
Arsène, S. (2015). Internet Domain Names in China. Articulating Local Control with Global Connectivity. *China Perspectives, 4,* 25–34.
Arsène, S. (2018). China, Internet Governance and the Global Public Interest. In S. Sieckmann & O. Triebel (Eds.), *A New Responsible Power China?* HAL Open Science.
Brady, A. (2017). Plus ça Change?: Media Control Under Xi Jinping. *Problems of Post-Communism,* 64(3), 128–140.
Brown, A. (2021, June 1). *Huawei's Global Troubles Spur Beijing's Push for Self-Reliance.* Mercator Institute for China Studies. https://merics.org/en/short-analysis/huaweis-global-troubles-spur-beijings-push-self-reliance (Accessed 18 June 2021).
Cai, C. (2018). Global Cyber Governance. China's Contribution and Approach. *China Quarterly of International Strategic Studies,* 4(1): 55–76.
Chen, H., & Greitens, S. C. (2022). Information Capacity and Social Order: The Local Politics of Information Integration in China. *Governance,* 35(2), 497–523.
Ciuriak, D. (2019). The US-China Trade War: Technological Roots and WTO Responses. *Global Solutions Journal,* 4, 130–135.
Creemers, R. (2020). China's Conception of Cyber Sovereignty: Rhetoric and Realization. In D. Broeders & B. Van den Berg (Eds.), *Governing Cyberspace. Behavior, Power, and Diplomacy.* Rowman and Littlefield.
Doffman, Z. (2020, March 20). Huawei Suddenly Gives Millions of Users This Surprise Google Alternative. *Forbes.* https://www.forbes.com/sites/zakdof fman/2020/05/20/huawei-surprises-millions-of-users-with-critical-google-replacement/#5cb6d66b6caa (Accessed 21 December 2020).
Drake, W. J., Cerf, V. G., & Kleinwächter, W. (2016). *Internet Fragmentation: An Overview.* World Economic Forum.
Dunford, M. (2022). The Chinese Path to Common Prosperity. *International Critical Thought,* 12(1), 35–54.
Flonk, D., Jachtenfuchs, M., & Obendiek, A. S. (2020). Authority Conflicts in Internet Governance: Liberals vs. Sovereigntists? *Global Constitutionalism,* 9(2), 364–386.

Flor Cruz, J. A., & Seu, L. (2014, April 24). From Snail Mail to 4G, China Celebrates 20 Years of Internet Connectivity. *CNN.* https://edition.cnn.com/2014/04/23/world/asia/china-internet-20th-anniversary/index.html (Accessed 20 September 2021).

Haas, B. (2017, July 19). China Blocks WhatsApp Services as Censors Tighten Grip on Internet. *The Guardian.* https://amp.theguardian.com/technology/2017/jul/19/china-blocks-whatsapp-services-as-censors-tighten-grip-on-internet (Accessed 20 September 2021).

Haggart, B., Scholte, J. A., & Tusikov, N. (2021). Introduction. Return of the State? In B. Haggart, N. Tusikov & J. A. Scholte (Eds.), *Power and Authority in Internet Governance. Return of the State?* Routledge.

Harcourt, A., Christou, G., & Simpson, S. (2020). Global Standard Setting in Internet Governance. Oxford University Press.

Hoffmann, S., Lazanski, D., & Taylor, E. (2020). Standardising the Splinternet: How China's Technical Standards Could Fragment the Internet. *Journal of Cyber Policy, 5*(2), 239–264.

Hofmann, S. C. (2019). The Politics of Overlapping Organizations: Hostage-taking, Forum-Shopping and Brokering. *Journal of European Public Policy, 26*(6), 883–905.

Ikenberry, G. J. (2018). The End of Liberal International Order? *International Affairs, 94*(1), 7–23.

International Telecommunication Union. (2020, November 26). ITU Completes Evaluation for Global Affirmation of IMT-2020 Technologies. *Press Release.* https://www.itu.int/en/mediacentre/Pages/pr26-2020-evaluation-global-affirmation-imt-2020-5g.aspx (Accessed 14 January 2021).

Internet Engineering Task Force. (2020). *Internet Standards.* https://ietf.org/standards/ (Accessed 5 February 2020).

Jiang, M. (2010). Authoritarian Deliberation on Chinese Internet. *The Electronic Journal of Communication, 20*(3), 1–22.

Jongen, H., & Scholte, J. A. (2021). Legitimacy in Multistakeholder Global Governance at ICANN. *Global Governance, 27*(2), 298–324.

Khan, R. (2023). The Impact of a New Techno-nationalism era on Eco-economic Decoupling. *Resources Policy, 82,* 1–16.

Kim, M., Lee, H., & Kwak, J. (2020). The Changing Patterns of China's International Standardization in ICT under Techno-nationalism: A Reflection through 5G Standardization. *International Journal of Information Management, 54,* 1–8.

Liu, J. (2020). China's Data Localization. *Chinese Journal of Communication., 13*(1), 84–103.

Meena, M. E., & Geng, J. (2022). Dynamic Competition in Telecommunications: A Systematic Literature Review. *SAGE Open, 12*(2), 1–10.

Ministry of Industry and Information Technology of the People's Republic of China. (2017). *Internet Domain Name Management Rules.* https://tinyurl.com/49bwc6fw (Accessed 17 September 2021) [中华人民共和国工业和信息化部. 2017. 互联网域名管理办法].

Mueller, M. L. (2010). *Networks and States: The Global Politics of Internet Governance.* MIT Press.

Mueller, M. L. (2017). *Will the Internet Fragment? Sovereignty, Globalization, and Cyberspace.* Polity Press.

Mueller, M. L. (2020, March 30). About That Chinese 'Reinvention' of the Internet… *Internet Governance Project.* https://www.internetgovernance.org/2020/03/30/about-that-chinese-reinvention-of-the-internet/ (Accessed 22 October 2020).

Nanni, R. (2021). The 'China' Question in Mobile Internet Standard-Making: Insights from Expert Interviews. *Telecommunications Policy, 45*(6), 1–12.

Nanni, R. (2022). Digital Sovereignty and Internet Standards: Normative Implications of Public-Private Relations among Chinese Stakeholders in the Internet Engineering Task Force. *Information, Communication & Society, 25*(16), 2342–2362.

Nanni, R. (2023). Journey to the East: Digital Sovereignty in China's East Asian Relations Through the Lens of Techno-Nationalism. The Mobile Telecommunications Case-Study. In M. Timoteo, B. Verri & R. Nanni (Eds.), *Quo Vadis, Sovereignty? New Conceptual and Regulatory Boundaries in the Age of Digital China.* Springer.

Negro, G. (2017). *The Internet in China: From Infrastructure to a Nascent Civil Society.* Palgrave Macmillan.

Negro, G. (2020). A History of Chinese Global Internet Governance and Its Relations with ITU and ICANN. *Chinese Journal of Communication, 13*(1), 104–121.

Negro, G. (2022). A History of Chinese Global Internet Governance and Its Relations with ITU and ICANN. In Y. Hong & E. Harwit (Eds.), *China's Globalizing Internet.* Routledge.

Plantin, J., & De Seta, G. (2019). WeChat as Infrastructure: The Technonationalist Shaping of Chinese Digital Platforms. *Journal of Chinese Communication.* http://eprints.lse.ac.uk/91520/1/Plantin_WeChat-as-infrastructure.pdf (Accessed 15 November 2021).

Poggetti, L. (2021, January 20). *EU-China Mappings: Interactions between the EU and China on Key Issues.* Mercator Institute for China Studies. https://merics.org/de/kurzanalyse/eu-china-mappings-interactions-between-eu-and-china-key-issues (Accessed 13 July 2021).

Pohlmann, T., Blind, K., & Hess, P. (2020). *Fact Finding Study on Patents Declared to the 5G Standard.* IPLytics and Technische Universitaet Berlin.

Pupillo, L. (2019, June 21). *5G and National Security*. CEPS. https://www.ceps.eu/5g-and-nationalsecurity/ (Accessed 20 October 2020).

Reuters. (2023, September 4). Teardown of Huawei's New Phone Shows China's Chip Breakthrough. https://www.reuters.com/technology/teardown-huaweis-new-phone-shows-chinas-chip-breakthrough-2023-09-04/ (Accessed 6 October 2023).

Russell, A. L. (2013, July 30). OSI: The Internet That Wasn't. IEEE Spectrum. https://spectrum.ieee.org/tech-history/cyberspace/osi-the-internet-that-wasnt (Accessed 27 November 2020).

Santaniello, M. (2021). From Governance Denial to State Regulation: A Controversy-Based Typology of Internet Governance Models. In B. Haggart, N. Tusikov, & J. A. Scholte (Eds.), *Power and Authority in Internet Governance. Return of the State?* Routledge.

Scholte, J. A. (2017). Complex Hegemony. The IANA Transition in Global Internet Governance. *GigaNet: Global Internet Governance Academic Network, Annual Symposium.*

Segal, A. (2018, August 13). When China Rules the Web: Technology in Service of the State. *Foreign Affairs*. https://www.foreignaffairs.com/articles/china/2018-08-13/when-china-rules-web (Accessed 10 November 2020).

Shen, H. (2016). China and global internet governance: toward an alternative analytical framework. *Chinese Journal of Communication, 9*(3), 304–324.

Shen, H. (2022). *Alibaba: Infrastructuring Global China*. Routledge.

Sin, B. (2020, April 1). What Google Ban? How to Get Huawei Phones Working with US Apps and Services Like Google Maps and Instagram. *South China Morning Post*. https://www.scmp.com/lifestyle/gadgets/article/3077689/what-google-ban-how-get-huawei-phones-working-us-apps-and (Accessed 21 December 2020).

State Council Information Office of the PRC. (2010). *White Paper on the Internet in China*. http://www.scio.gov.cn/zfbps/ndhf/2010/Document/662572/662572.htm (Accessed 17 September 2021). [中华人民共和国国务院新闻办公室 2010. 中国互联网状况].

Tang, M. (2020). From 'Bringing-In' to 'Going-Out': Transnationalizing China's Internet Capital Through State Policies. *Chinese Journal of Communication, 13*(1), 27–46.

ten Oever, N. (2022). 5G and the Notion of Network Ideology, or: The Limitations of Sociotechnical Imaginaries. *Telecommunications Policy*, 102442.

The Economist. (2016, August 6). WeChat's World. https://www.economist.com/business/2016/08/06/wechats-world (Accessed 20 September 2021).

Xinhua. (2017, March 1). International Strategy of Cooperation on Cyberspace (full text). http://www.xinhuanet.com/politics/2017-03/01/c_1120552767.htm (Accessed 24 July 2021). [新华社 2017 网络空间国际合作战略(全文)].

Zhang, L., Tandoc, E. C., Jr., & Han, S. (2022). Rage or Rationality: Exposure to Internet Censorship and the Impact on Individual Information Behaviors in China. *Policy & Internet, 14*(4), 807–823.

Zhong, R. (2019, April 25). Who Owns Huawei? The Company Tried to Explain. It Got Complicated. *New York Times.* https://www.nytimes.com/2019/04/25/technology/who-owns-huawei.html (Accessed 20 October 2020).

CHAPTER 7

Conclusion

7.1 Recap

This book has cast new light on the interaction between Chinese public and private actors, on the one hand, and Internet governance, on the other. It contributes theoretical and empirical innovation to IR-informed literature on Internet governance with new empirical nuances and a mixed methodological approach. Furthermore, it contributes to bridging gaps among IR Theory, STS, and China Studies. This book's findings go against a large part of the common wisdom available in the policy and media debates around China and Internet governance. Namely, this book rejects the idea of China as a catalyst of Internet fragmentation and finds Chinese stakeholders to be increasingly accepting vis-à-vis multistakeholder Internet governance. These findings are based on the evidence that Chinese stakeholders are not fully controlled by the Chinese government. Furthermore, these findings feed into the literature on digital sovereignty and the future of the Liberal International Order.

However, a number of research paths remain open. This concluding chapter addresses these aspects.

7.2 Empirical Findings and Their Academic and Policy Relevance

This research finds that Chinese stakeholders have adapted to multi-stakeholderism and refrained from establishing a *splinternet*. This entails acceptance of private-based governance at ICANN, IETF, and 3GPP, as well as no fragmentation at the technical level, whereby China adopts TCP/IP and the IANA-endorsed DNS in its domestic infrastructure. Furthermore, in the standardisation process of 5G, Chinese stakeholders sought to lead the making of a universally compatible standard at 3GPP instead of promoting a separate domestically implemented one as they did with 3G. To foster societal control, China resorted to alignment of the Internet to national regulation (Mueller, 2017), rather than establishing a separate network. This is to say, China has made an effort domestically not only to control information fluxes, but also to mitigate sensitive data flows as well as to harness those platforms that could possibly shape public opinion through the mass accumulation of data on users' (that is, citizens') behaviour online (Brussee, 2022; Shen, 2022). Notwithstanding this, Chinese companies retain a degree of autonomy in their choices as well as interests that may diverge from those of the state. Furthermore, they do not seek to establish a technically separate Internet.

This counters the narrative spread in part of the media, policy, and scholarly communities of China as a monolithic national actor that is rewriting the Internet's rules, its standards, and pushing for the creation of a separate *splinternet*. On the contrary, what emerges here is a portrait of Chinese stakeholders as norm entrepreneurs that push forward measures of contestation through such practices as forum-shopping (Leal-Arcas & Morelli, 2018), and also adapt to the existing normative settings when that allows them to influence decision-making. In this context, Chinese stakeholders prefer technical interoperability over a split network to retain scale economies (Mueller, 2017).

To be sure, underlying changes and tensions exist in the development of the Internet infrastructure and Internet-enabled technologies. While mobile connectivity is dependent on TCP/IP, it is in turn putting strain on the latter's functioning as anticipated in the introductory chapters. Furthermore, the growing reliance on 5G infrastructure for Internet-based connectivity is creating new forms of overlap and interdependence between Internet and mobile telephony infrastructure. For example, sectors of the literature observe that IOT development is bringing onto the market and among the usership myriads of Internet-connected devices based on the 5G infrastructure for Internet connectivity. As 5G is a telephony infrastructure, its network is centralised and fully determined as opposed to the Internet's traditional building-blocks architecture where intelligence is at the periphery (devices) as previously described in this book. This development therefore entails reliance on a more centralised infrastructure for a growing number of Internet connections, with potential implications for the future models of development of the Internet infrastructure itself (ten Oever, 2022). Multistakeholder, private-based Internet governance remains a site of contestation and China—along with other state actors—is seeking to reassert authority on the Internet architecture (Haggart et al., 2021).

The extent to which this will trigger the emergence of new actors and power dynamics within the existing governance settings and fora is unknown, as well as the potential changes in governmental influence through market actors in the near future. In the case of China, such influence could be enhanced through its ongoing antitrust crackdown on domestic *big techs* and the latter's growing dependence on China's domestic market amid the US-China technological and commercial competition. Furthermore, a trend towards centralised infrastructure could yield change in these dynamics (Allen, 2019; Douzet, 2021).

These aspects are open for further research in the forthcoming years. However, at this stage, the existing multistakeholder, private-based Internet governance regime complex centred on ICANN shows resilience and such powerful actors as China and its domestic stakeholders show interest in and gain advantage from participating in it. As norm entrepreneurs, Chinese stakeholders have adapted to and adopted the existing normative ecosystem to a large extent, while maintaining venues for contestation open (Negro, 2020).

This has important implications for the Liberal International Order at large. Internet standardisation and the distribution and management of CIRs are forms of liberal-informed global governance in that they take place across borders and feature a strong participation of and influence by private actors (Palladino & Santaniello, 2021). Therefore, they are a facet of the Liberal International Order in its free-market tenet as described in Chapter 2. To this end, this book's findings show that liberal-informed Internet governance can be characterised by such incentives as to favour the inclusion of emerging actors within the existing governance mechanisms and according to their existing rules (Ikenberry, 2018,

2020)—much like China moved from open contestation of multistakeholder Internet governance towards acceptance and growing influence within it as its capacity to influence decision-making from within was growing. This conclusion is, of course, not directly transferable to each individual facet of global governance. Nonetheless, all those governance ecosystems centred on the making of scalable solutions (whether technological or not) yield incentives that favour coordination among conflicting interests over closure and contestation, in turn yielding the inclusion of emerging powerful actors within the existing normative order. Indeed, an actor who can increase its influence within a decision-making ecosystem is less likely to engage in reforming or replacing it (Flockhart, 2020).

To summarise, contestation against liberal norms and the hegemony of liberal actors within global governance mechanisms is not fading, and indeed its part and parcel of global governance (Zürn, 2018). Those countries which historically hold leadership positions within the Liberal International Order, chiefly the US, will need to accept a loss of ground in leadership terms and potential changes in rules in favour of emerging actors. Indeed, the Liberal Order was founded at a time in which most independent states would not participate in the free market and most territories in the world were still colonies. As such, the Liberal Order has historically been bound to adapt to the emergence of new (state or non-state) actors (Flockhart, 2020). Nonetheless, the Liberal International Order's openness to domestically non-liberal actors provides incentives towards adaptation, rather than contestation, in several global governance ecosystems. Such openness lies at the basis of the aforementioned adaptability of the Liberal International Order to power shifts among actors, a key characteristic that makes such international order likely to be in place in the foreseeable future.

7.3 Theoretical Implications and Their Relevance

In theoretical terms, these findings show that the regime complex for Internet governance is characterised by such resilience as to incentivise emerging powers to adapt to and integrate in, rather than contest, the existing normative order (Leal-Arcas & Morelli, 2018). All in all, the concept of regime complexity proves useful in conceptualising Internet governance and in identifying the venues of influence in decision-making and how they intersect. It helped in making sense of normative rigidity and why norm entrepreneurs may choose adaptation over contestation. However, it must be acknowledged that such normative rigidity does not only stem from regime complexity in and of itself, but also from the specific characteristics of the regime complex in question. As illustrated, Internet standards and standards for Internet-based technologies need scalability to be economically viable. Thus, an extent of coordination on standards is better than no coordination at all for most actors. This creates an incentive for actors to integrate in existing standard-making processes when drifting or reforming them is not feasible.

All in all, these findings imply that, despite growing talk about digital sovereignty and growing attempts of governments to bring companies under regulatory control, private-led multistakeholder governance is here to stay for the foreseeable future. After all, neither companies nor governments have ever faded in Internet governance. Rather, historical periods in which one group or the other had more power in the governance ecosystem alternated (ten Oever, 2021). Arguably, at the time of writing, the digital sovereignty debate implies that Internet governance is experiencing a "return of the state", that is, a phase in which governments' power in Internet governance is growing amid calls for strengthening sovereignty over social processes taking place on and through the Internet (Haggart et al., 2021; Hong & Goodnight, 2020; Roberts et al., 2021), with companies still retaining a powerful and by no means dependent role in it.

In the specific case of China, calls for Internet sovereignty—as the Chinese term that more closely resembles the concept of digital sovereignty that is extensively discussed in European policymaking (Roberts et al., 2021)—imply growing governmental influence and regulatory control onto those sectors of the digital economy that influence citizens' behaviour the most (see, for example: Mueller & Farhat, 2022; Shen, 2022). On top of this, it implies further control on infrastructure—though refraining from fragmentation—and a stronger quest for technological autonomy in the form of Chinese tech manufacturers internalising the production chain to reduce vulnerability to a more rivalrous global political context (Brown, 2021; Nanni, 2023; Poggetti, 2021). In other words, it implies alignment of Internet-based activities to domestic regulation, but not fragmentation nor regime change in the multistakeholder global Internet governance ecosystem (Mueller, 2017).

Such findings carry implications for theorisation on the Liberal International Order: liberal-informed global governance mechanisms provide incentives for newly emerged (state or non-state) powers to act within the existing rules and maximise their influence in decision-making mechanisms rather than engaging in contestation and order-making (Ikenberry, 2018). In this view, this book contributes to the literature addressing normative contestation within the order itself (Ikenberry, 2018), instead of the existential challenges à la Mearsheimer (2019). After all, the latest literature on global governance has argued that contestation is part and parcel of global governance (Zürn, 2018, 2021). In doing so, this work gave a methodological and conceptual contribution. By systematically including technologists' views (through interviews) and behaviour (through network analysis) in this study, this book contributed to filling a gap in IR Theory, namely the tendency to overlook technologists' contribution to technology-related politics and its making (Hornsby & Parshotam, 2018; Tanczer et al., 2018). As a matter of fact, a tendency to treat technical aspects as separate from politics is very much present in society at large, with decades of technical as well as social scientific literature addressing the non-neutrality of technology (Polgar, 2010; Strate, 2012; Whelchel, 1986). Nonetheless, the need to combine technical expertise and social scientific approaches in studying the politics that affects the Internet infrastructure also emerges powerfully by reading the IETF's own mission statement: "The Internet isn't value-neutral, and neither is the IETF" (Alvestrand, 2004).

To summarise, this book contributed to theorisation on the Liberal International Order amid the rise of China from a regime-theoretic perspective. It did so by addressing critical conceptual aspects anticipated in other sectors of technology-related social scientific literature, such as STS, but not mainstreamed in IR Theory yet.

7.4 Caveats and Future Venues for Research

The findings of this book have been qualified all throughout the process by three major caveats. First, the author is not a technologist, which made access to technical knowledge more complicated and most often filtered through the eyes of interview participants possessing technical expertise. Nonetheless, the contribution of technical experts through interviews has proved essential in reducing such barriers to knowledge. Second, the author speaks Chinese but is not a native speaker. Linguistic barriers can be a major obstacle, especially when they involve languages with no common roots, such as Chinese on the one hand and English and Italian on the other. The use of sources such as DigiChina, however, helped the author in the interpretation of legal texts, where the misinterpretation of a single word can potentially yield the misinterpretation of the legal text as a whole. Third, the unknowns around public–private relations in China and the transformation in the relationship between Chinese state and big techs that is ongoing at the time of writing make some of this book's conclusions subject to potential revision in the near future. This, however, will always be an issue in research addressing politically sensitive topics such as digital infrastructure, as information on government policies and state-companies relations will never be complete to the researcher. These three caveats add to the ethical and positionality issues further addressed in Appendix A.

Furthermore, Russia's aggression to Ukraine in 2022 fostered new debates on Internet fragmentation, this time without China as its main protagonist (Internet Society, 2022a). During the early days of Russia's war of invasion reports were abundant about Russia's willingness to separate from the global Internet (Satariano & Hopkins, 2022), as well as Ukraine's attempts to pressure ICANN into cutting Russia out (Ministry of Digital Transformation of Ukraine, 2022). Nonetheless, while Russia did increase infrastructural and content control domestically, it did not establish a separate infrastructure (Ermoshina et al., 2022), much as the option of establishing a separate Russian-language DNS has been studied for years by the Russian authorities (Jee, 2019). On Ukraine's side, its attempts vis-à-vis ICANN and RIPE NCC to request the Russian namespace to be cut off the global Internet have been pushed back by the two bodies, both out of technical unfeasibility and normative undesirability vis-à-vis the political use of technical Internet governance bodies (Sullivan, 2022). While this conclusion has been debated in the Internet governance field (Various Authors, 2022), it is the leading one within the Internet governance practitioner community at the time of writing. Furthermore, the Russian aggression on Ukraine and subsequent political alignment (however partial) between Russia and China has renewed debates on power politics, spheres of influence, and the likelihood of rising powers to try and replace the Liberal International Order (Ikenberry, 2024).

The Russian invasion of Ukraine falls outside the scope of this book, but its implications for Internet governance and the debates on the Liberal Order suggest that future research would benefit from studies involving experts cutting across the areas of IR Theory, regional studies, media studies, and computer science. This is an issue of interdisciplinarity that this book sought to partially address. Furthermore, the Internet's and Internet-based technology's developments are path dependent but fast, with fewer than ten years separating the beginning of 3G rollout in most continents and the earliest 3GPP 5G-related release. Such changes, as well as changes in the power balance among those actors who most influence the future shaping of the Internet infrastructure and its protocols, have the potential to affect the future developments of the Internet infrastructure at a fundamental level, as mentioned throughout this book (ten Oever, 2022). The development of this latest aspect will also depend on the way in which the outcomes of the ITU's 2020 World Telecommunication Standardization Assembly (WTSA-20)—held in March 2022 owing to the Covid-19 pandemic—will concretise in standardisation terms in the near future. Held every four years, WTSA sets out the period of study for ITU-T. According to the Internet Society (2022b), the content of the Resolutions approved and modified at WTSA-20 on the non-radio aspects of telecommunications standards will affect Internet-based networking. Nonetheless, delays due to the Covid-19 pandemic worked against these standardisation activities, leaving their medium- and long-term assessment outside the scope of this book.

The same speed of change is visible in China's domestic environment and in the transforming relations between the state and its domestic companies, protected through the Golden Shield Project (Shen, 2022) and also controlled and cracked down upon through antitrust measures and new data protection mechanisms (Creemers, 2022; Zhong, 2021). Therefore, the empirical findings of this research will possibly need to be recurrently readdressed on the backdrop of emerging issues. What is granted, instead, is the need for Internet scholars (whether from Media Studies, IR Theory, or any other background) to familiarise themselves and engage in meaningful dialogue with China Studies when addressing questions related to the Chinese engagement with global Internet governance.

All in all, the theoretical claims advanced in this book and the empirical findings illustrated are durable in their relevance albeit subject to potential change. This is due to three main factors. First, the applicability of methods and findings about Internet governance regime resilience illustrated in the empirical chapters. Second, the long historical perspective taken by this book in exploring Chinese stakeholders' stances in their mutability make findings relevant in interpreting their current policy positions. Third, building on the previous one, findings on Chinese stakeholders' adaptation to and contestation of multistakeholderism and the technical foundation of the Internet feed directly into the emerging debate on digital sovereignty and the return of state in Internet governance.

7.5 Final Remarks

In conclusion, this book contributes to knowledge on Chinese stakeholders in Internet governance generating new data through both a variety of methods. It casts new light on the behaviour of such actors and their influence on norms in Internet governance. Furthermore, it contributes to regime theory and addresses conceptual and methodological loopholes pre-existent in the literature.

While several research venues remain open and unanswered questions are many, this book brings its own contribution to debates on China's rise and the future of the Liberal International Order, the future of multistakeholderism in Internet governance, and the question of Internet fragmentation. This book's contribution on state authority on the Internet infrastructure constitutes ground for future research on such emerging debates as the rise of digital sovereignty.

If the Liberal International Order accommodates China's rise, and assuming China chooses to adapt to the Order's rules by and large, questions will remain about whether such order can still be labelled "liberal" if the US (and/or Europe) were to lose central leadership positions. Nonetheless, while the US and the EU are losing power on the world stage in comparative terms, their demise is unlikely in the near future as demonstrated by Western stakeholders' strong position in Internet and mobile connectivity standardisation and resource distribution.

References

Allen, D. (2019, June 19). Analysis by Oracle Internet Intelligence Highlights China's Unique Approach to Connecting to the Global Internet. *Oracle Cloud Infrastructure Internet Intelligence.* https://blogs.oracle.com/internetintelligence/analysis-by-oracle-internet-intelligence-highlights-china%e2%80%99s-unique-approach-to-connecting-to-the-global-internet (Accessed 18 December 2019).

Alvestrand, H. (2004). RFC 3935. A Mission Statement for the IETF. *IETF Datatracker.* https://datatracker.ietf.org/doc/rfc3935/ (Accessed 10 January 2022).

Brown, A. (2021, June 1). *Huawei's Global Troubles Spur Beijing's Push for Self-reliance*. Mercator Institute for China Studies. https://merics.org/en/short-analysis/huaweis-global-troubles-spur-beijings-push-self-reliance (Accessed 18 June 2021).

Brussee, V. (2022). Authoritarian Design: How the Digital Architecture on China's Sina Weibo Facilitate Information Control. *Asiascape: Digital Asia, 9*(3), 207–241.

Creemers, R. (2022). China's Emerging Data Protection Framework. *Journal of Cybersecurity, 8*(1), 1–12.

Douzet, F. (2021). The Shrinking of Cyberspace: A Blind Spot of Cyber Policy. *The Hague Programme for Cyber Norms*. https://www.thehaguecybernorms.nl/conference-2021-speakers/frederick-douzet (Accessed 17 November 2021).

Ermoshina, K., Loveluck, B., & Musiani, F. (2022). A Market of Black Boxes: The Political Economy of Internet Surveillance and Censorship in Russia. *Journal of Information Technology and Politics, 19*(1), 18–33. https://hal.science/hal-03190007/file/Preprint_KEBLFM_JITP2021.pdf (Accessed 2 October 2023).

Flockhart, T. (2020). Is This the End? Resilience, Ontological Security, and the Crisis of the Liberal International Order. *Contemporary Security Policy, 41*(2), 215–240.

Haggart, B., Scholte, J. A., & Tusikov, N. (2021). Introduction. Return of the State? In B. Haggart, N. Tusikov & J. A. Scholte (Eds.), *Power and Authority in Internet Governance. Return of the State?* Routledge.

Hong, Y., & Goodnight, G. T. (2020). How to Think about Cyber Sovereignty: The Case of China. *Chinese Journal of Communication, 13*(1), 8–26.

Hornsby, D. J., & Parshotam, A. (2018). Science Diplomacy, Epistemic Communities, and Practice in Sub-Saharan Africa. *Global Policy, 9*, 29–34.

Ikenberry, G. J. (2018). The End of Liberal International Order? *International Affairs, 94*(1), 7–23.

Ikenberry, G. J. (2020). The Next Liberal Order. *Foreign Affairs, 99*, 133–142.

Ikenberry, G. J. (2024). Three Worlds: The West, East and South and the Competition to Shape Global Order. *International Affairs, 100*(1), 121–138.

Internet Society. (2022a, April 7). Defend the Internet, Stop the Splinternet. https://www.internetsociety.org/news/statements/2022/defend-the-internet-stop-the-splinternet/ (Accessed 12 April 2022).

Internet Society. (2022b, April 5). ITU World Telecommunication Standardization Assembly 2020 (WTSA-20)—Summary Issues Matrix. https://www.internetsociety.org/wp-content/uploads/2022/04/ISOC-WTSA20-Resolutions-Results-Matrix-Final.pdf (Accessed 15 September 2023).

Jee, C. (2019, March 21). Russia Wants to Cut Itself off from the Global Internet. Here's What That Really Means. *MIT Technology Review*. https://www.technologyreview.com/2019/03/21/65940/russia-wants-to-cut-itself-off-from-the-global-internet-heres-what-that-really-means/. Accessed 2 October 2023).

Leal-Arcas, R., & Morelli, A. (2018). The Resilience of the Paris Agreement: Negotiating and Implementing the Climate Regime. *Georgetown Environmental Law Review, 31*(1), 1–64.

Mearsheimer, J. J. (2019). Bound to Fail: The Rise and Fall of the Liberal International Order. *International Security, 43*(4), 7–50.

Ministry of Digital Transformation of Ukraine (2022, February 28). Correspondence: Fedorov to Marby. *Internet Corporation for Assigned Names and Numbers.* https://www.icann.org/en/system/files/correspondence/fedorov-to-marby-28feb22-en.pdf (Accessed 2 October 2023).

Mueller, M. L. (2017). *Will the Internet Fragment? Sovereignty, Globalization, and Cyberspace.* Polity Press.

Mueller, M. L., & Farhat, K. (2022). Regulation of Platform Market Access by the United States and China: Neo-mercantilism in Digital Services. *Policy & Internet, 14*(2), 348–367.

Nanni, R. (2023). Journey to the East: Digital Sovereignty in China's East Asian Relations Through the Lens of Techno-Nationalism. The Mobile Telecommunications Case-Study. In M. Timoteo, B. Verri, & R. Nanni (Eds.), *Quo Vadis, Sovereignty? New Conceptual and Regulatory Boundaries in the Age of Digital China.* Springer.

Negro, G. (2020). A History of Chinese Global Internet Governance and Its Relations with ITU and ICANN. *Chinese Journal of Communication, 13*(1), 104–121.

Palladino, N., & Santaniello, M. (2021). *Legitimacy, Power, and Inequalities in the Multistakeholder Internet Governance.* Palgrave Macmillan.

Poggetti, L. (2021, January 20). EU-China Mappings: Interactions between the EU and China on Key Issues. Mercator Institute for China Studies. https://merics.org/de/kurzanalyse/eu-china-mappings-interactions-between-eu-and-china-key-issues (Accessed 13 July 2021).

Polgar, J. M. (2010). The Myth of Neutral Technology. In M. M. K. Oishi, I. M. Mitchell, & H. F. M. Van der Loos (Eds.), *Design and Use of Assistive Technology.* Springer Nature.

Roberts, H., Cowls, J., Casolari, F., Morley, J., Taddeo, M., & Floridi, L. (2021). Safeguarding European Values with Digital Sovereignty: An Analysis of Statements and Policies. *Internet Policy Review, 10*(3), 1–28.

Satariano, A., & Hopkins, V. (2022, March 7). Russia, Blocked From the Global Internet, Plunges Into Digital Isolation. *The New York Times.* https://www.nytimes.com/2022/03/07/technology/russia-ukraine-internet-isolation.html (Accessed 2 October 2023).

Shen, H. (2022). *Alibaba: Infrastructuring Global China.* Routledge.

Strate, L. (2012). If It's Neutral, It's Not Technology. *Educational Technology, 52*(1), 6–9.

Sullivan, A. (2022, March 2). Why the World Must Resist Calls to Undermine the Internet. *Internet Society*. https://www.internetsociety.org/blog/2022/03/why-the-world-must-resist-calls-to-undermine-the-internet/ (Accessed 2 October 2023).

Tanczer, L. M., Brass, I., & Carr, M. (2018). CSIRTs and Global Cybersecurity: How Technical Experts Support Science Diplomacy. *Global Policy*, 9(3), 60–66.

ten Oever, N. (2021). The Metagovernance of Internet Governance. In B. Haggart, N. Tusikov, & J. A. Scholte (Eds.), *Contested Power and Authority in Internet Governance: Return of the State*. Routledge.

ten Oever, N. (2022). 5G and the Notion of Network Ideology, or: The Limitations of Sociotechnical Imaginaries. *Telecommunications Policy*, 102442.

Various authors. (2022, March 10). Multistakeholder Imposition of Internet Sanctions. *Tech Policy Press*. https://techpolicy.press/towards-the-multistakeholder-imposition-of-internet-sanctions/ (Accessed 2 October 2023).

Whelchel, R. J. (1986). Is Technology Neutral? *IEEE Technology and Society Magazine*, 5(4), 3–8.

Zhong, R. (2021, July 4). China Orders Didi Off App Stores in an Escalating Crackdown. *New York Times*. https://www.nytimes.com/2021/07/04/technology/china-didi-app-removed.html (Accessed July 6, 2021).

Zürn, M. (2018). *A Theory of Global Governance: Authority, Legitimacy, and contestation*. Oxford University Press.

Zürn, M. (2021). On the Role of Contestations, the Power of Reflexive Authority, and Legitimation Problems in the Global Political System. *International Theory*, 13(1), 192–204.

Appendix A

Elaborations on Theoretical and Methodological Aspects

This book addresses the following questions: *"(To what extent) are Chinese stakeholders reshaping the rules of Global Internet Governance?"*. In particular: (i) (To what extent) are Chinese stakeholders contributing to increased state influence in multistakeholder fora?; (ii) (how) is China contributing to Internet fragmentation?; and (iii) what are the main drivers of Chinese stakeholders' stances?

A key takeaway from this book is the multifaceted characterisation of multistakeholder Internet governance as a largely private-based regime complex where multiple actors cast their influence in a variety of loosely interdependent venues with partially overlapping competences.[1]

This appendix elaborates on the theoretical and methodological approaches adopted to conduct this book. Interactions within the three observed fora (ICANN, IETF, 3GPP) are studied through three methods: expert interviews, thematic analysis of standardisation documents, and the analysis of Chinese legal and policy documents.

Theoretical choices: Internet governance as a regime complex, norm entrepreneurship, and the question of digital sovereignty

---

[1] Nye, J. S. (2014). *The Regime Complex for Managing Global Cyber Activities.* Global Commission on Internet Governance Paper Series, 1. http://www.cigionline.org/public ations/regime-complex-managingglobal-cyber-activities (July 25, 2019).

© The Editor(s) (if applicable) and The Author(s), under exclusive license to Springer Nature Singapore Pte Ltd. 2024
R. Nanni, *Rising China and Internet Governance*,
https://doi.org/10.1007/978-981-97-0357-9

The author conceives the Internet governance ecosystem as a regime complex.[2] Addressing Internet governance under this lens allows one to make sense of the variety of venues of policymaking influence that can be accessed and leveraged by a multitude of public and private actors in a governance mechanism made of loosely interdependent and partially overlapping fora.[3]

This offers ground for this book's contribution to the emerging literature on digital sovereignty. In the ongoing dialectic between different forms of public and private power in Internet governance,[4] states are seeking to reassert their authority on the Internet infrastructure and its making.[5] Nonetheless, regime complexity blurs the lines of national interest and power relations among actors, thus limiting states' options for direct influence in Internet governance.

Digital sovereignty as a concept has experienced growing attention in the wake of the US–China technological competition. Nonetheless, definitions are blurred, ranging from individual empowerment vis-à-vis the collection and treatment of personal data to states' and the EU's quests for reduced dependence on foreign industries in technological innovation.[6] Owing to the concept's novelty, most literature has focused on the discursive characteristics of digital sovereignty, as practices are yet to emerge. However, studies on digital sovereignty practices are now emerging, often pinpointing a lack of consequentiality between digital sovereignty discourses and policy practice. For example, Perarnaud and Rossi[7] find that EU discourses on digital sovereignty have

---

[2] Nye, op. cit.

[3] Abbott, K. W., & Faude, B. (2022). Hybrid Institutional Complexes in Global Governance. *The Review of International Organizations, 17*, 263–291.

[4] Shen, H. (2016). China and Global Internet Governance: Toward an Alternative Analytical Framework. *Chinese Journal of Communication, 9*(3), 304–324; ten Oever, N. (2022). 5G and the Notion of Network Ideology, or: The Limitations of Sociotechnical Imaginaries. *Telecommunications Policy*, 102442.

[5] Haggart, B., Scholte, J. A., & Tusikov, N. (2021). Introduction. Return of the State? In B. Haggart, N. Tusikov, & J. A. Scholte (Eds.), *Power and Authority in Internet Governance. Return of the State?* Routledge.

[6] Pohle, J., & Thiel, T. (2020). Digital Sovereignty. *Internet Policy Review, 9*(4). https://doi.org/10.14763/2020.4.1532.

[7] Perarnaud, C., & Rossi, J. (2023). The EU and Internet Standards—Beyond the Spin, a Strategic Turn? *Journal of European Public Policy*. https://doi.org/10.1080/13501763.2023.2251036.

not been followed by policy shifts, with results being often unintended consequences of discursive shifts.

Notwithstanding the European context, digital sovereignty was introduced *ante litteram* in other political contexts. This includes China, which has officially introduced the concept of 'Internet sovereignty' in 2010, within the White Paper on the (state of) the Internet in China already discussed throughout the book.

Indeed, the focus on public authorities' enhanced quest for power in Internet governance is older than the digital sovereignty debate in academic literature. For example, states' turn towards the Internet infrastructure as a place of and tool for political contestation is a relatively longstanding issue.[8] Not only in terms of standards, but also in terms of architectural deployment: with the DNS4EU initiative, the EU seeks to strengthen its autonomy in and regulatory control on the process of DNS resolution.[9] However, the EU is not the first public authority to turn towards the DNS in its regulatory effort, as China established the so-called 'DNS Rules' in 2017.[10] Furthermore, the protectionist stances taken by world powers in 5G deployment amid concerns over China's undue influence over dataflows along new telephony infrastructures is also part of this broader trend on the market.[11]

[8] Musiani, F. (2013). Network Architecture as Internet Governance. *Internet Policy Review*, 2(4), 1–9; Musiani, F. (2020). Science and Technology Studies Approaches to Internet Governance: Controversies and Infrastructures as Internet Politics. In L. DeNardis, D. Cogburn, N. Levinson, & F. Musiani (Eds.), *Researching Internet Governance: Methods, Frameworks, Futures*. MIT Press.

[9] Claes, B. (2022, October 24). DNS4EU: A Future European Server to Resolve IP Address. *European Commission*. https://joinup.ec.europa.eu/collection/ict-standards-procurement/solution/dns-rfc-1034-rfc-1035-domain-name-system/news/dns4eu (September 19, 2023).

[10] Ministry of Industry and Information Technology of the People's Republic of China. (2017). *Internet Domain Name Management Rules*. https://tinyurl.com/49bwc6fw (September 17, 2021) [中华人民共和国工业和信息化部. 2017. 互联网域名管理办法].

[11] Ciuriak, D. (2019). The US-China Trade War: Technological Roots and WTO Responses. *Global Solutions Journal*, 4, 130–135; Poggetti, L. (2021, January 20). EU-China Mappings: Interactions between the EU and China on Key Issues. *Mercator Institute for China Studies*. https://merics.org/de/kurzanalyse/eu-china-mappings-interactions-between-eu-and-china-key-issues (July 13, 2021).

While such specific instances are better addressed in the empirical part of this book, they help to trace a few lines of digital sovereignty practices and how this book's focus on infrastructure politics feeds into this emerging literature.

As literature debates the return of the state in Internet governance, one must bear in mind that states have never left Internet governance in the first place.[12] For example, the US government played a central role in establishing and maintaining the Internet and then ICANN.[13] Rather, one should look at the debate on digital sovereignty as an attempt from public authorities to expand their share of power in Internet governance vis-à-vis private actors and competing state actors. In the Internet governance regime complex, no single authority is likely to emerge as the one regulator of the Internet, its infrastructures, and the technologies based on it. As anticipated, this is due to the variety of venues for policy influence that regime complexity creates.

Regime complexity is a late development in regime theory, which emerged in the early 1980s with Krasner[14] as one of its founders. According to him, a regime consists of "principles, norms, rules, and decision-making procedures around which actor expectations converge in a given issue area".[15] Criticised and transformed several times,[16] the concept of regime came to be closely connected to institutional liberalism.[17] In Krasner's view,[18] much as for liberal institutionalists,[19] the underpinnings of the international system are those recognised by realists: international anarchy and the incapacity of states to collaborate amid reciprocal mistrust. In this context, regimes are set up by states to create incentives and disincentives that can ensure collaboration on specific issue

---

[12] ten Oever, op. cit.

[13] Mueller, M. L. (2017). *Will the Internet Fragment? Sovereignty, Globalization, and Cyberspace.* Polity Press.

[14] Krasner, S. D. (1982). Structural Causes and Regime Consequences: Regimes as Intervening Variables. *International Organization, 36*(2), 185–205.

[15] Krasner, op. cit., p. 135.

[16] Strange, S. (1982). Cave! Hic Dragones: A Critique of Regime Analysis. *International Organization, 36*(2), 479–496.

[17] Keohane, R. O., & Martin, L. L. (1995). The Promise of Institutionalist Theory. *International Security, 20*(1), 39–51.

[18] Krasner, op. cit.

[19] Keohane & Martin, op. cit.

areas to avoid anarchy's suboptimal outcomes. To put in terms familiar with game theory, which characterised the early developments of regime theory, suboptimal outcomes are those deriving from such games as the prisoner's dilemma, whereby the individual incentive to defect prevents actors from collaborating and reaching an optimal outcome.[20]

Amid the emergence of constructivist approaches in the 1990s,[21] regime theory incorporated a cognitivist approach whereby actors' interests and actions gave form to regimes and the latter shaped and reshaped actors' interests and actions in turn. Other than adding a cognitivist component to the already existing rational one in regime theory, the 1990s witnessed the systematic incorporation of non-state actors as agents in IR theory.[22]

This opened the door to the concept of regime complexity which emerged in the early 2000s. Raustiala and Victor[23] were the earliest to elaborate this concept, which was later applied to such fields as environmental governance by Keohane and Victor[24] and Internet governance by Nye.[25] According to the latter, a regime complex is a set of loosely interrelated regime subsets with little or no clear-cut hierarchical relation. Regime complexity is a framework adopted to conceptualise the relations among subsets of Internet governance and among state and non-state actors within them. As for the three bodies addressed in this book, participants to one are often unaware of the details of the work conducted in other bodies. However, their activities are interrelated and influence each other. It is the case with 5G development and TCP/IP: the former is developed at 3GPP and the latter at the IETF, with different groups of people (often) from the same companies working on

---

[20] Axelrod, R. (1980). More Effective Choice in the Prisoner's Dilemma. *Journal of Conflict Resolution*, 24(3), 379–403.

[21] Wendt, A. (1992). Anarchy Is What States Make of It: The Social Construction of Power Politics. *International Organization*, 46(2), 391–425.

[22] Haas, P. M. (1993). Epistemic Communities and the Dynamics of International Environmental Cooperation. In V. Rittberger (Ed.), *Regime Theory and International Relations*. Oxford University Press.

[23] Raustiala, K., & Victor, D. (2004). The Regime Complex for Plant Genetic Resources. *International Organization*, 58(2), 277–309.

[24] Keohane, R. O., & Victor, D. G. (2011). The Regime Complex for Climate Change. *Perspectives on Politics*, 9(1), 7–23.

[25] Nye, op. cit.

them. However, 5G enables such technologies (such as Internet of Things devices) to put in question the efficiency of TCP/IP as a workable set of protocols, triggering debate on the development of additional and/or alternative ones. Despite this, technological path dependencies in Internet development make TCP/IP hardly replaceable and issues related with 5G-enabled IoT persistent. This research assumes a bidirectional relation between the regime complex and actors, whereby the former shapes the latter's interests and behaviour and the latter shapes the former's rules and norms.

This book maintains that regime complexes offer several venues for influencing policymaking to a multitude of public and private actors. As explained in Chapter 2, this creates a set of opportunities and constraints for state actors. On the one hand, states can cast influence in industry-based decision-making through state-owned enterprises or politically controlled private actors. On the other hand, such actors' interests may not be fully overlapping with those of the central government, especially when it comes to private actors, thus blurring the delineation of a clear-cut and coherent 'national interest'—however defined.

The complex interaction of several partially overlapping governance settings yields overlapping and potentially incoherent normative settings.[26] In this context, several public and private actors act as norm entrepreneurs in shaping the norms, rules, and principles of Internet governance, throughout and within the several hundred organisations involved in Internet norm-making.[27] The role of norm entrepreneurs in IR Theory has been explored at least since the 1990s, with the landmark publication by Finnemore and Sikkink[28] exploring norms' generation and development until adoption or failure thereof. In Internet governance, Hurel and Lobato[29] explored the role of private companies as norm entrepreneurs, focusing on cybersecurity norm-making as an aspect that

---

[26] Kettemann, M. C. (2020). *The Normative Order of the Internet*. Oxford University Press.

[27] Radu, R. (2019). *Negotiating Internet Governance*. Oxford University Press.

[28] Finnemore, M., & Sikkink, K. (1998). International Norm Dynamics and Political Change. *International Organization, 52*(4), 887–917.

[29] Hurel, L. M., & Lobato, L. C. (2018). Unpacking Cyber Norms: Private Companies as Norm Entrepreneurs. *Journal of Cyber Policy, 3*(1), 61–76.

is traditionally inscribed within states' competence. Radu et al.[30] coined the term 'normfare' to refer to the effort of norm-creation on a vast scale in which several (types of) actors are engaged in the several layers of the Internet infrastructure and its governance.

While regime complexity yields a multi-layered normative framework with no clear-cut hierarchy, an Internet normative order has taken shape according to Kettemann.[31] Such order consists of three layers: international norms, national norms, and transnational norms. Norms can be enshrined in law or be non-legal. In other words, norms are looked at in terms of functionality rather than legal formality. In Kettemann's[32] definition, norms can be either rules or principles: "rules 'encode' definitive commands (*Rechtsfolgen*), while principles only do so *prima facie*" (emphasis in the original).[33] While this definition of rules and principles resonates with political science literature, the latter tends to identify norms as a third separate category rather than a collective name for rules and principles. Finnemore and Hollis[34] define norms as "collective expectations for the proper behavior of actors with a given identity", a definition that identifies four elements for a norm to exist: "(1) identity, (2) behavior, (3) propriety, and (4) collective expectations".[35]

Departing from such three definitions of norms, rules, and principles, one can observe that the transnational layer of the Internet's normative order hosts a variety of private-based, non-legal norms that regulate both the process of Internet norm-making itself and its final outcomes. For example, the IETF creates voluntary industry standards with no *de jure* validity, but they bind industry to the adoption of certain protocols and affect users' rights (for example, privacy) and behaviour online. Norms elaborated transnationally are at the core of this book, which focuses on multistakeholder, private-based governance. Standardisation processes create influential technical rules, while ICANN bylaws and policies affect

---

[30] Radu, R., Kettemann, M. C., Meyer, T., & Shahin, J. (2021). Normfare: Norm Entrepreneurship in Internet Governance. *Telecommunications Policy*, 45(6), 1–7.

[31] Kettemann, op. cit.

[32] Kettemann, op. cit.

[33] Ketteman, op. cit., p. 256.

[34] Finnemore, M., & Hollis, D. B. (2016). Constructing Norms for Global Cybersecurity. *The American Journal of International Law*, 110(3), 425–479, p. 438.

[35] Finnemore & Hollis, op. cit., pp. 438–439.

the global management of the Internet's critical resources despite coming from a private organisation. The interaction of public and private norms is a bidirectional one, whereby state-sponsored actors by the rules of private governance, but governments' push to influence (infrastructural) policies limits private actors' actions.[36]

To summarise, regime complexes open a variety of venues for a variety of public and private actors to interact and participate in norm-making as norm entrepreneurs.[37] Based on the framework of norm entrepreneurship in regime complexes, the next section of this appendix illustrates the methods selected to conduct such analysis. The mix of qualitative methods selected reflects the need to analyse this phenomenon at many layers of interaction, coherently with the structure of the Internet governance regime complex. Such characteristics compel one to incorporate the views of those involved first-hand in standardisation and governance activities, especially when they possess such technical expertise whose understanding is beyond that of social science. This addresses the structural underrepresentation of such profiles in International Relations research on the politics of technology.[38]

In conclusion, through the regime complexity lens this book illustrated how the institutional settings and mechanisms of opportunities and constraints illustrated create venues for Chinese stakeholders' influence, contestation, as well as adaptation to the existing norms and institutions of global Internet governance. This raises two main theoretical expectations that have been addressed through the book. First, regime complexes blur the lines of national interest as they allow a variety of state and non-state actors to influence policymaking processes through a variety of venues. This reduces a government's capacity to cast control on national actors, despite quests for digital sovereignty, but also increases actors' capacity to contest norms through 'forum-shopping', that is, shifting competences from one forum to another.[39] Second, influence in a regime subset is never completely independent of influence in the other subsets of the same regime complex. Therefore, challenging norms in one subset

---

[36] Musiani, 2020, op. cit.

[37] Hurel & Lobato, op. cit.; Radu, op. cit.; Radu et al., op. cit.

[38] Tanczer, L. M., Brass, I., & Carr, M. (2018). CSIRTs and Global Cybersecurity: How Technical Experts Support Science Diplomacy. *Global Policy, 9*(3), 60–66.

[39] Hofmann, S. C. (2019). The Politics of Overlapping Organizations: Hostagetaking, Forum-Shopping and Brokering. *Journal of European Public Policy, 26*(6), 883–905.

entail challenging norms in others. This makes norms rigid and creates incentives for norm entrepreneurs to adapt to the existing normativity rather than contesting it.

Methodological Choices

On a methodological level, in order to explore China's contribution to the definition of Internet governance, two subset of global Internet governance were explored: *(i) critical Internet resources (CIRs) governance at ICANN and standardisation at the IETF*, and *(ii) mobile Internet standard-making at 3GPP*. Chinese stakeholders' interactions are observed within each forum and then analysed in conjunction, as regime complexity entails a form of interdependence among them.

This research adopts three different data collection methods: qualitative semi-structured expert interviews, thematic analysis of standards documentation, and thematic analysis of Chinese legal and policy documents. Each method brings information and serves as a control basis for the analysis conducted with other methods.

Semi-structured Expert Interviews

To start with, interviews help to gauge stakeholders' intentions and perceptions, as well as their understandings and interpretations of historical facts. In conjunction with other methods, they can both provide hints towards what is deemed politically important in a certain policy realm and serve as corroboration for findings obtained through other methods. To be sure, interviews do not provide a fully systematised interpretation of stakeholders' perceptions, but rather in-depth narratives from key profiles.[40] Nonetheless, their usefulness remains intact, especially in corroborating other research findings and gauging the views of key persons involved in processes otherwise too technical to be fully interpreted by social science researchers.

Other than playing this role, in this book's particular case expert interviews helped to explore the behaviour of Chinese stakeholders as norm entrepreneurs in Internet governance within the theoretical framework illustrated in the previous section of this appendix. Through the earliest

---

[40] King, N., Horrocks, C., & Brooks, J. (2019). *Interviews in Qualitative Research*. Sage.

interviews, this book's field of enquiry was fully defined, coming to identifying it with the ICANN, IETF, and 3GPP policy realms. Furthermore, interviews helped to establish the time references for documents and network analyses. Additionally, because such organisations meet few times per year (and in 3GPP's case meetings are not public), interviews represent a much more feasible qualitative study method than others, such as participant observation, which instead has been successfully used elsewhere.[41] Finally, when accompanied by the findings derived from the two other methods illustrated below, interviews help to gauge the drivers of Chinese stakeholders' actions and stances in the governance complex.

While necessarily carried out online owing to the Covid-19 pandemic, interviews proved proficient and were conducted coherently with recent methodological developments on remote interviewing.[42] Building on the two other methods described below, interviews allowed the author to interpret how Chinese stakeholders' stances within the Internet governance regime complex, and particularly within the three fora in question, changed in time, differentiating among different stakeholder groups. Collecting first-hand views from Chinese research participants, along with Westerners' perspective on Chinese stances, allowed the author to interpret how Chinese stakeholders' approaches and strategy within and towards the regime complex changed in time. Furthermore, this allowed one to gauge the relationship between Chinese stakeholders and norms within the fora in question, including how these actors adapted and adopted such norms.

The interview questions have been elaborated based on two pieces of secondary empirical data. The first is Chinese companies' leadership position in 5G standardisation, expressed in terms of standard contributions presented by Chinese actors-affiliated experts at 3GPP.[43] In particular, Huawei Technologies emerges as the single most important proponent of

---

[41] Cath, C. (2021). The Technology We Choose to Create: Human Rights Advocacy in the Internet Engineering Task Force. *Telecommunications Policy*, 45(6). https://doi.org/10.1016/j.telpol.2021.102144.

[42] Salmons, J. (2021). *Doing Qualitative Research Online*. 2nd. ed. Sage.

[43] Pohlmann, T., Blind, K., & Hess, P. (2020). *Fact Finding Study on Patents Declared to the 5G Standard*. IPLytics and Technische Universitaet Berlin.

5G standard contributions in absolute quantitative terms by the beginning of 2020 (26,372 by January 2020)—notwithstanding the various ways in which standard contributions can be quantified and qualified.[44]

The second piece of empirical evidence is Chinese actors' relative growth in contribution to the IETF's activity. The number of Chinese authors contributing to RFCs and Internet Drafts sharply increased between 2007 and 2010, then remaining relatively steady at 2010 levels thereafter. Furthermore, Huawei is on aggregate the second most important organisation in terms of 'active authors', slightly behind the US company Cisco, in the IETF by 2023.[45] These two companies hold the same position when looking at RFCs (co)published by their affiliates.[46]

The key informants participating in interviews are twenty-nine Chinese and non-Chinese (mostly Western) representatives of six Internet stakeholder communities: governments, international organisations, multinational enterprises, civil society, technical communities, and academia. This categorisation is drawn from DiploFoundation[47] and adds 'academia' to the five stakeholder groups often found in ICANN, Internet Society (ISOC), and UN institutional documents, as academics do not easily fit the other categories unless they carry governmental or business roles or hold strictly technical competences.[48]

To be sure, many taxonomies can be found in Internet governance literature.[49] Each one underwent criticism from other literature sectors as categories of stakeholders were excluded or overlapped conceptually. For example, it is challenging to distinguish between the technical community and multinational enterprises when around 80% of the technologists participating in the Internet Engineering Task Force are employed by corporations.[50] The global multistakeholder event held by the Brazilian

---

[44] Pohlmann et al., op. cit., pp. 25–26.

[45] Arkko, J. (2023). *Distribution of Authors per Companies. IETF Statistics.* https://www.arkko.com/tools/allstats/companydistr.html (July 21, 2023).

[46] Arkko, op. cit.

[47] DiploFoundation. (2015). *Multistakeholderism in IGF Language.* http://www.diplomacy.edu/IGFLanguage/multistakeholderism (November 25, 2020).

[48] Belli, L. (2015). A Heterostakeholder Cooperation for Sustainable Internet Policymaking. *Internet Policy Review, 4*(2), 1–21.

[49] See for example: Raymond, M., & DeNardis, L. (2015). Multistakeholderism: Anatomy of an Inchoate Global Institution. *International Theory, 7*(3), 572–616.

[50] Belli, op. cit.

government in the wake of the PRISM scandal, NetMundial,[51] proposed a six-fold distinction among stakeholders: governments, the private sector, civil society, the technical community, the academic community, and users. While possibly more encompassing, this definition does not avoid conceptual overlapping since 'users' could arguably fall under the category 'civil society'—after all, the latter's purpose is to represent citizens.[52] The UN-sponsored Working Group on Internet Governance's 2005 definition enshrined in the Tunis Agenda provides instead a threefold distinction among stakeholders: governments; the private sector; and civil society. This categorisation, while parsimonious, leaves out academia and the members of the technical community not affiliated to any of the three categories.

The six-fold categorisation adopted in this book is chosen as a good compromise between inclusiveness and parsimony.

As for the involvement of mostly Western (that is, mainly from the EU and the US) non-Chinese stakeholders, it is due to the fact that the main non-Chinese actors involved in the processes under analysis are Western (Cisco, Nokia, Ericsson, and the US government among others). Interviewing non-Chinese participants helped the author to gauge their views on Chinese actors' behaviour, stance, and policies. Interviews with Western participants were insightful as they held views on how they saw Chinese stakeholders entering into governance and standardisation venues and carrying their weight in them. This way, interviews with Chinese and non-Chinese, as well as interviews with exponents of different stakeholder groups, corroborated each other. The possibility to include actors from other national/regional backgrounds systematically in the analysis to address, for instance, China's relations to Latin American and African governments and stakeholders exists and would open the way to important analytical aspects, such as the role of China's relations to developing countries within its broader foreign and digital-infrastructural policies. Nonetheless, it also risked expanding the scope of this research project beyond feasibility. It goes without saying that key informants from other geographical areas of the world have been involved when their expert

---

[51] NetMundial. (2014). *Multistakeholder Statement*" https://www.cgi.br/media/docs/publicacoes/1/16570020190607-CadernosCGIbr_DeclaracaoNETmundial.pdf (October 16, 2020).

[52] Belli, op. cit.

position was deemed relevant within the scope and objectives of this research project.

The software QDA Miner was used to qualitatively analyse interviews. Interview texts are coded thematically through concepts found in literature: Internet fragmentation, compatible/incompatible standards, and normative change are the three crosscutting topics.

Thematic Analysis of Selected Internet Governance Documents

As for the second methodological approach, analysing documents allows a researcher to interpret the outputs of decision-making processes and thus the influence of specific (networks of) stakeholders. In terms of norm entrepreneurship, this method allows to gauge the efficacy and effectiveness of Chinese stakeholders' effort in policy- and norm-making within the analysed subsets of the Internet governance regime complex.

In this research's case, analysis has been conducted on selected documents of selected working groups within the three fora in question. As such working groups can produce several tens of documents per year, selected time references have been identified as illustrated in the next section.

The analysed documents contain specifications for selected releases (standards) of 3GPP[53]; RFCs for the IETF; and bylaws and GAC minutes and meeting transcripts for ICANN.

MaxQDA is used for qualitative document analysis. Each document is coded according to four themes derived from literature (influence, fragmentation, interoperable standards, East–West geopolitical divide are some of the crosscutting topics). A forthcoming section will illustrate the selected timespans and the targeted documents.

Through qualitative thematic document analysis, the author observes the policy impact of Chinese stakeholders in the selected multistakeholder governance fora. Document analysis provides good corroboration to interview findings, as one can observe whether interview participants' impressions and views correspond to policy outputs. Furthermore, it supports and corroborates the findings obtained through the other methods.

---

[53] Releases undergo several steps of re-elaboration and transformation, which complicates the retrieval of information. When reference to the content of a release is made, it points to its related specifications, a term that refers to both Technical Reports (TRs) and Technical Specifications (TSs) as defined by 3GPP in TR21.900 (3GPP 2021c).

Thematic Analysis of Chinese Legal and Policy Documents

To provide the historical context of China's domestic digital policies and connect it with Chinese stakeholder's engagement in global Internet governance, the author analysed legal and policy documents. The selection of these documents was based on their relevance for digital/Internet sovereignty debates in China. The selected legal documents are: Cybersecurity Law, Critical Information Infrastructure Security Protection Regulations, Internet Information Service Algorithmic Recommendation Management Provisions, Data Security Law, Personal Information Protection Law, and Outbound Data Transfer Security Assessment Measures. Connected legislation such as the Measures for the Management of Generative Artificial Intelligence Services and the Provisions on the Administration of Deep Synthesis Internet Information Services have been analysed. As for policy documents, the White Paper on the (status of the) Internet in China was selected as the starting point of China's discourse on Internet sovereignty in official policy,[54] while presidential speeches are analysed and reported in the book when they address doctrinal aspects of domestic Internet governance. These include, for example, Hu Jintao's remarks in a Party study session reported in Chapter 3.

As the author speaks Chinese but is not a native speaker, the website DigiChina[55] has been relied upon for legal translation. DigiChina is a joint project by the Cyber Policy Center of Stanford University and the Asia Centre of Leiden University. It provides English translations and original texts for Chinese policy documents and laws related to the digital ecosystem. As legal translation is a delicate matter where misinterpreting a word can lead to the full misunderstanding of a piece of legislation, the author relied on ready-made translations for this purpose. As per policy documents, instead, the author relied on his own translations except where official English translation was provided by the Chinese institutions in question. Mismatches between original and translated versions can exist

---

[54] Creemers, R. (2020). China's Conception of Cyber Sovereignty: Rhetoric and Realization. In D. Broeders & B. Van den Berg (Eds.), *Governing Cyberspace. Behavior, Power, and Diplomacy*. Rowman and Littlefield.

[55] Digichina. (2023). *Digichina. A project of the Program on Geopolitics, Technology, and Governance at the Stanford Cyber Policy Center.* https://digichina.stanford.edu/ (August 18, 2023).

also in official translation, often due to the difficulty of translating culturally bound concepts or to the need of appealing to different audiences.[56] For these reasons, the author always reports both the translation and the original text to allow Chinese-language readers to retain a benchmark for textual interpretation.

The analysis of these documents, along with a thorough literature review, allowed for a reconstruction of the evolution of digital policies within China. This is essential to discard simplistic views of Chinese stakeholders and the Chinese government as a monolithic entity fully controlled by the Communist Party. Along with the other two analytical approaches adopted in this book, namely interviews and thematic analysis of standardisation documents, this approach helped the author in providing an assessment of Chinese engagement in Internet governance that gives justice to the complexity of the Chinese stakeholders ecosystem and Chinese stakeholders' engagement with global Internet governance. Furthermore, the analysis of Chinese legal and policy documents, along with a strong reliance on both Chinese, European, and North American literature helped in reducing interpretation biases.

Building the Sample of Interview Participants

To summarise, the three data gathering methods illustrated in this section allow a threefold analysis of Chinese stakeholders' stance in Internet governance: their interests and drivers; their actions and strength through time within the selected fora; and the origins of the various stakeholders' stances in recent Chinese political history. This happens through a constant interaction between the three methods: interviews findings influence and help the interpretation of document contents and vice-versa, with the analysis of Chinese digital policies and regulations providing a gauge for the complexity of inter-stakeholders relations in China.

As analysable documents and working outputs are numerous, the author was bound to select significant documents in given timespans for feasible analysis: analysis on 3GPP, ICANN, and the IETF spans across decades and therefore needs to be trimmed down to a few nodal points in history. Different criteria have been applied in identifying time references

---

[56] Zhong, W. (2003). An Overview of Translation in China. *Translation Journal*, 7(2), 7.

and target groups for the three data collection and analysis methods illustrated above and summarised in Table A.1. However, the overall timespan ranges from 1998 up to the time of writing for each of them, being the founding year for both ICANN and 3GPP. These aspects are illustrated below in this chapter. Furthermore, different criteria have been adopted to sample interview participants within the six stakeholder groups identified above.

To begin with, interview participants have been selected through purposive sampling. Every participant has been first contacted by email. Earliest contacts have been made through senior members of the Department the author was affiliated to at the time the research was conducted, then each interview was concluded with a request for contacts with persons in key positions. Such contacts were either colleagues in the same organisation or structure as the research participants or representatives of other stakeholder groups with whom the participant was acquainted through their common activity at ICANN, the IETF, or 3GPP. Chinese and Western participants have been interviewed for every stakeholder group (governments, international organisations, tech companies, civil society, academia, technical communities), with the sole exceptions of governments and civil society. Only representatives of Western stakeholders could be involved from these groups, despite several attempts, arguably due to the autocratic nature of the Chinese governments and the sensitivity of the issues at stake.

Table A.1 A summary of this book's research methods and their objectives

Methods	Research objectives	Theoretical implications
Semi-structured expert interviews	Gauging stakeholders' views, interests, and drivers	Norm entrepreneurs' behaviour in the regime complex
Thematic analysis of standardisation documents	Observing Chinese actors' impact in policy and standardisation	Effectiveness of norm entrepreneurship
Thematic analysis of Chinese legal and policy documents	Observe the development of Chinese digital policy	Norm entrepreneurs act differently for domestic and international historical reasons

Government participants were familiar either with the GAC or Internet Governance Forum (IGF) processes, as public authorities are not represented in IETF and 3GPP. However, their familiarity with these bodies was investigated. Among academics, senior figures (assistant professors and professors) have been interviewed, all of which were Internet governance experts and/or participants. For all the other stakeholder groups, professional profiles engaged first-hand in ICANN, IETF, or 3GPP were selected. A strong emphasis was given to technologists' views, as they are underrepresented in IR literature but possess a privileged expert view on the politics of technical governance.[57] In ICANN's case, Western and Chinese members of staff have also been interviewed. It must be stressed once again that the stakeholder group categorisation is ideal–typical, and most interview participants fit more than one stakeholder group.

All interviews have been conducted between mid-March 2020 and February 2021. While interviews are kept confidential to allow participants to freely speak their mind, one can unpack the six Internet stakeholder groups illustrated above (government, international organisations, tech companies, civil society, academia, and technical community) and address the challenges encountered in categorising participants into one stakeholder group or the other. After all, categorisations are ideal–typical and stakeholder groups are overlapping—an element that is structural to multistakeholder Internet governance.[58]

The twenty-nine participants involved in interviews feature five between Chinese nationals and Chinese-born people. However, it must be stressed that non-Chinese people affiliated to Chinese corporate actors and Chinese people affiliated to Western institutions have been interviewed. In terms of stakeholder groups, the interview participants can be categorised as follows:

1. Three participants are affiliated to government, all from the Western hemisphere.
2. One participant is a member of staff of an international organisation. They are European.

---

[57] Tanczer, L. M., Brass, I., & Carr, M. (2018). CSIRTs and Global Cybersecurity: How Technical Experts Support Science Diplomacy. *Global Policy*, 9(3), 60–66.

[58] Palladino, N., & Santaniello, M. (2021). *Legitimacy, Power, and Inequalities in the Multistakeholder Internet Governance. Analyzing IANA Transition*. Palgrave Macmillan.

194 APPENDIX A

3. Nine participants are affiliated to the business sector, two of whom work for Chinese network manufacturers.
4. Two participants fall within the scope of civil society and both are Western.
5. Seven participants are members of the technical community, affiliated to both Western and Eastern organisations.
6. Seven participants are members of academic institutions, featuring both Western and Chinese people.

This taxonomy is imperfect for the reasons illustrated above. For example, the seven participants from the technical community do not encompass companies-affiliated technologists, who have been counted within the business community. Nonetheless, the knowledge and expertise they have access to, especially when their main professional role revolves around standardisation, is that of a member of the technical community.

Conversely, the seven participants classified within the technical community encompass ICANN staff members. This classification has been operated due to the role their organisation plays and its sui generis form that distinguishes it from public (state-based) international organisations. Nonetheless, the knowledge they possess and that they shared during interviews may originate from a business or civil society background rather than a technology one.

Furthermore, the only interview participant counted within the "international organisations" stakeholder group is an international organisation's staff member. Nonetheless, technologists employed by private companies participate in standardisation within such organisations as the ITU, thus adding a further layer of complexity to the classification operated. In this context, an organisation such as the EU, with both supranational and intergovernmental elements, falls in between the "government" and "international organisation" categories.

Briefly, Chinese and Western perspectives were obtained throughout the interview process from each stakeholder group, with the sole exception of government and civil society. No Chinese person affiliated—even non-exclusively—to one of these two stakeholder groups participated in interviews.

Analysing Standardisation Documents: Defining the Targets

Owing to the vast array of work conducted by ICANN, IETF, and 3GPP, selected working groups or sub-bodies have been targeted for document analyses.

For ICANN, the focus was on the Governmental Advisory Committee (GAC). The author analysed GAC transcripts and minutes from 2015 and 2016, namely the GAC documents from the three ICANN meetings that preceded the completion of the IANA stewardship transition in 2016. The work of governments in GAC showcases forms of collaboration that cut across usual geopolitical lines and displays each government's engagement with and position vis-à-vis ICANN. Observing GAC meeting transcripts and communiques helps to gauge a government's activeness in ICANN policymaking.

For the IETF, the focus was on three working groups (WGs): Inter-Domain Routing (idr); IPv6 maintenance (6man, which de facto took over the work conducted by the ipv6 WG); and Application-Layer Traffic Optimization (alto). These three groups are selected as they fit into three different areas of the IETF's work: routing (rtg), Internet (int), and transport (tsv).

Finally, within 3GPP, analysis was conducted on Releases 8 and 15, which contain the core technical specifications for 4G and 5G deployment, although implementation and standardisation continued with later releases. These documents allowed the author to observe both the evolution of Chinese companies' engagement in the standardisation process and the incorporation of standardisation work conducted elsewhere, which signalled convergence in standards rather than divergence.

Selected Timespans for Document Analysis

As mentioned, selected historical turning points have also been identified for document analysis. First, the end of the IANA stewardship transition in 2016 has been identified as a key moment for ICANN. The transition, ending the US's contentious supervision of the IANA functions, triggered reforms of ICANN's bylaws. Observing whether Chinese stakeholders had an influence on the 2016 text of the bylaws and in GAC bylaws in the three meetings (one year) preceding the end of the transition helps to gauge their normative influence on critical Internet resources governance. Coherently, network analysis is conducted on emails exchanged in the aforementioned ICANN subgroups in 2016.

Second, the beginning of Chinese company-affiliated authors' participation to IETF work (2007) and the freezing of the first 5G specification (Release 15, mid-2019) have been identified as key moments for the IETF. While the IETF is not competent for 5G standardisation, the latter has implications for the efficiency and maintenance of the Internet's basic protocols. Being Huawei the main Chinese actor in both the IETF and 5G standardisation at 3GPP,[59] a common interest at the basis of its activities can be assumed. Furthermore, 2007 and 2008 are key years in the roll out of IPv6: the closure of the ipv6 WG in June 2007,[60] de facto taken over by 6man as mentioned above, signalled an up-step in IPv6 implementation following the end of its standardisation process.[61] For these many reasons, mail interactions and RFCs presented throughout the years in question (June 2007 to June 2008; June 2018 to June 2019) are analysed.

Applying the same criterion of relevance, the freezing of Release 15 in mid-2019 has been identified as a key moment in 3GPP's history, preceded by the freezing of Release 8 on 3G Long-Term Evolution (LTE) (that is, the first 4G-related specification) in March 2009.

To be sure, further elements could be added. For instance, one could analyse contents of Releases 15, 16, and 17 to have a full panoramic of 5G development. However, that would broaden the scope of this research beyond feasibility. Furthermore, the technical nature of standards and technical documents (IETF's RFCs and 3GPP's Releases) makes them often unintelligible to non-technical readers. Alternative ways to study actors' impact on policy and technical outputs have been considered. For instance, output documents of the Internet Governance Forum could prove useful to reconstruct the public position taken by Chinese actors and stakeholder groups. However, given the authoritarian characteristics of the Chinese government, public documents from policy fora may not reveal deeper aspects of Chinese stakeholders' stance on specific topics. While this may also hold true for the aforementioned documents and mailing list exchanges, the deeply technical nature of standards makes

---

[59] Arkko, op. cit.; Pohlmann et al., op. cit.

[60] Internet Engineering Task Force. (2021). *Datatracker*. https://datatracker.ietf.org/ (January 6, 2022).

[61] Internet Corporation for Assigned Names and Numbers, op. cit.

them less exposed to public scrutiny and therefore more likely to show dynamics and dialectics in Chinese public and private actors' relations.

Conclusion

To summarise, this book builds on literature on regime complexity and norm entrepreneurship to bring IR Theory into dialogue with STS and China studies in the field of Internet governance. Methodologically, this book pursues its objectives through a qualitative analysis of China's domestic factors and Chinese contributions to the Internet governance processes at the international level.

Interviews play a major role in this research as they are the main key to interpreting Chinese behaviour in Internet governance through the last two decades of history.

Notwithstanding the positionality issues and linguistic barriers discussed above in this appendix, this book provides a balanced analysis that seeks to make justice to the complexity of Chinese stakeholders' engagement in global Internet governance.

Appendix B

Sample Interview Questionnaires

While interviews retained a similar structure across the research process, two slightly different lists of questions were drafted: one related to critical Internet resources and one related to the mobile connectivity realm. Questions were then adjusted to the interview participant's experience, background, and affiliation.

One element that influenced the length of the question list was the time available to the interview participant. While the general duration of an interview was one hour, the author conducted interviews as short as twenty minutes and as lengthy as three hours.

While the questionnaires contained prompts and follow-up questions, new unanticipated questions have emerged time and again throughout an interview.

The following are two sample interview lists of questions. Numbered questions are main questions, while questions listed through letters are prompts and follow-ups. It must be stressed that, while the questionnaire looks "rigid", interviews flowed more like a semi-structured conversation with the questionnaire used by the interviewer as a guide. Questions were shared in advance at the request of the interview participant.

A Sample Interview Questionnaire on Critical Internet Resources

On China's engagement in the governance of critical Internet resources:

1. Has China's participation in ICANN GAC increased since its reaccessions in 2009?
2. How does China's participation in GAC compare to Chinese stakeholders' participation in other ICANN bodies and constituencies?
3. How does Chinese participation in ICANN compare to Chinese stakeholders' participation in IETF?
4. What activities are China's government and Chinese non-state stakeholders conducting in the ITU?
5. What types of proposals are generally advanced by the Chinese government in critical Internet resources governance bodies (ICANN GAC and ITU mainly)?
6. How does it compare to the proposals advanced by Chinese non-state stakeholders in ICANN, ITU, and IETF?
7. Between 2007 and 2010 there was a steep increase in CN proposals at IETF, which later remained more or less stable at 2010 level: what is in your view the reason of this steep increase?
8. How did China's participation change in ITU, ICANN, and IETF throughout the periods below? What is your opinion?

    a. Before and after the GAC boycott
    b. From Jiang Zemin's presidency to Hu Jintao's (2003–2013), to Xi Jinping's (2013–now)
    c. Before and after the IANA stewardship transition

9. In critical Internet resources management body:

    a. What is your view on the way in which governments react to Chinese (both government and non-state stakeholders) actions in CIRs governance bodies?
    b. What is your view on the way non-state stakeholders react to Chinese (both government and non-state stakeholders) actions in CIRs governance bodies?
    c. Can patterns of reaction be identified (e.g. along stakeholder community lines, along nationality lines, etc.)?

10. Do China's government and Chinese non-state stakeholders influence ICANN's decisions? Can you please provide an example?

11. Do Chinese stakeholders influence IETF's decisions? Can you please provide an example?
12. Have you seen changes in relations among states and stakeholder groups in critical Internet resources governance bodies (main reference: ITU, ICANN, IETF) through the last two decades? Can you please provide an example?
13. Have critical Internet resources governance rules and norms changed throughout the last two decades? Can you please provide an example?
14. (If the answer to questions 13 and/or 14 is 'yes'), do you think China's non-state stakeholders and government had an influence in shaping rules and/or relations?
15. Is there any further important information that you would like to add?

A Sample Interview Questionnaire on Mobile Connectivity Standardisation

1. Have Chinese actors become more proactive in standardisation processes in time? (e.g. more present in ETSI, ...)
2. Was there a change in attitude by the various actors in the standardisation processes? What is your view?
3. What is your opinion on Chinese companies' actions in the standardisation of 5G?

    a. Which is stronger in the standardisation process: government or companies?

    b. Which relationship do you see between Chinese companies and the Chinese government?

4. Is there a single aspect of 5G standardisation that attracts Chinese stakeholders' attention more?
5. What is your opinion on non-Chinese actors' reactions vis-à-vis Chinese companies in telecommunications standardisation?
6. How did Chinese governmental policies vis-à-vis telecommunications standardisation change from 3 to 4G to 5G?

    a. Is there more state control on companies?

    b. What is your view?

7. Did standard-making rules change in time in your perspective?

8. Did you see power relations in telecommunications standardisation changing in time?
9. Do you think there is a political will (in both the "East" and the "West") to make/keep standards universal?
10. Do you think there is the likelihood of incompatible standards being established in the future?

Index

A
Alibaba, 58, 59, 62, 88, 90, 149, 154

C
China, 1–13, 21–23, 27–32, 35, 40, 41, 44–49, 57–79, 88–93, 95–101, 104–112, 119–137, 143, 145–158, 165–173, 177–179, 185, 188, 190, 191, 197, 200
China Communications Standards Association, 44, 123
CIRs. *See* critical Internet resources
critical Internet resources, 2, 3, 9, 12–14, 23, 24, 46, 48, 88, 111, 112, 134, 136, 143, 145, 156, 185, 195, 199–201
Cybersecurity Law, 71, 73, 153, 154, 190

D
Data Security Law, 71, 72, 190

digital sovereignty, 3, 8, 11–13, 27, 33, 46, 66, 68, 71, 87, 151, 158, 165, 169, 173, 177–180, 184
Domain Name System, 25, 26, 40, 65, 74, 75, 92, 96, 107, 151, 152, 154, 156, 157, 166, 171, 179

E
EU. *See* European Union
European Telecommunications Standards Institute, 43, 44, 103, 128, 201
European Union, xiii, xix, 68, 71

F
Facebook, 40, 58, 61, 66, 67, 78, 106–108, 112, 153, 154
5G, 2, 9, 30, 31, 37, 38, 44–46, 60, 104, 106, 119, 120, 125, 126, 128–132, 134–136, 145, 147–149, 166, 167, 172, 179, 181, 182, 186, 187, 195, 196

4G, 44, 46, 90, 98, 109, 120, 122, 125–129, 134, 135, 145, 147, 154, 195, 196

G

global governance, 4, 5, 8, 10, 21–23, 46, 137, 167–170
Golden Shield Project, 58, 61, 62, 77, 105, 106, 108, 111, 112, 122, 152, 154, 172
Google, 34, 40, 66, 67, 77, 106–108, 112, 145, 146, 153, 154
government, 3, 4, 11, 13, 14, 24, 25, 27–29, 31, 32, 35, 36, 40, 46, 47, 57–59, 65, 68, 70–72, 74, 77–79, 88–93, 95, 96, 98, 99, 107, 110–112, 121–127, 131, 132, 146, 148–150, 152, 155, 157, 158, 165, 171, 180, 182, 184, 188, 191, 193–196, 200, 201
Great Firewall of China. *See* Golden Shield Project

H

Huawei, 1, 31, 34, 37, 44, 46, 57, 60, 62, 77, 87–91, 97–102, 104–106, 110, 120–136, 145–148, 151, 154, 156, 157, 186, 187, 196

I

information sovereignty, 8, 68
International Telecommunication Union, 23, 27–29, 33, 35–38, 44, 45, 97, 102, 108, 109, 112, 124, 129–131, 134, 147, 152, 157, 172, 194
Internet Assigned Numbers Authority, 24–27, 29, 30, 34, 40, 46, 70, 75, 88, 93–96, 100, 103, 111, 136, 149, 150, 166, 195, 200
Internet Corporation for Assigned Names and Numbers, 9–14, 24–30, 32–35, 39, 42, 45, 46, 48, 65, 70, 75, 87–97, 99, 100, 103, 107–112, 121, 125, 143, 144, 147, 149–152, 154–157, 166, 167, 171, 177, 180, 183, 185–187, 189, 191–195, 200, 201
Internet Engineering Task Force, 9, 12–14, 24, 25, 27, 33–39, 42–46, 48, 87, 88, 92, 94, 97–106, 108–112, 123, 125, 133–135, 143, 144, 147, 149, 151, 154, 156, 157, 166, 170, 177, 181, 183, 185–187, 189, 191–193, 195, 196, 200, 201
Internet fragmentation, 2, 3, 10, 11, 13, 14, 21, 32, 38, 39, 41, 42, 49, 119, 136, 137, 143–145, 149, 151, 155, 156, 158, 165, 171, 173, 177, 189
Internet governance. *See* multistakeholder global Internet governance
Internet Protocol. *See* Transmission Control Protocol/Internet Protocol
Internet sovereignty, 8, 61, 66–68, 70, 71, 154, 158, 169, 179, 190
IP. *See* Transmission Control Protocol/Internet Protocol
ITU. *See* International Telecommunication Union

L

Liberal International Order, 3–8, 10–12, 14, 21–24, 32, 33, 35, 38, 41, 42, 46, 49, 137, 143, 145, 151, 165, 167–171, 173

INDEX   205

Long-Term Evolution, 44, 196
LTE. *See* Long-Term Evolution

M
multilateralism, 31, 33, 35, 111
multistakeholder global Internet governance, 3, 65, 75, 109, 143, 158, 169
multistakeholderism. *See* multistakeholder global internet governance

P
Personal Information Protection Law, 71, 190
platform regulation, 2, 8, 67, 77, 78

R
regime complex. *See* regime complexity
regime complexity, 7, 13, 14, 23, 46, 168, 169, 178, 180, 181, 183–185, 197
regime resilience, 110, 172
Requests for Comments, 34, 43, 46, 88, 97, 100–102, 110, 147, 151, 187, 189, 196

S
state, viii, 1, 2, 4, 6–8, 10–12, 22, 23, 25, 27, 30, 32, 33, 35–37, 41, 45–48, 57, 58, 60–64, 68, 70, 71, 73–75, 77, 79, 87, 89, 90, 92, 93, 99, 100, 104, 105, 110, 120, 122, 123, 127, 131, 133, 135, 136, 147, 148, 151, 157, 158, 166, 168, 169, 171, 173, 178–180, 182, 184

T
TD-SCDMA, 45, 122–124, 126, 134, 137
techno-nationalism, 31, 157
Tencent, 58
3G, 24, 37, 43, 45, 63, 98, 99, 106, 109, 120–127, 129, 132, 134–136, 144, 145, 147, 148, 154, 166, 172, 196
3rd Generation Partnership Project, 9, 12, 24, 33, 36–38, 42–46, 48, 98, 99, 105, 110, 120–125, 127–137, 143–145, 147–149, 154, 157, 166, 172, 177, 181, 185, 186, 189, 191–193, 195, 196
Transmission Control Protocol/Internet Protocol, 26, 38, 39, 41, 102, 103, 107, 120, 144, 151, 156, 166, 181, 182
Twitter, 58, 61, 66, 67, 78, 108, 154

U
United States, 1–3, 6, 8, 11, 22, 26, 29, 31, 58, 62, 70, 71, 90, 99, 100, 102, 120, 131, 155, 167, 180
US. *See* United States

W
WhatsApp, 40, 58, 62, 106, 108, 112, 154

Z
ZTE, 37, 87, 90, 99, 121, 124–128, 130, 132, 133, 148

Printed in the United States
by Baker & Taylor Publisher Services